JOB SEARCH
THE TOTAL SYSTEM

THIRD EDITION

Kenneth M. Dawson
Sheryl N. Dawson

Published by

TOTAL CAREER RESOURCES
Houston, Texas

Dedication

*To our client companies who have entrusted
their employees to us;*

*To our individual transition clients around the world
who have proven that The Total System works;*

*To our staff who serve as a model of the qualities and techniques
that create success;*

*To our parents who taught us to excel and
encouraged us to achieve;*

*To our many friends who inspire and
encourage us on our journey;*

*To each other for believing in our vision and
persevering to its fulfillment.*

Foreword

Dear Reader –

Whatever caused you to open this book, *Job Search: The Total System*, you have found a superb resource and support system to assist you in visualizing your optimum future and, even more importantly, attaining that future! You will appreciate this invaluable guide as you study, learn and apply the time-tested principles of *The Total System* book and accompanying audio program. You will realize its power when you are swept up and taken under the experienced wings of the authors Ken and Sheryl Dawson and learn to soar for yourself. They have dedicated their lives to helping tens of thousands of people like you and me achieve their dream jobs during the past thirty years. They truly care that you as a unique individual become the success story that you can be!

I am one of Ken and Sheryl's graduates from their corporate transition program. Among many things that have continued to impress me over the years since then, has been their ability to develop and maintain their successful core process while incorporating changes happening in the workplace and enhancements through ever advancing technologies. They have accomplished this relevance to today's work place in a manner that provides value wherever you are in your own personal career cycle -- a newcomer to the work force, college graduate, in transition from military service to the civilian job market, mid-career seeking advancement or career change, or seasoned worker considering pre-retirement work options. Add to these possibilities a whole range of entrepreneurial options including independent business, contract work or consulting, as well as not-for-profit and academic directions and you have an appreciation for the comprehensiveness of *The Total System* for guiding your career quest! Having worked internationally, I may add that wherever you reside or whatever your geographical preference, *The Total System* applies! Finally, whether you are motivated by your own desire to seek a new opportunity, or involuntarily released by your former employer, you have found the best resource to help you transition successfully regardless of your organizational level.

As you begin the process of identifying your job and career goals and then marketing yourself to achieve them, you need to realize that you are in a very competitive world and that success involves a lot of hard work. A vignette from my own experience might be valuable to help you gain perspective on your challenge. Keep in mind that I am an engineer by profession, had retired from the Army and worked internationally for seven years as a corporate officer of an international engineering and construction firm, and with my wife had decided to relocate to Atlanta to be nearer to our children and their growing families. While I was still working in the Balkans, my company had extended to me the opportunity of transition support by the Dawsons. I eagerly read *Job Search: The Total System* and listened to the audio program several times before returning state side.

For me the single most important element of my experience was thinking through what I really wanted to do with the remainder of my professional life. Making that decision was essential to creating a game plan for success and carefully developing the components – including resume, letters of references, networking letters, practice interviews and a growing list of network contacts – necessary to reach my objective. The unique concepts of *The Total System* such as linkage and psychological leverage coupled with positive thinking provided me with an effective framework within which to create my personal game plan. Rather than implementing isolated plays or steps in a haphazard or reactive way, this framework enabled me to develop an integrated plan and play book, one that would win the game!

As an introvert, I required considerable coaching and prodding to be comfortable "selling myself" in the marketplace. In addition, I found it difficult to develop a resume and interview technique that truly reflected what I could achieve for a future employer or client rather than simply reciting past experience. Don't minimize that point, as it is at the heart of what *The Total System* is all about and what makes *The Total System* unique in the plethora of job search advice! It challenges you to envision the future that is right for you, enables you to communicate your value to a potential employer, and then propels you to achieve your dreams.

I was able to use the tools and the knowledge gained from *The Total System* to bring three desirable job opportunities to the point of decision at the same time and select the one that provided the most overall value for me. Applying the negotiation techniques, I was successful in increasing my compensation package by about twenty-five percent above the initial offer and have leveraged my earning potential substantially by applying these principles with subsequent job advancements.

The most wonderful thing about *Job Search: The Total System* is that it really works! Just as it has enabled me to achieve my career and life aspirations, *The Total System* will work for you and your family as you soar into your future. Good luck and enjoy the journey!!

Bob Bunker
Atlanta, Georgia

Bob Bunker is a retired major general, Army Corps of Engineers. After retiring from the military, he created and managed an international engineering and construction organization for Asia based in Singapore and was then Theater Director for support to deployed military forces in the Balkans. Relocating to Atlanta, Bob became Co-Owner and CEO of TGA Technologies, a small and entrepreneurial communications-electronics firm. He presently is Senior Vice President of Brookwood Group, an international corporation with project/construction management expertise.

Table Of Contents

Introduction

The third edition of *Job Search: The Total System* is your guidebook to your next challenging, meaningful and profitable position. Whether you are unemployed, dissatisfied with your present position, or merely considering a job change, this book will prepare you to achieve your ultimate career goal. Even if you are new to the workplace or looking for a post-retirement career, the principles of *The Total System* are for you – there is no generational gap when it comes to job search success!

Specializing in career transition for over 30 years, we have assisted individuals at all organizational levels, in a wide spectrum of functional areas, and across many industries with excellent results. Our clients' average time-to-placement is 3.2 months, almost half the all-industry average of six months. Although we also have a recruiting division in our company, the primary role in helping our transition clients is to provide the resources and coach them on how to find better jobs for better pay. Their successes in implementing *The Total System* have demonstrated that our proven techniques can make all the difference in the success of your career transitions as well.

Since publishing the first edition of *Job Search: The Total System* in 1988 and the second edition in 1996, tens of thousands from many backgrounds have attained their career objectives whether as an employee, independent business person, or contractor/consultant. Those who diligently applied the principles set out in *The Total System* achieved their job search goals and moved to the next step in their career progression.

While the essential techniques of *The Total System* are unchanged, this third edition presents a technology update, many more examples and illustrations, revised forms and exhibits, and new strategies in every step of the process. Throughout the third edition, the application of *The Total System* techniques are explained for individuals from entry level to executive seeking to advance their careers, new graduates, return-to-work situations, military transitions, and other special situations. Whatever your circumstance, *The Total System* is your ticket to success in job search as well as career transition and advancement.

The techniques and skills presented in this book apply to every job seeker.

The earlier in your career that you develop effective job search skills, the more quickly your career will advance. For the senior executive who thinks that his or her needs are unique, consider the fact that whereas once only 40 percent of executives responded to search firm inquires, now 90 percent respond to such calls. However, this book will enlighten you to the fallacy of relying strictly on executive search firms as your sole source for finding jobs, and will provide a dynamic system by which you can take control of your next job search.

HOW TO PLAY THE ODDS IN YOUR FAVOR

In case you are contemplating a passive approach to your job search, bear this statistic in mind: in spite of the dramatic increase in the use of the internet for connecting people with jobs, less than 30 percent of job opportunities are found through internet sites, listings and placement agencies. While initial contact for openings may originate via an internet listing or source, invariably to accomplish placement, networking is essential. The odds are greater than 70 percent that your next job will be found through networking and not simply responding to job listings. Are you prepared to apply that ratio to your job search? On these pages we will challenge you, stretch you, and force you into an eyeball-to-eyeball confrontation with yourself. To that end, we are unrelenting in our approach to teaching job search techniques. Why? Because in so doing you have the best opportunity to achieve your goals, your potential and your career destiny. Whether you are between opportunities or seeking the next step in your career, it is in your best interest to embrace *The Total System* and follow it to the letter.

Be proactive, better prepared, more aware, always anticipating your next action!

Every job search technique that we teach relates to the concept of psychological leverage. At each step of your job search, you must be mentally a step ahead. Psychological leverage enables you to be proactive, better prepared, more aware, always anticipating your next action. Begin now to build psychological leverage by making up your mind to take control of your job search. When you realize that placement is up to you, the job hunter, this book will become an indispensable guide. *Job Search: The Total System* provides the tools for your successful job search and will never let you down.

Psychological leverage is an integral concept in our Cycle of Success. Simply stated, one must combine positive thinking with our concept of linkage to achieve psychological leverage. Throughout *The Total System* you will learn how to link each step of the process to maximize your control and ability to get the job you want. While it sounds easy, it takes planning, practice and perseverance to implement the system. In each chapter of this book we present the essential elements of a successful search and career transition. When we say link every step, we mean leave nothing to chance, incorporate every step of the process, and do everything with excellence. We challenge you to set high standards for each step of your campaign.

The Total System "A+" formula:

A+ Resume
A+ Letters (Reference, Cover)
A+ Lead Generation Plan
A+ Research (Target Companies)
A+ Networking
A+ Interviewing
A+ Negotiating
Equals Better Job for Better Pay!

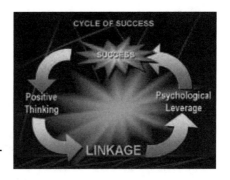

SUCCESS FACTORS

Short cuts, gimmicks, and dramatic innovations simply do not exist. If you accept this reality, you've taken a giant step toward thriving in your job search. No doubt you'll find many sources in the bookstore and online that peddle a variety of search techniques promising to simplify and expedite your job campaign. We stand on our previous statement. Information is out there in abundance, but much of it is ineffective and even counterproductive to your success.

Make no mistake about this—you'll not find any "warm fuzzes" or meaningless "feel-goods" on these pages. Suggestions such as "Take a couple of weeks off to rest and let your psyche heal" or "Go to the beach, sit on a pier, and watch the tides or contemplate where you want to go next" are commonplace in the job search world. We won't challenge the idea that you need time for reflection and assessment; you have an important decision to make in your immediate future. However, you don't arrive at realistic solutions by sitting at the end of a pier, awaiting a message in a bottle to wash in with the tide. You prepare for important decisions by researching, planning, analyzing, and networking.

In any challenging situation we all must rely on our subconscious minds for guidance and direction. You also probably understand that you get out only what you put in. Unless you spend time putting valid information in, you won't get any substantive conclusions in return. The most valid information about job search is traditional and time-tested. The tactics that work best today are those that have worked for 50 years and will continue to work best into the future. Dedication, discipline, courage, preparation, self-confidence, consistency, and professionalism are key. These qualities are the drive wheels for career and life success. But their importance expands exponentially during job search, when emotions are taut, time is pressing, and

> Dedication, discipline, courage, preparation, self-confidence, consistency, and professionalism are key success factors.

financial needs and commitments are of concern. As a result, we seek— demand —an intensive short-range time and energy commitment from you, coupled with a pledge to plan and use your time efficiently.

TIPS TO MAXIMIZE YOUR RESULTS

Are you beginning to sense the power you will gain when you master these concepts, principles and techniques? If you would like to harness some of this power for yourself, you have only to decide that *The Total System* is for you and begin today! Here are some practical tips to maximize the value of *The Total System* for you, your entire family and friends:

1) Take *The Total System* as seriously as you can and work smarter, harder and longer to gain the maximum benefit from it.

2) Resist the temptation to disregard information just because you do not agree with it or think it's not important for you.

3) Be open to new ideas and techniques and consider how they may be adapted to your situation and increase your ability to achieve your goals.

4) Read the book and listen to the audio version actively and think creatively; sometimes an isolated idea will "springboard" into many more which in turn starts a chain reaction of thoughts and inspirations.

5) Take notes as you read and listen.

6) Optimize the value of repetition and reinforcement provided through *The Total System's* many resources, leading to greater understanding, improved skills, increased confidence and success.

7) Involve your entire family and friends to help and encourage you and also to benefit them as they seek job opportunities of their own.

8) Utilize the complementary resources for *The Total System* to leverage your job transition and career advancement.

If you are feeling a bit intimidated by the journey ahead, let us assure you that each element of *The Total System* is sound and, even more importantly, linked into a powerful overall process. The more resources you utilize, the more techniques you activate, the more intensely you apply the principles, the greater success you will experience. You will be in control, more confident and more competent! And you will beat out your competition at every step.

Following this Introduction is a Personal Commitment Contract for you to sign as a way to hold yourself accountable to these success principles. Sign it now and let's get started on your first step to career success! You may like to have your spouse or other family member or friend acknowledge your self- contract to affirm your commitment, to encourage you along the way, and hold you accountable when your resolve may weaken. This is another way of validating the impact of your commitment, decisions and actions not only on your own career and life, but on your family's and friends' as well. By your commitment you can be like the courageous salmon swimming upstream, battling the current to achieve success!

One Percenters Club
Successful job hunters are like salmon swimming upstream. The one percent courageous enough to battle the current achieve success.

We guarantee that those who won't buy into our principles, who can't make a commitment without reservation, will simply be swept away by the current, floating downstream on wishful thinking. But the good news is that survival in the world of job search isn't based on luck or good fortune. Everything you need to know to succeed is learnable. And we are the teachers. As the student, continue reading and applying our guidelines to career and job search success and you will not be disappointed!

CHANGE HAPPENS – BE PREPARED!

With companies restructuring because of acquisitions, mergers, divestitures, re-engineering, right sizing, and other organizational changes, it's a fact of life that job security has gone the way of the dinosaurs. The phenomenon of the dual-career couple also has made it increasingly difficult for individuals to plan their careers in only one organization, which may frequently demand relocation for promotion. Rapid technology advancements and the wholesale shift in employment opportunities from manufacturing to service and information-oriented jobs have made job and career change a way of life for virtually every worker. Add to these global trends the emphasis on personal career advancement, the prevalence of the contingency workforce as well as entrepreneurial ambitions and you can appreciate the need to develop a sound strategy for ongoing job and career self marketing. A generation ago, an individual may have looked for a job only a few times in a career. Now job and even career changes occur numerous times throughout one's working life.

As professional career consultants, we have helped thousands of employees develop their careers within organizations and find new jobs and career opportunities when their current employers eliminated their positions. In case such services are new to you, they are called outplacement, career transition or redeployment. Termination is no longer considered a notice of incompetence and being jobless is not like wearing a badge of dishonor. Today career transition is an accepted reality not only of a constantly changing work force but as a part of doing business. Corporate conscience has motivated many organizations to recognize that it is their responsibility to assist their transitioning employees. As part of their severance packages, terminated employees often are provided professional assistance to find new employment in another company, a consulting opportunity, or start their own business. Key phases of transition support may include career assessment and counseling, professional resume preparation, job search organization, networking and interviewing skill development, as well as spouse and financial counseling. The objective of transition support is to enable the displaced employee to find the right position within the shortest period of time and with a minimum of trauma. These services are exactly what our firm offers organizations to assist their employees who are transitioned or redeployed. Through *The Total System* you gain the benefit of our experience so you are prepared for a life-time of career change.

In addition to reading the book, access the complementary online resources of *The Total System* to optimize the application of the principles and techniques. Wherever you are in the world, what ever stage in your career, whether voluntarily or involuntarily seeking a change, you can benefit from the proven techniques and resources of *The Total System* to find your next best opportunity and advance your career.

Kenneth M. Dawson
Sheryl N. Dawson

Note: Throughout *Job Search: The Total System*, we provide examples to illustrate specific techniques. All names used in our examples and the testimonials in chapter 10 have been changed to respect the confidentiality of our clients.

THE TOTAL SYSTEM
PERSONAL COMMITMENT CONTRACT

I, _____, totally commit to read, listen, and learn my entire *Job Search: The Total System* materials – book, audio, study guide and organizer – and review it as often as necessary to effectively implement my job search or career development campaign.

I further acknowledge that my success depends on *my dedication, discipline, courage, preparation, self-confidence, consistency, and professionalism* and hereby commit to developing these qualities day-by-day throughout my career and life.

I will embrace the Cycle of Success, thinking positively and using linkage to achieve psychological leverage throughout my career and job transitions. To energize this commitment I will work harder, smarter and longer to achieve my goals and vision.

I will take on the challenge and opportunity to:
- Become the Chairman of the Board of my own career (whether entrepreneur or intrapreneur).
- Be positive, hopeful and goal-directed at all times.
- Be diligent in my efforts and never, never give up.
- Believe I am going to do bigger and better things.
- Be a "One-Percenter" courageously applying the entire system.

I will be accountable to myself to establish short term and long term goals for my career development and job transitions; I commit to stretch myself to achieve my full potential.

In exchange for my commitment, Total Career Resources has committed to providing the best transition and career advice available based on 30 years of research and experience. I accept the challenge to apply these proven principles and techniques to achieve a better job for better pay. Each job and career transition I make in the future shall result in a life time of success, happiness, and prosperity for me and my entire family.

_____   _____
Your Signature   Date

_____   _____
Acknowledged by (Family Member or Friend)   Date

Technology Update

I. Using Technology for Career Success

Just as technology has impacted every aspect of the work place, it has affected how one seeks job opportunities and conducts job searches as well as career development. Recent statistics reflect that about 32% of hires connect through the internet; 28% by employee referrals; and 40% by other means, primarily traditional networking sources. Of those 32% through the internet, 68% are via company web sites, 14% through job boards, and 18% through other sites. Those are dramatic percentages in light of the fairly recent advent of the internet. What are the key areas which technology has impacted job and career transition? There are primarily three categories:

- Communications

- Research

- Record Keeping

These three areas impact each step of the job and career development process. In keeping with our concept of linkage, technology must be linked to each step to optimize effectiveness, efficiency and ultimate success. Following is an overview of how technology is linked to the various job search steps.

COMMUNICATIONS

Communications is listed first for a reason – technology has revolutionized how we communicate! Within just a few years the internet, email and cell phones have changed our communications in ways we never dreamed! Through the internet and email we communicate worldwide instantaneously. The integration of internet technology with cellular technology has further accelerated the use of these communication technologies.

With any revolutionary change come good and bad effects. On the positive side, communications are easier to send, faster, and global. On the negative side, communications are easier to send, faster and global. No, that is not a typographical error! It may sound contradictory, but consider that in communications there is both a sender and receiver. What is easy for the sender may be challenging for the receiver and vise versa. Being able to send communications quickly does not mean the answer comes as quickly – processing the communication and decision-making around it can often be as slow as in the days of snail mail! Global communications challenge us due to multiple languages and cultural differences. In many ways, technology is a blessing and a curse to the job search process. Regardless of one's perspective or preferences, however, it is a reality and you must be knowledgeable of how to effectively use technology in communications. Let's take a look at some of the key communications in job and career transition.

COMPANY USE OF TECHNOLOGY FOR TALENT MANAGEMENT

In human resources lexicon, talent management is the latest buzz word. Companies manage the flow of talent in their organizations with a number of technologies. Talent may represent employees, contract personnel, and consultants. First of all, most companies now have a website with a job and career portal. Many human resource departments require communications regarding potential work with the organization to initiate through that portal. Again, that is good and bad for you! It is good in that you can efficiently get your application and resume to the human resources department. It is bad in that it may go into a black hole or cyberspace never to materialize again! In all honesty, that is not much different from the days when you manually sent a resume or application. So what has changed? It is simply the MEANS of communication, not the result.

Nevertheless, the job seeker must often comply with each company's portal requirements to enter their talent management world. Later we will discuss how the tried and true techniques of networking mitigate the black hole syndrome.

These talent management systems include resume data bases and screening devices which also affect the resume writing process. Resumes should be formatted to be "friendly" to these technologies, and at times you may be required to submit a special format or even online format to comply. Again, this may be easy for the company, but makes your application process time consuming. In most cases, The Total System's straight forward, professional resume format is user friendly for the talent management systems. Using key words for your function and industry, including all skills and competencies, and listing all credentials are essential to be "selected" in a technology based screening process. We will cover the particulars to maximize your potential to be selected for interviews in the resume chapter.

E-MAIL

Email has become a communications blessing and nightmare depending on one's perspective and reliance upon it. Extroverts wish it had never been invented! For introverts it is the best thing since the creation of the quill! Certainly, one's style and communication preferences color one's view of email. What does that mean in practical terms in job and career transition? Ask your contact what they prefer — it is as simple as that. Blasting out 100 resumes to all your contacts may not be effective at all. Sending out email to executives who have their assistants monitor their email may not be effective either. Certainly, if someone asks you to email your resume, you have a green light to do so, otherwise use email for sending your resume cautiously. In addition, you will need to follow up to be sure they received it and reviewed it. Sound familiar? When you study the networking techniques, you will see that this is another fundamental that has not changed follow-up, follow-up, and follow-up!

CELLULAR TECHNOLOGY

Cell phones are viewed as good and bad in the same way that email is. When you can't get away from a ringing phone even in the bathroom, you know technology has become a bit ridiculous! Never-the-less, cell phones have accelerated our receipt of messages, both voice and electronic. In terms of receiving those important calls from potential employers, it means being prepared for a call at all times. That can be very challenging, especially if you have a vast network and you have communicated with many potential employers. Being organized and having your list of contacts readily accessible is essential to your ability to handle calls effectively. Being prepared with your 30 second commercial or background summary and message is also critical. Where ever you may be, having the ability to take notes is also important... perhaps, waiting to take a cell call until you are out of the bathroom may be the best practice! In terms of calling others, courtesy and common sense is the best policy. Ask if it is a good time to talk and if not, find out what would be a good time.

With regard to networking, these communication technologies have become increasingly dynamic. Company internet websites, association sites, college and alumni sites, job sites, job boards, web crawlers, blogs, networking sites and forums such as Linked-in have proliferated. Networking online has its advantages and disadvantages. It can expand your network dramatically, but it can also be impersonal. Regardless of how many contacts with whom you connect, if you do not follow up personally, they will have limited effectiveness. We will cover more on the use of all these sites under the topics of networking and lead generation.

RESEARCH

That brings us to the next key area in which technology has impacted job and career transition – research. From researching specific companies, to industries, to finding network contacts, the internet has revolutionized the process. In terms of getting information it has dramatically reduced the time and effort required. Sifting through manual directories in the days of old would often take days! Now in a few minutes, contact lists in various industry segments, names of contacts in specific companies, and detailed information on contacts and companies can be accessed with a click of one's finger! Clearly, that is a huge benefit. On the other hand, one can get so bogged down in lists and details, that it can be overwhelming. Learning to use the search engines, data bases, web crawlers and career sites effectively and efficiently is very important to job and career success. The kind of information you can find goes beyond industry and company information and job listings. You can also research:

- Opinions of insiders and former employees about specific organizations

- Insight into an organization's culture and how they are treated in the media

- Legal filings against an organization

- Information on officers and key personnel

- Analyst opinions on organizations

More on internet resources will be covered in the networking and lead generation chapters.

RECORD KEEPING

Finally, the third key area in which technology has affected job and career transition, is in record keeping. We alluded to this earlier. Managing your contacts is essential and technology has certainly improved the methods for contact or data base management. However, whether or not you are organized depends not on the methodology as much as it depends on one's use of it! So, whether you choose the ol' fashioned manual system, or an electronic contact manager, you must have it set up for job search specifics and you must USE it! Tracking calls, letters, email and dates for follow up are essential elements of a successful record keeping system. Set it up from the beginning of your campaign and consistently use it. There are suggestions for what to track and how to track it in the networking and lead generation sections. The organizational and tracking forms throughout *Job Search: The Total System* are available in electronic format in the complementary *Total System Organizer*.

THE FUNDAMENTAL STRATEGY

In summary, whether you love it or hate it, technology is an essential part of job and career success. While it has changed the pace and manner in which we communicate, conduct research and keep records, it has not changed the importance of the foundational principles of The Total System – positive thinking, linkage and psychological leverage. As we address the ten steps of the job and career transition strategy, we will mention more specifics about the use of technology. Also, in our complementary online career portal, we offer many of the tools to efficiently and effectively utilize technology in the job and career transition process. In conclusion, it is wise to keep in mind that it is people who make job offers and whatever technological means you may utilize to connect with them, ultimately you must sell them on your value to the organization in order to win the better job for better pay you seek.

II. Internet Basics for Your Job Search

There are some basic categories of internet sources that are helpful to review prior to discussing specific job step applications. First of all, recognize that the old adage, what you read does not make it gospel truth, is still applicable. You will want to verify information obtained over the internet, just as you must verify information from other sources for accuracy. Also, since internet cyberspace is so porous, be careful what information YOU list on internet sites and by email. Once it is out there, whether well intentioned or not anyone can access it. Now, let's review some basic kinds of sites.

SEARCH ENGINES

To find information you seek, there are many search engines available. However, Google commands about 80% of internet searches. The engines reduce your search time for various topics related to your search including industry, company, and career related information. Some of the popular search engines include:

www.google.com

www.excite.com

www.msn.com

www.lycos.com

www.infoseek.com

www.yahoo.com

BLOGS

The latest craze seems to be the blogs and discussion boards where you can share information and access expert (and not so expert) information on every topic under the sun. A blog is like a personal journal and is short for web log. They contain content, commentary, links and contacts. To find blogs that mention an organization you may be researching, use one of the search engines and look for the organization's name and the word "blog."

NETWORKING SITES

These sites such as Linked In are useful to advance your networking and access people who work in industries and companies and who may otherwise not be available to you for networking.

COMPANY DATA BASES

The publisher sites for company information are excellent for gathering information on public companies as well as private companies and not-for-profit organizations. Some are free and some fee based. The best known are:

Dunn & Bradstreet (fee based ratings)	www.dnbmdd.com/mddi/
Standard & Poors (Stocks & ratings)	www.standardandpoors.com
Moody's (Stocks & Bonds)	www.moodys.com
Hoovers (Free Basic Company Info)	www.hoovers.com
Edgar (SEC & Annual Reports)	www.edgaronline.com
Wall Street Research Network	www.wsj.com
Forbes (Business & Finance)	www.forbes.com/200best/
Inc. (Small Business)	www.inc.com
Biz Web	www.bizweb.com
Companies Online	www.companiesonline.com
Fast Company	www.fastcompany.com
SEC Information	www.secinfo.com
Thomas Register	www.thomasregister.com
Corp Tech	www.corptech.com

INDUSTRY INFORMATION SITES

Industry information can be found in many association sites. The following are survey and statistical sources along with business rankings:

Industry Surveys	www.investools.com
Labor Statistics	www.jobstar.org
Business Week	www.businessweek.com
Forbes	www.forbes.com
Fortune	www.fortune.com
Value Line	www.valueline.com

NAICS - North American Industry Classification System
http://www.census.gov/epcd/www/naics.html
(Numerical codes assigned to virtually any kind of business in the U.S.)

SIC – Standard Industrial Classification System
http://www.osha.gov/pls/imis/sicsearch.html
(Numerical codes assigned to virtually any kind of business in the U.S.)

WEB CRAWLERS

There are innumerable job sites and web crawlers to help minimize the time you spend searching through these sites for potential opportunities that match your background and job goals. That is a good thing because you can expend all your waking hours on surfing the net for job leads! The problem with that strategy is you would not have any time to follow up on them. With web crawlers, you can reduce your time investment and focus on networking and follow up on potential leads. A couple of user friendly crawlers for job leads include:

www.simplyhired.com

www.indeed.com

CAREER AND JOB SITES

There are a vast array of career sites sponsored by independent sources, universities, associations, geographical regions, and publishers. Many also have associated job boards. In addition, there are many separate job boards. The web crawlers can minimize your time on these sites; however, there may be some industry-specific, job/career-specific, or executive and college level sites that are particularly useful to you. These you may wish to routinely check, or they may incorporate a web crawler to send you listings in your area of search. In addition, many of these sites contain salary information useful in negotiations. Following are some of the popular sites:

CAREER SITES/SPECIALTY SITES:

www.monster.com
www.hotjobs.com
www.nationjob.com
www.careerjournal.com
www.ajb.dni.us/   America's Job Bank
www.wetfeet.com
http://www.headhunters.com/
www.jobbankusa.com

www.ceweekly.wa.com Contract Employment Weekly
www.net-temps.com
www.classifieds.yahoo.com
www.craigslist.org
www.career.com
www.careermag.com
www.brassring.com
www.careerpath.com
www.cweb.com Career Web
www.careerbuilder.com
www.ComputerJobs.com
www.Computerwork.com
www.Dice.com
www.eFinancialCareers.com (Europe - based)
www.EmploymentGuide.com
www.HEALTHeCAREERSNetwork.com
www.Jobsinthemoney.com
www.jobster.com
www.LatPro.com
www.MarketingJobs.com
www.TalentZoo.com
www.TrueCareers.com
www.vault.com
www.VetJobs.com
www.Workopolis.com (Canada – based)
www.Zoominfo.com

EXECUTIVE LEVEL:

www.execunet.com

www.netshare.com

www.6figurejobs.com

www.theladders.com

COLLEGE LEVEL:

www.SnagAJob.com
www.Teens4Hire.org
www.CollegeRecruiter.com
www.CampJobs.com
www.SummerJobs.com
www.Craigslist.org

COMPENSATION RESEARCH:

www.salary.com

www.salaryexpert.com

www.wsj.com (Career Journal)

SEARCH CONSULTANT SITES:

www.kennedyinfo.com   Directory of Executive Recruiters

www.tapc.org Houston Association of Personnel Consultants

www.recruitinglife.org   National Association of Personnel Consultants

III. Technology Impact on Job Search Steps

STEP 1: ASSESSMENT

One of the advantages of technology in the area of assessment is the availability of computerized career and behavioral assessments. The development of these assessments in recent years using computers has facilitated their accuracy and usefulness in career planning and targeting the best fit for various types of jobs. In addition to career assessments, there are entrepreneurial fit assessments that can be useful in assessing the likelihood of one's success in running an independent business or consulting. Career consultants and universities are good sources for these instruments. Some employers may also make these available to their employees as part of career planning. You may also access high quality career, professional fit and entrepreneurial assessments in the complementary resources of *The Total System* online.

It should also be pointed out that some organizations are using behavioral assessments as part of their selection process. In fact, with the improvement in accuracy of instruments which can be customized to predict success in various roles and positions, they have become an additional source of information beyond experience and interviews to determine fit. When asked to complete behavioral or work place preferences assessments, you should not be concerned about or try to prepare for them. Getting plenty of rest is the best preparation. Simply respond to questions honestly and do not attempt to second guess what answers they may be seeking. In most cases, that strategy results in an inconsistent score which would not be helpful to you or to the organization.

STEP 2: ENTREPRENEURIAL OPTIONS

The internet is a fabulous source of information when considering independent options including whether to own a business or consult. In terms of learning about how to run a company, buy a company, start a company, or consult, the availability of information is endless. In particular, you may wish to check out the US Small Business Administration's website. There are also many franchise sites to explore. Often associations also provide consulting information in their industry.

STEP 3: RESUME & COVER LETTERS

As outlined in part I of this technology update, the format of your resume should comply with technology requirements for scanning and for loading on the internet. Use an easy-to-read font – we recommend Arial in 10 point. Many organizations now require applying online with the attachment of your resume. This can be time consuming, however, if it is an organization in which you are interested, you may have to comply to be placed on the company resume data base for consideration.

In terms of content, you will want to be sure to use all the key words appropriate to your function, industry, and credentials to facilitate selection in a computer search. Proofing is always essential whether for purposes of the human eye or computer sort. Companies also key in on competencies and skills, so be sure to include words that are very descriptive of your expertise.

Your cover letter may be sent by mail or email or both depending on the situation. In many cases, email is preferred since it facilitates the speed of delivery and the ease of filing electronically as well as forwarding to appropriate company contacts.

The key technique here is to be professional and proof! Email has become so quick, that we often send messages that are cryptic and riddled with errors. In job search, that spells disaster. Take extra time to formalize the letter which you can then attach as well as use in the body of the email as appropriate. In addition to spell check, you should carefully proof all communications and have someone you trust help you proof – a second pair of eyes for proofing is always your best safe guard against an embarrassing mistake. We also recommend preparing some generic letters for various types of contacts to reduce your time in letter writing. However, be sure to customize and re-proof each letter for accuracy. In many ways, email has increased the chances of making mistakes in communications, so beware! Chapter 3 also has an exhibit with additional emailing recommendations.

When sending mail or email, you should always follow up to be sure your contact has received the message. We all know how easy it is to miss email in the deluge we receive. Asking for confirmation of receipt by your contact can also be helpful. Automatic confirmation is not always adequate, since they may receive but not recognize it or follow up as they should. A reminder by calling is your surest way of ensuring your message was received with the appropriate action.

Your follow up on resumes may be both by email and phone — again, accuracy and persistence are essential. Your contact may make their cell number available and often email is received by phone as well. In the barrage of electronic messaging, it is essential that you keep good track of your messages for appropriate follow up. In the chapter on networking and campaign organization we will cover some tips on effective record keeping.

STEP 4: REFERENCES

Most reference contact lists and letters are provided following an offer. You should have them in your "tool kit" so you can provide them in hard copy. The company may request these be sent by email as well for ease of processing. In most cases, references will be called for their comments. It is best to alert them by a call to explain the offer you have received and to be sure they are aware of an impending call. This procedure is really not affected by technology in any significant way. If your references give permission to use their cell numbers for contact by potential employers, then you may do this. Be careful to ask before you do, however. If they receive a call unexpectedly on their cell or in their office, it could reduce the effectiveness of their response. Never assume the reference checks are perfunctory!

STEP 5: NETWORKING

As outlined in part I and II of this update, networking is significantly impacted by technology. One of the greatest advantages is in targeting companies. We have listed many of the search engines, data bases, and other sources of industry and company information. The key is to set a strategy for their use and systematically explore the best ones for your career and job goals. Set a time frame for review of various sources and your goals for establishing your target lists. It is natural to start with those that are most familiar to you, but do not overlook others that may be recommended to you or which are discovered as you research various sites.

Developing a tracking and electronic filing system to manage all the information you access is key to success in networking. It is easy to spend hours reviewing information in which you discover useful information, but if you fail to save it to facilitate your next steps, your time could well be wasted. It is also very frustrating when you know you saw a lead or information you later need, and then can not locate it again! In the old days one could usually rummage through notes or files to come up with such gems, but when it comes to internet bits and bites, it is far worse than a needle in a hay stack! Organization in our electronic world is more crucial than ever.

Job postings on the internet are everywhere it seems and we have listed a number of the popular sites. Once again, we caution against spending all of your time browsing these listings. Limit your time surfing the net to 20% and spend 80% of your time on calling, face-to-face networking and follow up.

The networking sites have also proliferated and can be very useful in uncovering contacts you may not have found in other ways – blogs, Linked-in, association networking boards, and other networking boards are invaluable in expanding your network. Just remember that follow up by phone and face-to-face are important to maximize the value of these contacts to your search.

STEP 6: SEARCH FIRMS

The agencies value internet sources as well. Many use Monster and other sources to access resumes, so be careful how much information you put on public resume data bases. Besides agencies which may submit your resume without permission, there are other unscrupulous people who gather information from the internet. To protect your privacy, be careful with personal data and contact information. Professional firms will always contact you before submitting your resume to a company.

Communications with the search agency during the selection process is critical just as with potential employers; keep in close touch with and be responsive to an agency which has submitted your resume. Cell phones and email are usually big time savers in this process. As with all your contacts, keep good records of these contacts and the companies to which they are submitting your resume; typically an employer is obligated by contract to pay the agency or firm for up to a year after submission of your resume, so should you or such an employer reconnect regarding a potential opening it is important to immediately alert the agency through whom you were initially presented.

STEP 7: LEAD GENERATION BY TELEPHONE

As discussed in networking, follow up by telephone is essential regardless of the source of your leads. The acceleration of electronic messaging has made "telephone tag" as challenging as ever. People are really busy and tough to reach by phone! Professionalism and persistence are essential to succeeding. Once again, if you have someone's cell phone, be sure they can talk when you reach them. Everyone has their moments when they answer, yet may not really be able to take your call at that time. Courtesy is the watch word in those awkward moments and do not take it personally if the sign off is not as courteous as yours!

Whether or not you get a returned call from your voice mail can depend on many factors, some you can control and others not! You can control your tone of voice, the selection of your words, and professionalism. Even when you are well prepared and at your best, your contact may not have the time or be ready to return your call. Try not to get rejection remorse and just follow up at an appropriate time based on your compelling need to speak with them and the potential opportunity. As in any sales activity, you need to prioritize your contacts and stick to your plan. Managing your calendar and tracking calls is essential to your success in ultimately reaching your contact and turning the potential opportunity into an offer.

STEP 8: INTERVIEWING

Interviewing may not seem as susceptible to technological changes, but there are some things to note. We mentioned in step 1 that organizations may request an assessment as part of the selection process. Under resumes, we observed that many organizations require online applications which are also part of the selection process. Reference checking is typically done by phone, but background checks often involve internet searches of information on you. You may wish to "Google" yourself to see what is out there in cyberspace in your name. There could be someone with your name who is not as hirable – it may be good to just be aware of that. If a company does a background check, they will ask for written permission from you to do so. Some also do credit checks, so knowing what is on your record would be good as well.

The latest technology is video interviews. These are usually reserved for long distance situations and are not very prevalent at this time. Short video resumes have also developed but have limited acceptance by companies who are concerned regarding potential discrimination claims. With home video so popular, you may appreciate the advantages and disadvantages of this technology! For an interview it can complicate your ability to feel comfortable and natural. If you should be scheduled for one, it would be good to practice interview with a video camera in preparation. Playing it back can be helpful in preparing for any interview since you will observe body language and responses that will help you improve your interview skills overall.

STEP 9: NEGOTIATING

As pointed out under research sources, salary and compensation information is readily available on the internet. It is very useful to do this research prior to entering negotiations. Determining your market value is essential to maximizing your leverage in the process. We have seen companies that request documentation of your former salary, so while negotiating from value is the best strategy, keep in mind that you may be asked to verify your former income. We know you would never fudge on quoting this figure – honesty is the best policy as we have stated throughout The Total System! Compensation packages can be complex with the many bonus schemes including signing bonuses, profit sharing plans, stock plans, relocation and other factors, so having a spreadsheet to compare multiple offers is important. Finding someone who is familiar with compensation in your industry is very helpful in this important step of your search. Remember, your future salary increases will be based on your initial salary, so informed negotiating is key to your future income.

STEP 10: PLACEMENT

When the offer is submitted in writing, it may very well be sent by email. However, once the negotiation is complete and you have accepted, we recommend getting an originally signed copy of the agreed upon offer. You may also wish to consider writing an acceptance letter which should be signed but may also be saved electronically.

A TANTALIZING FORE TASTE

This quick overview of the technological impact on each step of the job search process is just a teaser for what will be covered in The Total System. Read the entire book and avail yourself of the The Total System complementary resources available online to optimize your career and job search potential.

Setting the Stage: Where You've Been, Where You Are, Where You're Going

In the pages of this book, you'll learn more about the nuances of job search and your career than you ever thought existed. To categorize the information, we can say that all we know, all we teach, fits under the umbrella of our two great commandments of job search. If you have a stone tablet handy, carve these down: *linkage and positive thinking*.

THE FIRST COMMANDMENT: LINKAGE

Typically, job search is approached as a series of freestanding, unrelated events. Resume writing, networking, interviewing, and negotiating are generally written about or taught as a series of independent occurrences. This should not be so. By adopting our principle of linkage and putting it into action, you'll begin to see job search as a series of interlocking steps, each inexorably linked to the previous event and the subsequent one.

Linkage means that you approach your job search with a specific game plan. A series of unrelated plays, no matter how great, is not likely to result in a win. Linkage requires that each step in your job search be thought through and carefully planned, for itself and in relation to the other steps, just as athletes look at each play as part of an overall strategy to win the game. A great resume may get you an interview, but if you are unprepared to back up your accomplishments with solid evidence during that interview, you've failed to use linkage. Or if you've obtained a reference letter from a former employer but didn't prepare him for a reference check by a potential employer, you've failed to use linkage. In effect, linkage in job search is a tightly structured plan of action to achieve a specific career objective or objectives. Nothing is left to chance as you take control of your job search game plan.

> Linkage in job search is a tightly structured plan of action to achieve a specific career objective or objectives. Nothing is left to chance as you take control of your job search game plan

For example, although you want to impress a potential employer during the interview that your skills and strengths are limitless, your answers to interview questions don't come from a box of granola — they come from your resume. Likewise, when you wonder what one of your references might say about you, stop wondering and use linkage to take control: Prepare a draft of a reference letter for each of your references for their approval and signature.

When you're negotiating compensation, you don't throw a number on the table and expect the employer to go after it like a famished German shepherd. Your research should have already firmly established your negotiating position as fair, reasonable, and consistent with industry and company norms. Moreover, your interviewing performance will have so impressed the hiring authority that you will be aggressively pursued as a valuable member of the team. Consequently, you will have psychological leverage to negotiate a mutually satisfactory compensation package.

THE SECOND COMMANDMENT: POSITIVE THINKING

If you do not think positively, you will not succeed at job search. We recognize that losing a job can be a tough blow psychologically. Typically, a termination will drag you through a five-step process:

1. *Denial*—This can't be happening to me.
2. *Anger*—How can they do this to me when others do only half the work I do?
3. *Bargaining*—Can I take another job at lower pay?
4. *Depression*—No one's hiring; there's no use trying.
5. *Acceptance*—OK, they cut me loose. Where do I go from here?

For a few people—generally those with serious disorders predating their career disruption—that process is a steep slide downhill. They never rise to step 5. For those cases, we recommend a therapist or a psychologist to help sort out the problems. But for the rest of us—the vast majority of people—we can reach the point of "Let's get moving." This is a problem of attitude, and it's controllable. We believe your attitude can be controlled as surely as your behavior can be controlled. We stress to clients that there are three time periods to life: the past, the present, and the future. Two of those you can control, but the past is history. So why get depressed and confused for weeks following termination? Certainly, you can work through the five-step process, but we believe that's a task measurable in hours or perhaps days, not weeks or months. Go beyond the past—deal with the present and your future.

> There are three time periods to life: the past, the present, and the future. Two of those you can control, but the past is history.

Don't lay more psychological weight on this event than it need carry. Have you ever experienced the death of a child, a spouse, a best friend, or a parent? Those are truly devastating psychological traumas; each could be a life-shattering event. Moreover, they are irreversible. Not so your job loss—that is a salvageable situation. Remember, you've lost your job, not your talent or your career. Consider how many other organizations you can target who can benefit from your skills. Think about how many other industries might use your talent and background in areas you haven't yet investigated. Don't get depressed, get busy. That's the best cure for any attitude problem. Don't allow yourself to wallow in self-pity. Don't get angry, get assertive. When you do, you begin to build momentum, which begets positive thinking, which begets hard work and effort, which begets success.

> *Rather than the worst thing, this could be the best thing that's ever happened to you!*

We watch the scenario unfold every day with our transition clients. In fact, we see it happen so often that we like to suggest to just-terminated clients: *Rather than the worst thing, this could be the best thing that's ever happened to you*....if you follow our system and advice! We base that belief on the notion that termination is seldom a surprise. If indeed you're shocked by it, it's probably an indication you just haven't been aware of what's happening around you. More important, however, we have the evidence; we see a consistent pattern of placement that verifies our proposition. Our clients who utilize these principles of job search do land better jobs—for more money. The application of our principles of positive thinking and hard work boosts these displaced workers to their next career step—frequently without a hitch. Often that next step is another (usually better) job. Occasionally, a person who is released from a position will decide to become an independent business owner or a consultant, or change careers completely.

Witness the experiences of three former clients in our program, who represent very different but typical examples. They entered our program weighted down with fear and uncertainty about their future.

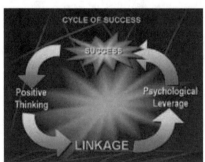

Joe Williams, an introverted engineer in his early 40s, was so paralyzed over the prospect of making cold calls to seek out job opportunities that he had trouble picking up the phone, let alone talking into it. Initially, Joe came to us to ask if we'd be willing to place that first, tough telephone call to break the ice for him.

Hank Turner, a former operations vice president over 60, was conditioned to believe that he'd have to slide into retirement after his termination because no one, anywhere, was being hired in his area of expertise—and especially not people over 60. The market was too overpopulated with young hotshots for that to happen.

Tracy Miller was a recent college graduate with a computer degree. All of her work experience was unrelated to her chosen field and performed in short-term spurts to help put herself through school. Tracy was concerned people would not take notice of her, especially with competition from foreign candidates.

Rather than succumbing to the deceptive warnings of many so-called experts who say that it will take one month of searching for every $10,000 you earn, let's look at the facts instead as they relate to our three clients and how they applied the Cycle of Success:

Joe Williams applied himself fully to our program, bought into our concepts and within two months was working the phones as though he'd done it all his life. More important, within another month he'd generated three fine job offers. Incredibly, Joe orchestrated the pace and timing of those offers so that all three were on the table on a Friday afternoon—every *t* crossed and every *i* dotted, ready for his evaluation and final answer. He took the weekend to discuss the offers with his family, came back on Monday and said yes to the company he thought offered the best opportunity with significantly more money.

This was a textbook case—in three months, he'd progressed from ground zero to the top one percent of all job hunters. Joe transformed the worst event of his life into a turning point in his life—for the better. Now he's living in a community of about 20,000 people—just what he and his family had wanted. He's working for a small engineering company, which he preferred over a multinational corporate giant. And he's working in municipal construction, where business and the new company is booming—away from the stressful atmosphere of an industry in transition.

Hank Turner, the former Operations Vice President, took his search in another direction but nonetheless generated similar positive results. Cut loose from his firm, Hank spent the first 45 days networking, re-establishing contact with people all over the world. Ultimately, he didn't have to accept early retirement. Instead, he was placed in a senior operations consulting role with a foreign steel manufacturer.

The startling part of Hank's story is that his new employer had an absolute, international hiring freeze in force. Yet Hank networked his way into the firm, leveraged his contact—in this case, the Chairman of the Board—to the limit, and got the offer. So not only did he get another job, but it was a better job, with more responsibility and more money and with a better company. Even the term *better job* doesn't touch upon the magnitude of his accomplishment, however. What Hank created was his *ideal job.* He analyzed what the steel company needed in order to get where it had to go. Then he built a scenario detailing how his skills could help it get there, by utilizing our requirements/qualifications letter (see Exhibit 28, pages 206-207). When he was ready, he sold the idea to the Chairman. He created his own new job, structuring for himself a position of duties that included those he had always enjoyed performing while eliminating those he didn't enjoy. What might have been the end of his career had been transformed into an opportunity to make the last five years of his career the best years of his career.

One aside: During his job search, Hank kept hearing one objection repeatedly, "You're over qualified." Of course, that's a polite and legal way of telling an applicant "You're too old." So Hank conceived the best answer we've ever encountered to the underlying objection. When he sensed that the interviewer was building toward the stock objection, he would preempt it by saying, "Well, I have thirty-five years of operations experience and that's what you need. The fact is, if you want someone with thirty-five years' work experience, you're going to have to hire an older person." Not only was his response clever, it met the test of any selling statement. Rather than trying to shield or minimize a negative perception, Hank faced the potential objection head-on and diffused it by transforming it into a positive with a bit of humor. And he sold the chairman by demonstrating, through his accomplishments on his resume, what his five-year contribution to the bottom line would be.

In our third client example, Tracy Miller followed our advice outlined in Chapter 3 on presenting her work experience in the most favorable light. While unrelated to her chosen field, it showed many other desirable attributes and skills. Tracy was conscientious and hard working and had demonstrated her willingness to perform any task necessary to get the job done. She was thorough and cared about the quality of her work. Finally, her resume reflected the skills she had acquired through school, not only her technical computer skills, but her writing and problem-solving skills. Tracy was surprised that employers cared about her background and skills. As a result of her networking, she received two offers, one with a small computer marketing firm and one with a larger computer applications development company. After considering the pluses and minuses of each offer and negotiating the best offer with each, she selected the marketing firm position because she felt it would give her the greatest exposure to multiple roles; it would be her best first professional experience. In addition, it was for considerably more money than she expected!

All three of these former clients met our test of what makes people succeed in job search. Just as thousands of our clients whom we've helped over the years have done, they organized and implemented a personal assault on the job market. We take considerable pride in contributing to that success. All were placed within a three-month period. But we don't presume to take all the credit, because we didn't conduct their job searches for them. We push, pull, lead, and counsel—whatever is most needed. The individual does the work, investigates the company, conducts a needs analysis, then devises a sales presentation designed to convince the company that he or she can solve their problems.

Just as these clients did it, you can do it. We can't tell you the precise words to say, because it's *your* background you're selling. We can't tell you precisely which companies are hiring or which to select as networking contacts—that's your role. If you do it well, you'll have access to those jobs a step ahead of the rest of the job search world. You'll catch those jobs before they "go public" with listings in state employment services, search firms, and online.

You will have identified the company's needs, you will have orchestrated a scenario establishing that your skills and background can benefit the company in an area of need, and you will communicate those facts in your networking, cold-calling, and interviewing opportunities. This is how you find jobs. In subsequent chapters, we'll discuss extensively how each element works. But prepare yourself to accept the fact that *you* must do the work. We'll put up some signposts, guardrails, and speed limits to help you through the tough parts and keep you on course.

It's central to our philosophy of job search that you take on this responsibility for your own campaign. Remember, you will find a job. Anyone can do that—almost everyone does eventually. That's not an issue in your search. What job you find is an issue. Now we're getting into variables. What job you get and how long your search takes are controlled primarily by you, not by market conditions. It doesn't take a mathematical genius to figure out that if you work five hours a day and find your new position in six months, you might find that same position in three months if you work ten hours a day. What you do with those hours is as important as the basic decision to use them for work. For example, during prime business hours, you work the telephone, networking and cold-calling. In the evenings and on weekends, you read, research, answer newspaper ads, search the internet, and otherwise use the time when you won't be able to reach most people by phone. That's how you build a winning job search formula. And that's how you achieve placement in record time.

**Build Your Own...
Cycle of Success!**
If you work hard, you'll take pride in what you're doing. When you're proud, you're confident. And when you're confident, you become more proficient at job search and more attractive to employers. That's linkage in action.

THERE'S NO MAGIC FORMULA

We know our principles work. They work so well, in part, because they're so old. Like bad cars, bad ideas never have a chance to get old. Don't assume that you must "reinvent the wheel" to find a job. People search endlessly for the final solution—some internet solution that will replace the traditional methods of job search. The fallacy of this approach, however, is that there's nothing wrong with the traditional steps. People fail with them not because of the methods but because of the implementation. In other words, they don't find new positions because they don't work hard and long enough and because their ability to communicate their skills and attitude aren't yet ready for a nose-to-nose and toes-to-toes session with an employer. In contrast, you can build your own *Cycle of Success*. If you work hard, you'll take pride in what you're doing. When you're proud, you're confident. And when you're confident, you become more proficient at job search and more attractive to employers. That's *linkage* in action. You eliminate negative attitudes because you're busy locating job openings or networking into new companies. If you follow our advice to the letter, you'll start your search a step ahead of about 99 percent of all job hunters.

Let's look briefly at some concerns with which job hunters must deal.

SEPARATION BENEFITS

You negotiate going into a job, so don't think it out of place to negotiate when you go out. You should initiate discussions with your immediate superior and provide a list of what you need to make the transition to your next position easier. At the top of most lists would be salary continuation and health insurance coverage. Outplacement is one of the most valuable negotiable separation benefits— ask for it if the company has not included it in your package. Whether in an employee's or an employer's job market, transition services are valuable to the organization to retain good will and a positive reputation, as well as to the individual transitioning.

BUDGET

You probably already have a workable budget for your household. If you don't, institute one immediately. You'll need it now, more than ever, during your job search. For your current purposes, however, you don't use a budget simply to monitor income and outgo. During job search, your budget becomes a key player in the goals and time periods you establish for each step in your campaign. For example, if your budget calculations indicate that your household can continue operating for three months on reduced income, you can plan on establishing a three-month job search campaign. Like every other phase of our instructions, your budget links with the time frame you've set to regulate your entire job search calendar.

GOAL-SETTING

We're assuming that you've utilized goal-setting as an important component of your professional success to this point. Don't abandon it now. Like all goals, your job search goals should be realistic, specific, timed, and measurable. To assist you in goal-setting from the beginning of your job campaign, Exhibit 1 provides a form for getting started. As you read the chapters that explain the tasks outlined on the form, set your goals for completion and monitor your own progress.

SPECIAL SITUATIONS

In addition to these concerns, following are suggestions for applying *The Total System* to a diversity of career and life situations. Whatever your particular circumstance, the techniques throughout this book can be adapted to ensure your success whether or not the following situations apply to you.

NEW COLLEGE GRADUATE

As we learned from Tracy Miller's case described earlier, the new college graduate has more to offer than he or she usually realizes. While it may seem that experience in minimum wage and part-time jobs, as well as in co-curricular activities and organizations, is impossible to translate into skill-based accomplishment statements, it is not. And doing so is essential to properly and effectively market or sell yourself to an employer. Your resume at the kick-off of your career is just as important as it will be at mid-career and in your pre-retirement years. Take time to evaluate your work history in terms of employers' needs and requirements and you will be surprised at your own capabilities. Also respond to the assessment questions in this chapter to assist you in this evaluation. Finally, review the sample accomplishment statements for new graduates in Chapter 3 and in the Sample Resumes as you draft your resume.

ENHANCING CREDENTIALS

If you have reached a plateau in your career, or lack skills or requirements essential for continued advancement in your industry or functional responsibility, now may be the time to consider enhancing your credentials. Taking certification courses, completing skills training, or entering a degree program may be just the boost you need to energize your career. When employed, check with your manager and/or human resources department to identify what learning opportunities are available internally, what the educational reimbursement policy is, and what other training or support resources are available. Plan carefully to ensure that the programs you select will enhance your credentials for the long term as well as the short term.

When between jobs, and considering your next employer, you may wish to review their developmental and training opportunities before accepting an offer.

Once you have completed the training and educational plan, use your accomplishment as one more negotiating tool for advancement when employed, and to market yourself when you are job searching. Be sure to include credentials, education, and training on your resume. You may also wish to highlight recent enhancements of credentials in your resume summary and/or in your cover letter. The point is, when you are better qualified, your value to a company increases along with your *psychological leverage*.

EARLY RETIREE

Whether you voluntarily opt for an early retirement package or are faced with separation that includes an involuntary retirement option, if you still want to work and financially need to work, then you can work! With the aging of the population worldwide, companies are learning to take advantage of this growing segment of the workforce. To prepare for the inevitable — no one can stop the clock — follow these recommendations:

- Keep your skills current—continue to learn.

- Do not allow yourself to become complacent in a job, "coasting to retirement."

- Keep your network current, including younger contacts.

- Maintain your health and fitness.

- When job searching, emphasize your maturity, experience, energy, work ethic, and flexibility.

- Consider contract/consulting options as an "early retirement" career opportunity; if benefits are not a concern to you, then let companies know — it will build your leverage with them.

Age is not a problem unless you think or act "old." We have had clients in their seventies who successfully placed because they followed these tenets for remaining marketable at any age.

RETURNING TO THE WORKFORCE

The fear and lack of confidence felt by a just-terminated employee is often insignificant compared to that felt by the individual returning to the workforce after raising a family or returning to school for a degree. Out-of-step with the workforce for a number of years, the returning candidate feels that he or she is no competition for seasoned workers or younger graduates. If you are in that circumstance, take heart! You too have more to offer than you think. First, is your maturity. Yes, that is a plus and you should use it to your advantage as you present yourself. Whether or not you've just received a degree, you must take stock of your skills, both technical as well as interpersonal, and your organizational skills. Do not overlook experience in the nonprofit or volunteer association arenas. While you may not have been compensated for these roles, no doubt you did make significant contributions and developed skills. In particular, communication, organizational, presentation, fund-raising and team building skills are often highly developed through such associations and assignments. Just because they were achieved part-time or were uncompensated makes them no less valuable to an employer. Some examples of return-to-work successes follow.

> Martha had raised her family and traveled extensively as her husband pursued his career. She had been active in PTA as well as volunteer organizations, including the Red Cross and a hospital. She sought to begin a career in health care by emphasizing her exposure to this industry through her volunteer activities. Martha's resume reflected excellent communication and leadership abilities, which were demonstrated by her accomplishments in various volunteer projects. Her contacts in these various organizations were also very helpful as she networked into a position in the patient relations department of a hospital. Her international travel and exposure to other cultures was also an asset in obtaining the job offer since many patients were from other countries.

> After teaching for several years following graduation, Connie had focused her energies on her family for many years. She was ready to return to work, but was terrified of the prospect because she had not participated in any significant activities outside the home since her teaching years. She developed a resume from her early teaching experience and began to contact her seemingly limited network. To her surprise, a friend suggested contacting the school's credit union where she successfully interviewed for a part-time position. Her confidence boosted, Connie began working. She discovered that her organizational and communication skills were well-developed compared with her younger co-workers. Connie quickly became a full-time employee and after establishing an excellent performance record and learning the credit union's procedures, she was promoted within 18 months to a supervisory role.

Examine the return-to-work and nonprofit *A+ Sample Resumes* in *The Total System* online complementary resources for examples of how to present these experiences. If you were not involved in these activities and primarily focused on family needs, then your sales task is a greater challenge. But if you want to work or must work, you can. First, believe in yourself, then evaluate your capabilities through the assessment in this chapter, and finally utilize the techniques throughout the book to get off to the best start possible as you return to work. Once working you can rebuild your experience, prove yourself to your employer and move on to bigger and better opportunities in the future using the same techniques.

CHANGING CAREERS

Career change is certainly a viable option for someone coming out of a stagnant industry. But be sure that you comprehend the parameters. If you have grown tired of industrial engineering for the automobile industry because there has been too little new product development, and you are thinking of aeronautics, think again. That may not be a profitable or wise career change. Jump from a declining industry if that's best for you, but be certain that you pick a landing spot that can best utilize your skills. Otherwise, you'll walk into a lineup with the rest of the rookies. Build on what you've done, and what you can bring to the bottom line in terms of results and accomplishments as presented in your resume. Don't hastily chuck it all just because of a transitory economic slowdown.

On the other hand, if you have in mind a change of careers for other personal reasons, then building on past experience may not be as relevant. For instance, if you have been in manufacturing operations for many years, have grown tired of the repetition of your work, and now would like to enter health care, your technical manufacturing skills will probably not help you make the transition. This type of career change may require additional training or degree work and may necessitate beginning at the entry level to make the transition. This is a personal choice only you can make, but researching the alternatives and evaluating your potential for success based on your self-assessment and discussions with others in your field of interest are essential before making the change.

To assist you in evaluating the possibility of changing careers, answer these questions:

- What specific careers hold the most appeal for me?
- What are current market conditions in those careers?
- Are there related occupations I need to learn about?
- Whom do I know in this field? Whom do they know?
- What about other options — independent business, entrepreneurial organization, consulting?

INDUSTRY/FUNCTION TRANSITIONS

The key to changing industries or functional areas is transferable skills. If you desire a change or the marketplace necessitates a change, use self-assessment to identify your skills. Then research viable areas to which your skills are transferable and build your job search campaign strategy around them. Using linkage, highlight those skills in your resume, cover letter, networking, and interviewing. Be sure to do your homework on the industry, function, and companies that you target. Reading the literature of the industry or function and talking with professionals in those areas is essential to learning the unique language of the field, understanding its goals and needs, and identifying how your transferable skills apply.

MILITARY TO CIVILIAN

Making the change from the military to the civilian workforce is similar to the career change process, but can be even more challenging and perhaps disconcerting. The questions relating to changing careers outlined earlier should be answered initially. Use the self-assessment section in this chapter and research the fields and industries of primary interest to you or to which your skills most readily apply as the next essential steps. Translating your military experience into language that civilian employers can understand and relate to is critical to a successful transition. Your technical and management training and experience coupled with the military's strong results-oriented focus are highly marketable attributes to emphasize. Be prepared too for very different relationships between employee and employer, manager and subordinate. No longer will there be a rigid chain-of-command and strict structure to the workplace. But, while the civilian workplace has more informal structures, you may have much to offer in terms of valuing teamwork and applying team principles to achievement of organizational goals. Be sure to emphasize these assets as you present your skills to employers. An example of a military transition follows.

> Howard was a pilot who had completed his service and was floundering in presenting himself to civilian employers. His father-in-law suggested he visit with us. He applied *The Total System* from restructuring his resume to networking to interviewing. Emphasizing his work ethic, strong technical skills, maturity, and professionalism, Howard landed a position as a pilot with a commercial airline. Within two years, he realized that he was ready to change careers and continued to apply *The Total System* principles. Howard successfully made another job and career transition to purchasing.

Be sure to examine the military-to-civilian Sample Resumes when writing your resume as recommended in Chapter 3.

ADVANCING YOUR CAREER

Besides these special situations and the inevitable loss of a job that one faces from time to time in a volatile job market, everyone wants to advance their career! Let's face it, if you want to improve your job or your pay, YOU must take responsibility for making that happen. The company you work for may offer assistance along the way, but ultimate responsibility lies with you, and no one else. Have you reached a plateau? Been passed over for promotion? Lost out to a younger employee? Have you been pigeon-holed because you are "too important" to the company in your current role? Considered a threat to your boss? Side-lined because of competition? Whatever the reason for your dissatisfaction, you can do something about it.

If you want to advance in your current company, visit with your boss, mentor, or human resources manager about your options. Often companies are very committed to retention and will do their best to help you prepare for another role in the company.

If you want to change companies, than begin to put your job search strategy together through The Total System. All of the steps and techniques outlined here are applicable. Just because you have a job does not mean you can take short cuts in advancing your career. You must have a well designed game plan and implement it deliberately. Let's get started!

ASSESSING STRENGTHS AND WEAKNESSES

Ideally, career assessment should be done professionally. We offer highly accurate and effective behavioral and career assessment resources to our clients and frequently, universities and colleges have assessment centers where you can complete a professional career assessment very cost-effectively. If you must do it yourself, first make a list of your likes and dislikes. When you've identified a potential direction, then the work really starts. Do your research and networking to discover the career possibilities in the chosen area.

SELF-ASSESSMENT

To evaluate *where you've been, where you are,* and *where you're going,* complete the following self-assessment questionnaires. They are designed to help you focus on the factors that are important in targeting your job search.

PERSONAL ASSESSMENT

1. How do you feel about your current situation?

2. How does your family (spouse, children, parents) feel about your current situation?

3. What people or groups do you feel will be most supportive of you at this time?

4. How would you describe your energy level at this time? (Consider physical and psychological factors.)

5. What three personal qualities do you consider to be your greatest strengths?

   a.

   b.

   c.

6. What three personal qualities would you most like to change about yourself?

   a.

b.

c.

7. Have you begun to make these changes? (If not, why not?)

8. How do you use your personal time?

9. What topics do you enjoy reading and talking about?

10. What must you achieve during your lifetime in order to consider yourself a success?

11. What are your short-term personal goals (for the next 1 to 5 years)?

12. What are your long-term personal goals (for the next 6 to 20 years)?

PAST CAREER ASSESSMENT

Also critical to this process is a self-analysis of what you've done in the past. This is a good time to separate personalities from actual occupational problems. For 10 years, you might have thought you were out of place as a computer programmer. Now, in retrospect, you might discover that programming is fine — it's the ingrate you worked for all those years that made your life miserable. Part of our conviction that job search is a positive experience is rooted in the idea that this is the perfect time to sort out all these emotions. Evaluate all the data, then set a new course.

1. Why did you select the career opportunities or jobs you have held in the past?

2. Have you been doing what you felt you wanted to do or what you had to do?

3. List the titles of the jobs you have held throughout your career, in order, from the first job to your most recent.

4. Do you feel you were well suited to your most recent position? (Why or why not?)

5. What did you like about your most recent position, job, or other activity, such as volunteer work or co-curricular associations?

6. What did you dislike about your most recent position, job, or other activity, such as volunteer work or co-curricular associations?

7. What skills or personal qualities have you been complimented on by previous employers, professors, or association affiliations?

8. What, to your knowledge, have employers, co-workers, and/or subordinates found fault with? Did more than one person have the same complaint?

9. Have you held a position in the past that you would describe as your ideal job? (If so, what was this position and what characteristics of this job made it ideal for you?)

FUTURE CAREER ASSESSMENT

1. Which of the following occupations or functions are of special interest to you? (Circle your choices.)

Accounting/bookkeeping

Acting

Administration

Advertising

Agriculture

Anthropology

Archeology

Architecture

Art (fine, commercial)

Athletics

Aviation

Banking

Biomedical technology

Biological Sciences

Building, construction and maintenance

Business development

Communications systems/ technology

Community service

Computer technology – software/ hardware

Consulting

Customer relations/service

Dancing

Decorating

Dentistry

Distribution

Domestic and personal services

Ecology/natural sciences

Economic analysis

Education

Electronics

Engineering/technical specialties, industrial applications, design

Entertainment

Environmental technology

Finance

Financial planning

Fine manual work

Firefighting

Food/restaurant

Forestry

Geology

Government contracts/relations

Government and public service

Graphic arts

Health care

Health and safety

Home economics

Human resources

Information technology

Insurance/risk management

Internet technology

Landscaping

Languages

Law

Law enforcement

Library

Machine operation and repair

Maintenance

Management

Manufacturing

Mathematics

Mechanical design and construction/repair

Medicine

Military

Ministry

Music

Non-profit associations

Oceanography

Operations

Organization planning

Packaging

Performing arts

Photography

Physical services

Policy development

Product/process design, development

Production (planning, scheduling controls)

Psychologist/counselor

Public relations

Publishing and printing

Purchasing/procurement

Quality control/assurance

Real estate

Research/investigation

Retail/merchandising

Safety/housekeeping

Sales/marketing

Scientist

Securities

Security

Social services

Social work

Strategic planning

Systems analysis (methods, procedures, control)

Taxes

Teaching

Technical services

Technician

Telemarketing/call centers

Telecommunications

Therapy

Training

Transportation

Travel and leisure

Warehousing/inventory

Waste management

Wholesaling

Word processing/clerical

Writing/journalism

Other: _____

_____

_____

2. How do you rank the following in terms of importance to you? (Rank the most important as 1 and the least important as 12.)

_____   Earnings

_____   Working conditions

_____   Tasks of the job

_____   Status of the job

_____   People I'd work with

_____   Chance to do important work

_____   Supervisor I'd report to

_____   Job security

_____   Opportunity for advancement

_____   Benefit program

_____   Opportunity to use abilities and interests

_____   Opportunity to learn

3. How would you describe your ideal job today?

_____

_____

_____

_____

_____

_____

_____

4. Which of the following *skills* and *abilities* do you have that would make this an ideal job for you? (Circle your choices.)

Analyzing/synthesizing

Artistic design

Communications/verbal (speeches, presentations, teaching, languages, writing, etc.)

Conceptual

Controlling

Coordinating

Creative

Data/details (figures, records, systems, controls, research)

Decision making

Idea generation (ingenuity, original thinking)

Interpersonal (people sensitivity)

Intuitive

Innovative

Judgment, strategic

Leadership (directing, motivating)

Listening

Making money

Management/supervisory

Mechanical/manual

Memory

Negotiating

Observant

Organizational

Planning

Problem identification/solving

Resourcefulness

Teamwork

Technical

Other: _____

_____

_____

_____

_____

5. What special *knowledge* and *experience* do you have that would make this an ideal job for you? (Circle your choices.)

Accounting/bookkeeping

Acting

Administration

Advertising

Agriculture

Anthropology

Archeology

Architecture

Art (fine, commercial)

Athletics

Aviation

Banking

Biomedical technology

Biological sciences

Building, construction and maintenance

Business development

Communications systems/technology

Community service

Computer technology – software/hardware

Consulting

Customer relations/service

Dancing

Decorating

Dentistry

Distribution

Domestic and personal services

Ecology/natural sciences

Economic analysis

Education

Electronics

Engineering/technical specialties, industrial applications, design

Entertainment

Environmental technology

Finance

Financial planning

Fine manual work

Firefighting

Food/restaurant

Forestry

Geology

Government contracts/relations

Government and public service

Graphic arts

Health care

Health and safety

Home economics

Human resources

Information technology

Internet technology

Insurance/risk management

Landscaping

Languages

Law

Law enforcement

Library

Machine operation and repair

Maintenance

Management

Manufacturing

Mathematics

Mechanical design and construction/repair

Medicine

Military

Ministry

Music

Non-profit associations

Oceanography

Operations

Organization planning

Packaging

Performing arts

Photography

Physical services

Policy development

Product/process design, development

Production (planning, scheduling controls)

Psychologist/counselor

Public relations

Publishing and printing

Purchasing/procurement

Quality control/assurance

Real estate

Research/investigation

Retail/merchandising

Safety/housekeeping

Sales/marketing

Scientist

Securities

Security

Social services

Social work

Strategic planning

Systems analysis (methods, procedures, control)

Taxes

Teaching

Technical services

Technician

Telecommunications

Telemarketing

Therapy

Training

Transportation

Travel and leisure

Warehousing/inventory

Waste management

Wholesaling

Word processing/clerical

Writing/journalism

Other:_____

_____

_____

_____

6. Which of the following *personal qualities* do you have that would make this an ideal job for you? (Circle your choices.)

I am:

Accurate	Energetic
Alert	Enterprising
Analytical	Enthusiastic
Assertive	Extroverted
Authoritative	Fair
Calm	Flexible/adaptable
Cautious	Friendly
Charismatic	Gregarious
Compassionate	Growth-oriented
Competitive	Humorous
Concept-oriented	Idealistic
Conceptual	Independent
Confident	Individualistic
Consistent	Ingenious
Content to be alone	Innovative
Cooperative	Insightful
Courageous	Inspiring
Creative	Intelligent
Decisive	Introspective
Dedicated	Introverted
Deep thinking	Intuitive
Deliberate	Knowledgeable
Dependable/reliable	Likeable
Diligent	Logical
Direct	Long-range planner
Discreet/tactful/diplomatic	Lucky
Easy to converse with/share with	Magnetic
Economical	Methodical
Effective communicator	Objective
Empathetic	Open/flexible

Organized

Original/imaginative

Participative

Patient

Perceptive

Persistent

Persuasive

Practical/realistic/pragmatic

Professional

Prudent

Punctual

Quality conscious

Rational

Receptive

Reflective/quiet

Responsible

Resourceful

Results oriented

Sensitive to others

Solid/unwavering

Sparkling

Spontaneous

Stabilizing

Thorough

Uncomplaining

Understanding

Versatile

Well-organized

Other:_____

_____

_____

_____

I can:

Anticipate problems

Appreciate excellence

Commit to cause

Cut through emotional smokescreens

Delegate well

Develop systems

Draw out feelings

Follow through

Get things done

Get to the core of the problems

Impose high standards

Increase cooperation/teamwork

Keep current (knowledgeable)

Keep others informed

Meet deadlines

Resolve conflicts

See inter-relationships

See the "big picture"

Strive for excellence

Take calculated risks

Take and give orders

Take responsibility   Weigh alternatives

Think quickly   Work well under stress

Use time effectively   Work with minimal supervision

Value ideas

Other:_____

_____

_____

_____

I have:

Energy/drive

Initiative

Preference for people, variety, action

Rich friendships

Sense of timing/priorities

Other: _____

_____

_____

_____

7. What additional capabilities, experience, or educational qualifications would you need to acquire in order to be well prepared for your ideal job?

8. What are your greatest strengths which apply to the job?

9. How can these strengths benefit an employer?

10. What are your potential weaknesses which apply to work?

11. How can you eliminate these potential weaknesses or turn them into a benefit for an employer?

12. What is your short-term career goal (for the next one to five years)?

13. What is your long-term career goal (for the next six to twenty years)?

14. How do your career goals relate to the career and life goals of your family members?

15. Do you believe that your ideal job is attainable today? (If so, please explain.)

16. If not, what major obstacles stand in the way?

17. Can you overcome these obstacles to achieve your career goals? (If not, please explain.)

18. Would you relocate for the right career opportunity? (If so, where are you prepared to relocate?)

19. What specific jobs have you targeted for your employment search?

20. Are the jobs you have targeted realistic career goals, given the nature of the current marketplace?

21. Do you prefer a small, medium, or large firm?

22. Do you want to work in a highly charged environment or a more evenly paced one?

23. What leadership style is compatible with yours?

24. Are you willing and able to risk joining a relatively new company?

25. Have you targeted specific companies you would like to join? (If so, list these companies and state the factors that attracted you to them.)

26. How hard would you be willing to work to join one of these companies?

27. Do you want to explore consulting, independent business, or other opportunities? (If so, why?)

28. Using the pie diagram, how would you divide your level of interest in three options:

a. Company position/employment
b. Consulting/Contract Work
c. Independent Business

Example   **Your Priorities**

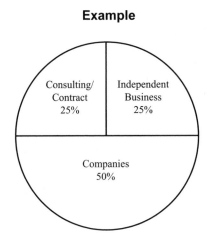
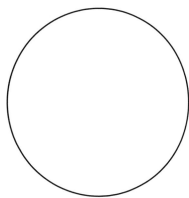

29. Based on your priorities, how do you plan to allocate your research/
    networking time among these three options?

    a. Company position/employment   __ %
    b. Consulting/Contract Work   __ %
    c. Independent Business   __ %

30. Have you set a personal goal regarding when you expect to be employed
    or earning income from consulting or a business venture? (If so, what is
    the date? If you have not set a date, please explain.)

31. How many hours per week do you plan to work to achieve this goal?

SET YOUR GOAL

Having completed your self-assessment, review it carefully and set your goal for
the position or independent opportunity you desire. Illustrations of how important
goal setting is to achieving the right job for you follow:

Vance was a new college graduate who wanted to go on to medical school. Unfortunately, he had not yet been accepted, so he needed work. He was depressed about his situation, but we encouraged him to target medical research institutions to strengthen his ability to gain acceptance in medical school. He was skeptical about his marketability, but after putting a winning resume together and identifying institutions to target, he found employment in 6 weeks with a research institute.

Phillip had progressed from technical positions to Vice President of Business Development when a merger eliminated his position. At 57, he wondered what he could do as a next step in his career. After reviewing the self-assessment, he realized that he could market himself either for another corporate position with a medium-sized firm or pursue consulting opportunities. He chose to explore both simultaneously, dividing his networking time equally initially, but remaining flexible to reallocate his time as opportunities arose.

These are just two examples of how the assessment process links to the job campaign. If Vance had merely looked in the classifieds or took the first job that was available, he probably would have settled for a job unrelated to his degree or career aspirations. For Phillip, pursuing multiple objectives gave him greater flexibility and increased his ability to market his capabilities. Setting a goal based on your assessment is an essential step in landing not just a job, but the *best* job for you and your career.

CAUTIONS

Although we set world records for emphasis on positive thinking, a few *don'ts* can help eliminate grief and streamline your search.

• *Don't take time off.* You don't deserve a reward until you have accepted your new position — then take the time you need before you start.

• *Don't assume that your closest networking contacts know all there is to know about you.* Even your best friend may have misconceptions about what you can do and where you've done it. You must tell them explicitly what you're aiming toward and what you want them to do for you.

• *Don't take rejection personally.* It's a normal by-product of job search. Learn to transform an initial no answer into a positive conclusion for you. Obviously, the majority of the contacts you make will not have an opening, and if you stop there you will be wallowing in negative feedback. We insist that your contact shouldn't stop with a *no*. Push the phone call forward. If you can't get a job offer or a lead, get additional names you can contact. In that way, almost every call becomes positive. One of the job search theories we dislike most is the Mickey Mouse exercise called "the rule of no's." The idea is to write the word no on a piece of paper several hundred times, then write yes at the bottom, and paste the paper on your wall. Then, each time someone tells you no, rejoice and cross one no off, because you're even closer to your yes. We dislike that because it's a cop out. If your phone calls are all ending in no's, the problem is you. Learn to cold-call (Chapter 7), improve your technique, and meet your goals. If you won't be satisfied with a *no,* we guarantee you won't hear it as often in your job search.

- *Don't count on one hot lead working out.* The most encouraging network contacts—the hottest leads—turn up stone cold more often than not. Never wait on one contact to bear fruit. Keep working and keep making your contacts. Remember, you don't have a job, and your search isn't completed until you have an offer, have accepted it, and have started working in your new position.

- *Don't expect search firms, and online job listings or resume data banks to do all your work.* Combined, these sources account for at most 10 to 30 percent of job placements. Yet most people spend 100 percent of their time working these sources. When you read about rejection, depression, and endless searches for new jobs, the victimized people are almost without exception the people who rely on agencies, search firms and online listings. That is the easy way, the lazy way. But it usually doesn't work, because you're competing with the whole world. Also, be aware that when you use a search firm, although you're dealing with someone who professes to be able to assist you, in reality he or she is an agent of the employer and is looking out, first, for the interests of the company. The people who network are the people who get the best jobs first.

> The people who network are the people who get the best jobs first.

- *Don't keep the bad news to yourself.* If you've been terminated, don't be embarrassed about telling close friends and family members. They can help in two ways. During the initial period, when you're dealing with your emotions, they are your best support system. Then they become the first names on your networking lists.

- *Don't call a lawyer.* We teach job search as a win-win proposition. Filing suit against your former employer violates every rule of positive thinking and smart planning that we teach. By engaging in a lawsuit, you're focusing on the past. Remember, that's beyond control. Even if you win a lawsuit — and ten years from now get back pay, reinstatement, or a settlement — so what? You've wallowed in bitterness and anger for all those years, and that's not any way to live and work. Termination isn't a disaster; it's an opportunity. Get on with your future. Let your former employer be an asset to your future through an excellent reference.

Now for the last caution before you begin structuring your job search:

Let your former employer be an asset to your future through an excellent reference.

- *Don't fall prey to unprofessional agencies.* In every field there are those who are in it to take advantage of others' situations—job search and career counseling is no exception. When people are unemployed they can be vulnerable to agencies that overcharge for the services rendered. Anyone who wants your money up front for job *placement* is suspect in our view. Frequently, they are called retail placement firms, but whatever their title, if they want your money first, be certain you know what services you are getting in return.

A reputable search agency is paid by the company listing a job. In some cases, the individual job hunter pays the freight—but only after services have been rendered and you have a job. Certainly there are legitimate career counselors who can support you in resume preparation and other steps in the job search process. Our caution is, buyer beware--check references and credentials before considering these services. Don't get hooked up with some fast talking charlatan who'll give you a resume and a computer printout, and promises of placement that have no basis for credibility. If you feel pressured to sign on the bottom line and write a check for more than you are comfortable paying, than take time to go home and consider the value of the services and your need for them. Often these operations will use psychological tactics to make you feel inadequate to find work on your own merit or efforts.

If you are unemployed and your income has stopped, you need to monitor your cash flow more than ever. It is disheartening and embarrassing to spend money on services that do not help your job search. We recall one client whose experience sums it up best:

> After completing our outplacement seminar as a corporate-sponsored client, Bill Brown commented that several years before, he'd fallen prey to one such job search consulting service. The experience cost him nearly $6,000. Bill told us, "You people actually do what they promised they would do. I spent all that money and got nothing but a half-baked resume in return. I'm really ashamed to admit I did that. I'm a lawyer and I'm supposed to know better than that."

If you would like professional assistance from a reputable career counselor or outplacement firm, the following criteria distinguish the pros from the peddlers:

1. Seek good, solid references, credentials, and a proven track record of success.

2. Review services carefully; they should be clearly defined with samples of resumes, letters, and materials.

3. Evaluate whether services promised can be met by their staff, facilities, and credentials.

4. Evaluate the environment and sales approach—if it makes you feel pressured and uncomfortable, leave!

5. Avoid high-pressure techniques or psychological hooks which make you feel inadequate. You should be encouraged, motivated, and energized by professional and knowledgeable assistance.

Now, with the main issues and cautions on the table, let's move on to the first actual step of job search — deciding if *a job* is really what you want!

EXHIBIT 1
Personal Marketing Plan: Getting Started

TASKS TO COMPLETE	GOAL	DATE COMPLETED

(1) ASSESSMENT
   (A) Evaluate career goals
   (B) Explore independent
      business options
	(A) _____
	(B) _____
		(A) _____
		(B) _____

(2) RESUME
   (A) First draft
   (B) Second draft
   (C) Final draft
	(A) _____
	(B) _____
	(C) _____
		(A) _____
		(B) _____
		(C) _____

(3) GENERIC LETTERS
   (A) Cover
   (B) Search Firm
   (C) Ad response
	(A) _____
	(B) _____
	(C) _____
		(A) _____
		(B) _____
		(C) _____

(4) REFERENCE LETTERS
   (A) Boss
   (B) Boss's boss
   (C) Peer and others
	(A) _____
	(B) _____
	(C) _____
		(A) _____
		(B) _____
		(C) _____

(5) NETWORKING
   (A) Personal/professional
      contact list
   (B) Target companies (initial list)
      (i) A priority (high)
      (ii) B priority (medium)
      (iii) C priority (low)
	(A) _____
	(B) _____
		(A) _____
		(B) _____

(6) SEARCH FIRM LIST		
(7) IDENTIFY AD RESPONSE SOURCES		
(8) PRACTICE INTERVIEWING		
(9) IMPLEMENT PERSONAL MARKETING		
(10) PLACEMENT (NEW POSITION)		

Electronic Forms are available in *The Total System Organizer*

Before You Search: Explore Independent Options

It's only Chapter 2, and already we're telling you not to look for a job—at least not yet. (We promised this wouldn't be run-of-the-mill career advice.) The fact is that we want everyone who's looking for a new position to consider contract, consulting, or entrepreneurial ventures first, before plugging into the traditional employee environment. We don't want to push anyone into a field for which he or she is not suited, but it's imperative that you look at entrepreneurship now, if you've ever had an interest in it. After you're in a new position, you'll only be second-guessing whether you might have succeeded independently. So stop now and analyze whether or not your skills and personality might successfully drive a small business, consulting operation, or contract work relationship. Whether you are faced with a voluntary or involuntary change, military-to-civilian transition, return to work, early retirement, seeking to advance your career, or other work change scenarios, do not skip this chapter.

Independent work options are becoming increasingly important in our changing economy. The advent of the information age and globalization of industries has changed the way work is done and forced companies to restructure, reengineer and redefine their missions. As a result, the contingent workforce has grown dramatically. Part-timers, self-employed, temporary workers, freelancers, consultants, leased employees, and independent contractors may represent as much as 35% or more of the workforce. This market place reality suggests that you may be forced to consider these options, whether or not you prefer them. Taking control of your career and planning for your next inevitable change is more important than ever to your career success.

> 35% or more of the workforce is contingent!

BE YOUR OWN BOSS

Self-reliance and individualism are values that the new work trend promotes. Adapt them to your career and you will discover a whole new realm of possibilities opening up before you. If you seek only a traditional job, given the contingency work trend, you've eliminated about one-third of work alternatives! To help you adapt to being your own boss, acquire or develop the following:

1. Ability to identify the value of your work to an organization in terms of bottom line results.
2. Ability to demonstrate your value in each work situation you find yourself.
3. A view of yourself as an external vendor, rather than a traditional employee — if you become a contingent worker, you will be anyway!
4. A perception of being in business for yourself. Even if you are an employee, consider that your company has "outsourced" certain responsibilities to you.
5. A commitment to career-long self-development. Look for ways to develop your skills, expand your responsibilities, and learn new functions.
6. Responsibility for your health insurance, retirement funds, and negotiating your compensation as your work situation changes (whether as an employee or independent worker).
7. Ability to work effectively in teams, to be flexible, to work without a clear job description and without close supervision, and to handle multiple tasks. (Sounds like a small businessman or entrepreneur!)
8. Self-marketing skills to promote yourself internally and externally. *The Total System* is your textbook to develop these skills.

If these recommendations are uncomfortable for you or seem risky, or too demanding, you are not alone. While change is never easy, the alternative can be far worse — becoming obsolete, stagnated, bored, or simply jobless!

INDEPENDENT CONTRACTING

This option has become very viable in today's contingent workforce. While once the domain of low level, repetitive functions, contracting is common in virtually all functions and all organizational levels.

> Katherine wanted to begin a family and continue to work part-time. As a public relations manager, she decided to market herself as an independent. She used her extensive network to present her capabilities and services. Operating out of a home office, she succeeded in developing a number of ongoing client relationships and, by referrals, accepted short-term assignments as she had time.

Even executives are sought for temporary or contract assignments. Organizations may have a project that requires short-term leadership, or restructuring may have left holes in various functions, or an organization may seek to test the abilities of a new executive prior to offering a permanent role. Interim contracts for executives are on the rise.

Outsourcing is another trend that has fueled the need for contract workers. Beyond basic support services, companies are outsourcing functions more critical to operations such as internal auditing, management of computer systems, benefits, and even manufacturing. While a major company may outsource a function and downsize, job opportunities are created by the firm that wins the contract for providing the services outsourced. If you have the skills and capabilities to perform the outsourced function, it may also present an opportunity for you to be an independent contractor!

> Kevin had managed the computer operations of a large firm for five years when they decided to outsource the operation. In negotiating with several alternative companies to take over the function, he decided he could best meet the company's needs for the least cost. He prepared a proposal and negotiated an arrangement with his company in which he provided the services required as an independent business. When the transition took place, there was minimal disruption to operations or personnel. Everyone won.

We won't attempt here to outline and clarify all the legal, financial, and technical elements of creating your own business. Rather, we will share our ideas on the personality and motivational aspects of life as a free agent. Our hope is to give you a better understanding of what you're looking at—why some people succeed and others fail—when you consider independent options.

Before all else, however, you'd best discover if you have the personality suited to an independent career. That's what we'll attempt to help you sort out first.

Consider the following traits you'll need to be a successful contractor, consultant, or entrepreneur:

- *Enthusiasm and energy level:* Success as a consultant, contractor or entrepreneur may require that you have the stamina to work long hours for sustained periods.

- *Self-reliance:* You need self-confidence, a belief in your ability to achieve goals, and a sense that events in your life are determined primarily by you.

- *Calculated risk-taking:* Entrepreneurship is generally equated with risk-taking, and properly so. You don't have to act like a riverboat gambler, but much of the dependability regarding income and benefits will be eliminated from your professional life, at least for the short term.

- *Aiming for high goals:* You need the ability to set and reach goals and objectives that other people might consider too challenging.

- *Enjoyment of problem solving:* You must have an intense and consistent desire to drive toward completion of a task or solution of a problem.

- *Long-range commitment:* You must be able to commit yourself to completing projects that will require two to five years of intermittent work.

- *Ability to set the tempo and take charge:* You need the desire to seek and assume initiative and to put yourself in the middle of situations in which you are personally responsible for the success or failure of the project.

- *Growing from setbacks:* You must be able to use failures as learning experiences. Setbacks must not discourage or frustrate you.

- *Maximum utilization of talent:* You must be able to effectively identify and nurture the expertise of others. You can not be so intent on meeting your goals and independent accomplishments that you fail to delegate responsibility.

- *Optimism:* If you can't be totally positive about yourself, your skills, and your business ideas every day, why in the world would you want to be an entrepreneur? Starting and running a new business successfully is one of the most difficult propositions you'll ever face in your professional life. You must believe in yourself without equivocation before you start and every day you operate your business.

- *Sales skills:* You must either have sales skills or learn them if you expect to succeed in any venture. Businesses don't survive unless someone is selling the products or services. And make no mistake — when you're independent, that someone is you.

Those are only a sampling of what's required to operate independently. We suggest that you approach any assessment of your personality more thoroughly than any book can profile you. For example, part of our transition counseling process is a thorough personal, behavioral and work preferences assessment. Our clients receive a professional, accurate, introspective look at how they work at work. With this comprehensive assessment, they can go forth confident that they've picked the best of the three options available — another company, independent business, or consulting/contracting.

You must also look at the marketplace potential before you jump.

But you're making a fatal error if you assume that only your personal characteristics, attitudes, and aptitudes dictate success as an independent business operator. You must also look at the marketplace potential before you jump. For example, our favorite illustration of a marketing disaster in the flesh is the story of a geologist who opened a fishing camp because he liked to fish. And then there was the systems analyst who bought into a hot dog restaurant franchise because he always loved to eat hot dogs. That is not proper targeting in the marketplace, let alone market research. Use all your networking contacts (Chapter 5) and your cold-calling skills (Chapter 7) to learn how your ability and background will sell in the marketplace before you venture out.

As for the specific building blocks of a small business, you can find an enormous amount of information online to guide you through the creation and operation of a business. That's why we've elected not to review those resources here. So do your homework — and be as certain as possible before you make a decision.

FINDING HELP

For guidance in the mechanics of going into business for yourself, we recommend that you consult an attorney, an accountant, and other professionals concerning legalities, accounting, financing, taxes, patents, contracts, copyrights, and the like. Do not rely on books and online resources as your sole source of information. That would be like performing a triple coronary bypass with a scalpel in one hand and a medical text in the other. If you expect to succeed in your new business, get an attorney as well as a CPA who can advise you regarding legal, tax and financial matters.

Then utilize all the educational materials. Remember that most chambers of commerce have small business or entrepreneurial committees that sponsor workshops and business lead sessions. Moreover, the Small Business Administration conducts frequent seminars for independent business owners. For perhaps the first time, you will have ultimate responsibility for finance and accounting, marketing, sales, production, managing growth, human resource administration — in short, every event that comes up in small business (and then you come to the second hour of the day). Given the fact that four out of five new enterprises go out of business in the first year because of mismanagement or under capitalization, commit yourself, first, to doing the necessary research to get your embryonic business off of the ground and running in the proper direction.

If you feel that you fit the mold thus far, perhaps you're ready to consider some of the positives and negatives of contract work, consulting, or entrepreneurship.

SOME POSITIVES

- It is a chance to be truly your own boss, with minimum involvement in organizational politics and red tape.

- It can allow you to control your time — the number of hours you work and the time of day or night you work.

- It presents the opportunity for varied work settings and travel.

- Consulting can require minimal capital investment.

- It does not have a mandatory or traditional retirement age.

- It has great potential to be financially very lucrative.

SOME NEGATIVES

- It is so attractive, the competition is intense.
- You are on your own, so you do not have the support system of an organization.
- You are outside the power structure of an organization, therefore you lack the authority to impose solutions on others.
- You can control your time, however, you do not have the aid of a regimen or schedule with which you must conform.
- Your time is your own, yet you may find that the distinction between working time and leisure time is lost; your time may actually become your client's time.
- Financial resources are frequently difficult to obtain, so cash flow can be a serious problem in a small business.
- Due to the risks, job security is very low and the potential for failure is high.

BASIC SKILLS

In addition to weighing the pluses and minuses of contract work, consulting, or entrepreneurship and considering whether your personality traits match those of successful independent professionals, you must bring to the table a basic set of skills before you bet your career on independence. We like to consolidate them into the following four categories.

INTERPERSONAL SKILLS

You must be able to relate well to the client or customer and to his or her staff. Your communications skills must be sufficient to persuade the client that your analysis, problem identification, and proposed solution are valid and worth acting upon. You must assume responsibility for reducing any friction in the client's office or plant that results from your presence, positioning yourself as a problem-solver who will benefit the company and its employees. Finally, you must communicate effectively in the jargon of the industry and the company, and you must be prepared to do this with all levels of the organization.

MARKETING SKILLS

You must have confidence in yourself and in what you're doing. And it's imperative that you communicate that confidence always, everywhere. As an independent consultant or entrepreneur, you not only maintain a formal marketing program for your company and utilize sales skills to generate new business, but you also become a spokesman for your business in every phase of your life. Whenever and wherever you meet people — at parties, conventions, or professional meetings, or across a backyard fence — they become potential clients or leads to potential clients.

TECHNICAL SKILLS

Your skills in a professional discipline are, of course, the basis for your confidence and marketability. Quite naturally, these skills should be a given for anyone opting for independence. But, be aware that if your employment background portrays you as a *generalist* — the type of person whose versatility and flexibility are invaluable to organizational efficiency — perhaps corporate life is just where you belong. Your potential client most likely doesn't need a generalist. Someone like that is probably already on staff. You must have specific technical skills — preferably on the cutting edge of technology — to be able to attack the client's problems successfully.

CONSULTING SKILLS

At first glance, a requirement for consulting skills may seem a redundancy. Actually, however, consulting skills and technical skills can differ dramatically. For example, simply because you're the finest reservoir engineer in the world doesn't mean that you're worth a three-legged alley cat as a consultant. The difference lies in the consultant's communications skills, leadership, problem-solving ability, and personal motivation. A consulting engineer's area of concern is not just the reservoir — how much is there and how to get it out — but in focusing that expertise on how it relates to the client's company and strategy.

Following are just two examples of how the independent business option can breathe new life into a career and expand one's financial prospects.

Bert had decided that being outsourced was a signal to take control of his career. He evaluated his options and decided a small business was his best route. He researched the purchase of a number of going concerns and settled on a franchise operation. A thorough review of the market and financials further convinced him that he was ready to become a small businessman.

Matthew had been an architect with major companies for many years and was considering starting his own business. However, he was unsure of how to get established since his financial resources were limited. Involving his family, he developed a plan of action based on his research and assessment. The family agreed to reduce their standard of living and relocate to the desired location. Matthew marketed himself for short-term consulting opportunities to meet immediate cash flow needs. In the interim, he developed his business plan and began marketing his new business service. Within 6 months, he had relocated and begun implementing his plan. After 2 months, he projected matching his old salary within a year and achieving significantly increased revenues thereafter.

MAKING YOUR DECISION

We've given you a great deal to evaluate before you leap to independence. Although much of the information we've provided may seem like pitfalls, we don't mean to discourage you from considering the independent/entrepreneurial/ consulting options. The dramatic changes in the work world have accentuated the need to evaluate these options more carefully than ever. In some cases, successful consultants may be reluctant to provide you with a favorable picture of their operation — for obvious competitive reasons. So don't be scared off, but do evaluate fully what you're walking into before you take the first step. Remember that the correct answers for your life and career aren't in this book or any other book. Nor are they found in what the members of your network advise. Until you thoroughly assess your personal preferences, attitudes and aptitudes, you're not ready to hang out your shingle. Until you've researched the market and worked in conjunction with a lawyer and an accountant or financial analyst, you're not ready to unlock the door under that shingle.

If all signals are go, however, we'd like to share with you — as a potential cornerstone of your fledgling business — our custom-designed consulting proposal. Quite naturally, we like it because we created it, but also because it's simple, it works, and it has contributed to the success of many of our clients.

The necessary elements of a consulting proposal include:

- A brief heading used as a title.
- A synopsis of the client's problem, supported by a brief analysis of your documentation.
- A brief outline of your proposed solution.
- A statement of the benefits the client will realize as a result of following the course of action you recommend.
- An outline of the first step of the solution, which should be simple and should involve you personally.
- An estimate of the time to completion for the first stage of the project.
- A full description of your ongoing role — gathering further information, overseeing the first stage of the solution, diagnosing other manifestations of the problem, analyzing results following completion of your suggestions, and so on.
- A statement of your fees.

Our clients have successfully used straightforward, bottom-line proposals to begin their consulting careers and so can you. Here's just one example:

> Theresa had been restructured out of her job in health care manufacturing. Two months later, she was tempted to take her first job offer which would have involved a lateral move and relocation. Recognizing her talent and marketability, we cautioned her to go more slowly and consider a consulting option. Using the consulting proposal model, she approached the firm that had extended her the offer with the idea of meeting their needs as a consultant. Rather than losing her, they accepted, and it was only the beginning of Theresa's successful independent business.

See Exhibit 2 for an example of a consulting proposal which will get a company's attention and commitment.

Whether your answer is yes, no, or maybe to the contract/consulting or independent business option, don't stop reading. Whether you're a consultant, a small business owner, or a corporate employee, you'll need a resume. Turn one more page, and you'll discover a new world of resumes — resumes which get results, to be precise. We are confident that our approach to resumes is the best in the entire job market because we have thousands of success stories to prove it!

Likewise, whoever you are, wherever you go, you'll need our networking, cold-calling, interviewing, and negotiating skills. Although you may already be a world-class consultant or a proven, fast-tracking corporate employee, over the next eight chapters you will become a world-class job campaigner.

EXHIBIT 2
Consulting Proposal

NAME
Address
City, State Zip
Cell/Office Phone
Email Address

Consulting Proposal
Date:

- **Objective:**
  To provide a management consulting service to DELTA HEALTH CORP., a new health equity resource company.

- **Synopsis of requirements and needs:**
  Based upon my initial understanding, I recommend three (3) areas of concentration:
  (1) Providing needed consulting services to develop a business plan for Delta Health Corp.
  (2) Assisting in presentations to potential clients with the Delta Health Corp. team.
  (3) Providing technical coordination and evaluation of potential facility programs in support of analysis.

- **Proposed solution:**
  Based upon the above stated problems, I recommend an initial 12-month contract as Health Care Consultant to provide the necessary consulting services to identify and solve any problems related to 1, 2, and 3 above.

- **Benefits the client will realize as a result of following the course of action recommended:**
  At the conclusion of a 12-month time frame, the client will have a completed business plan with a five year strategy plan; plus, a marketing effort that produces awarded projects to initiate the capitalization of Delta Health Corp.

- **First step of the solution:**
  My first step of the solution will involve working in various locations convenient to your team to review the concept and develop a proposed schedule and plan to resolve these problems for your review and approval and to assist in contracting with your funding source.

- **Completion time for the first stage of the project:**
  My estimated time for the first stage of the consultant work will be 12 months, which can than be monitored and extended as necessary.

- **Ongoing role:**
  My ongoing role will be determined during the development of the business and strategy plan.

- **Fees:**
  My monthly consultant fee is $12, 000 per month, which amounts to $144,000 for the initial 12 month period. In addition, all expenses will be reimbursed at cost.

Accepted by: (company)   Accepted by: (consultant)

_____   _____
Name   Name

_____   _____
Title   Title

_____   _____
Date   Date

Beyond Resume Platitudes:
The Foundation for Goal Setting

Before you even think about writing a resume, do yourself a favor. Purge from your mind any advice you've ever heard or read about the subject — how to write a resume, how to avoid writing one, how to get a better job without one. When you put pencil on paper to create a resume, make sure your brain is free of clutter.

Much of the advice you've ever received about resumes is useless. When you go looking for any kind of information, you're going to find some good, some not so good, and a small percentage downright bankrupt. It is no different with resume advice. As the reader, your greatest responsibility is to discern quality advice from bankrupt advice peddled by unemployed hucksters. If you've learned a bunch of "trendy" junk from such pseudo-career counselors, exorcise it from your brain and your library.

If you've done any serious research on conducting a job campaign, you're familiar with the verbal effluent with which many "authors" or "consultants" flood the job marketplace. The theories parallel this line of thought: Resumes don't work. . . . Corporations get hundreds, or thousands, every week. . . . Yours won't be read. . . . so don't use one. The rationale continues that a "savvy" job hunter makes direct contact with the hiring authority, uses an alternative marketing letter to generate interviews, and never presents a resume to the company. Online applications replace the resume, so just have your experience outlined and prepared to upload.

There's a grain of truth in that scenario: It acknowledges the value of networking. But networking doesn't replace your resume; they are two tools that complement one another. So if you swallow the trendy line that resumes don't work, you're not as savvy as you think. You're listening to people who don't understand resumes, who probably have never written or read a truly good resume, and who can't even conceive of the multiple benefits an effective resume can produce for your job campaign. In short, our conviction is that *your resume drives your entire job search.* Certainly it will if you'll agree to do it our way. Any other suggestion will not provide legitimate guidance for your campaign.

> A resume is not just a calling card… it sets the tone and direction for all that you do in your job search.

HOW THE RESUME WORKS FOR YOU

Honor your resume; understand that it summarizes your work life and charts your future. A resume is not just a calling card. That's one of its important functions, but many people limit it to that. Nor does the resume simply attract the employer's attention and allow you access to the hiring authority, although that is one of its primary jobs.

More important, however, the procedure you use for creating an effective resume reinforces the process of self-evaluation and goal setting. Your resume sets the tone and direction for all that you do in your job search. When you complete the preparations for creating a resume, you will have on paper how your skills and experience can benefit both you and your next employer.

Properly prepared, the resume will introduce you and sell your skills. Moreover, it will be an ally that will never fail you in any facet of the job campaign. In particular, the resume will assist during interviews, provided that you write it correctly and learn how to use it.

WHY MOST RESUMES ARE OVERLOOKED

The one overriding reason that 95 out of 100 resumes don't work is that 95 out of 100 aren't worth reading.

Admittedly, the platitudes that some people peddle as job search advice are based on a truth—corporations are inundated with resumes. It's therefore logical to assume that when you submit a resume you're playing a numbers game, with the odds stacked against the job hunter. In fact, only five out of every hundred resumes survive the corporate cut. The problem, though, isn't with the concept. It's not the pieces of paper or bits and bites of your electronic version that render a resume ineffective. Nor is it the competition from hundreds of other resumes on the same desk that makes yours get lost in the shuffle.

What renders resumes useless is what's in them. The world of job hunting may be smothering in a choking cloud of resumes, but it's a cloud of bad resumes. In general, they are as poorly written and ill-conceived as the "expert" advice that tells job hunters to ignore them. The one overriding reason that 95 out of 100 resumes don't work is that 95 out of 100 aren't worth reading. Here's an example:

> Recently a company downsized their procurement department, sending three of their professionals at various levels to our outplacement program. Having developed their resumes in our recommended format, they began to market themselves with confidence. All three learned of a job opening and separately submitted their resumes. All three were selected to be

interviewed. During the process, the interviewer revealed that over 200 resumes had been received for the position, and that 6 were selected for interviews. It's no coincidence that our three clients were among the 6. Chances are that of the 200 applicants they were not really in the top 3% of candidates in terms of credentials and skills. Yet, because of the strength of their resumes, they were interviewed.

This is just one illustration of the importance of an effective resume. Can you buy into our approach? Can you commit the next two or three days of your life to writing the best resume you've ever seen? That's just what you'll get from this chapter. But if you can't follow our advice by burying all the disinformation about resumes you've heard previously, our relationship, writer to reader, is in deep trouble for the rest of this book. Without an effective resume, built according to the formula provided on the following pages, nothing works. Our approach to job search is driven by our approach to resume writing.

THE GOSPEL OF RESUMES: THERE IS ONE WAY, ONE TRUTH, ONE RESUME

- *The format is chronological order* (most recent experience first).

- *The resume is two pages long.* (Exception: On occasion, new graduates, entry levels, administrative support people, or workers in a trade can fit their professional lives into a one-page resume.)

End of resume alternatives—beyond that single exception, never deviate from the formula. You could probably list many different resume formats—most people say five or six. Some "resume services" offer a menu with choices of ten or twelve different styles. Please, don't fall into the trap of selecting your resume from a list of alternatives. If you write any other resume format— functional, hybrid, targeted, or our favorite aberration, the "alternative marketing letter"—you're not acting in your best interest.

RESUME VARIATIONS

Beware: All variations in format are designed to accomplish one goal—to smokescreen weaknesses in your background. A termination? A new job at a reduced salary? A cut in responsibility? Job hopping? A gap between jobs? A functional resume, for example, can effectively create the illusion that you had management experience with IBM, when in fact it was as a board member of a PTA school group. On the surface, that's great. But guess what? The person who reads resumes in companies isn't easily fooled. The reviewer's first thought upon picking up a functional or targeted or hybrid resume is, "Let's see what we're hiding here."

Aside from resumes with different formats, there are the gimmick resumes. You know the scenario. A candidate wants her resume to stand out from the others and wants to catch the employer's eye, so she sends it inside a tiny coffin, with the note, "I'm dying to get this job." Or a guy sends a resume rolled up inside a shoe, with a note on the sole, "I'd walk miles to get this job." Don't waste your time. Those are gadgets. They have no place in a professional job search. More ominously, they suggest to the employer instantly that you are a promoter who needs to embellish the facts on your resume to compete with other, more qualified, candidates. A resume introduces and sells you to the employer, so a gimmick won't work—unless you're applying for a job as a ringmaster with Barnum & Bailey or a bouncer in a Tijuana strip joint.

> Your resume gets only about 15 or 20 seconds of reading time. You get one chance to make a good first impression.

Remember, your resume gets only about 15 or 20 seconds of reading time. You get one chance to make a good first impression. And you do that best with a resume illustrating your credentials, experience, accomplishments, competencies, knowledge, skills, professionalism, and maturity. When you think about sending a resume to an employer, keep one thought uppermost in mind. It's as though the company is asking, "What can you do for us?" You can't be there to answer the question, so your resume must speak for you. To that end, a two-page, chronological format serves you best.

ONLINE RESUMES

But you say, how about the resume data bases and the company resume portals that request an alternative resume? What should I do to utilize those search avenues? First of all, recognize that when you place your resume online you are entering a data base with millions of other applicants. So you have to ask yourself, is it worth the investment of time to place your data in with theirs? Is it a specialized data base matching your background? Is it a private data base where your resume is secure? Or, is it a company that you have specifically targeted? If your answer is YES to these questions, than you may indeed wish to take the time necessary to complete the online resume form. If not, steer clear and stick with your professionally designed resume.

Whenever possible in using online resume portals, upload your professional resume if provided that option. Be very cautious about placing your resume on the massive data bases that give the world access to your data. Remember that privacy and control of your resume are significant issues in your job search. Not everyone who has access to such data bases is ethical or concerned about your goals and objectives.

SELECT A SAMPLE RESUME

We won't ask you to invest time in picking a resume format. Instead, the Sample Resumes provide a template to help you get started. This is not a contradiction since they're all in the same format—chronological. But each represents a different function, industry, level or special circumstance in the workplace. Moreover, we are confident that they are the best examples of resumes you've ever seen. We call them "A+" resumes because they optimize the ability of the job seeker to market and sell his or her experience, accomplishments, skills, knowledge and competencies and to link the resume to all steps in the job search process. This is the quality of resume to which you should aspire as you draft your own.

If you're a chemist, look at the sample resume for chemist. A manufacturing manager can follow one example, a computer programmer another, a corporate planner another. The point is, that's the only choice you need make. Pick the industry, function and level that fit your career, insert your professional information into the format, and be confident that you have a real heavy-hitter on your side in your job search. Your resume will serve as the basis for your entire campaign.

If you haven't yet referred to the Sample Resumes, do so now. Concentrate on the occupational function or level that fits you. You'll probably be able to borrow phrases and ideas from them. Plan to spend a couple of dozen hours preparing your resume. But please, don't try to write it yet. There's more to learn. If you don't also understand how to utilize the resume in your job search, you might as well send the employer that old shoe or the miniature coffin.

> Recall our First Commandment of Job Search: **Linkage...** Your resume is the key link.

Remember our all important *First Commandment of Job Search: Linkage.* Restated, it means that every step you take in job search ties in with the previous step you took and the next one you plan. Each phone call, each networking contact, each letter of reference, each resume you send, each interview—they are all linked. And *your resume is the key link* in this process.

FORGING THE FIRST LINK

If you think ahead to the interview as you write your resume, you will see that what you put in the resume, and how you structure it, determines how you will answer the most important questions put to you when you're sitting across the desk from the hiring authority.

To be sure you grasp the importance of your resume as a critical link in your entire job search let's consider the alternative. In most job searches, job hunters prepare their resumes independently of the other job search activities. Consequently they send a resume, follow up with a phone call, get an interview appointment, go to the interview and talk for an hour, and go home without an offer. That's how job search works when you don't understand or use linkage.

In Chapter 8, we'll discuss in detail all the facets of interviewing for a job — including, of course, the tough questions. But consider for a moment the traditional opening question in a job interview—and for many candidates the toughest—"Tell us about yourself." That's a signal for most people to launch into a rambling, disjointed biographical statement. More often than not, this response is a self-incriminating litany of every reason why no one, anywhere, would ever want to hire this person. But you can be different. When you complete your resume a couple of days from now, you'll be able to answer that opening question with a response that gets you off and winging with confidence on your interview. It's really not difficult when you link your resume to the interview. To give you a preview of how linkage works in your favor, let's look at the correct way to respond to this typical interview question.

Your answer should consist of four parts, and you should talk roughly two minutes. All you really have to do is state what's in your resume starting from the bottom of page two and moving to the top of page one.

1. Start with your *early history*—where you were born, where you grew up. If you served in the armed forces, mention that here.

2. Part two is your *education*. Tell where you went to school and what degree you received.

3. Part three is *professional experience*—a brief description of your jobs since leaving school, explaining the transitions between jobs. Then quickly move to your most recent (or current) position, *explaining how your skills, experience, and accomplishments relate to the opening.*

4. Finally, part four is a *career plan*—a brief explanation of why you and this company would be a *good match,* reflecting facts you learned in your advance research on the firm. In closing, mention what a *first-rate company* this is and that you are *pleased to be interviewed* for a position in the firm.

Voila! Your answer is complete. You not only got through—in all likelihood, you knocked them out of their chairs. Confidence boosted, you're ready for the subsequent interview questions. It's so simple it mystifies us why more people don't do it.

The resume will serve you equally well all through the interview. Any time you get into trouble (you will—we all do, sooner or later), count on the resume to rescue the interview, as surely as a lighthouse guides a floundering vessel to port. For example:

> Beth found herself straying from the interviewer's question. Realizing that she was losing the interviewer's attention, she said, "I've given you more detail than your question asked for, but as my resume reflects, my attention to detail has enabled me to achieve significant results." The interviewer used Beth's cue to ask his next question concerning her accomplishments.

This is just one example of linkage in action. That's how a powerful resume sets the stage for a winning interview. But enough about interviewing for now—you have an A+ resume to write!

IT'S TIME TO START WRITING

To answer the tough interview questions so adroitly, you must know your resume and what's in it —forward, backward, upside down, and inside out. You're dead if you try to read from it during the interview, so you must know every word that's in it by heart. Obviously, it follows that you must write it yourself. Paying someone else to write your resume may short-circuit the process but will likely guarantee a bad start for your job campaign. It's your life, your career. And it must be your resume if you're to utilize it to full advantage. We're not suggesting professional help is not an advantage – certainly our coaching support facilitates our clients' success in achieving an A+ resume. But remember, the process of writing your resume is linked to your assessment of where you have been and where you are going; the more you take ownership of that process, the greater value you will receive from it and from your final resume.

Write it. Rewrite it. Cut it down and rewrite it again. Polish it. It's probably still five pages long, so let it cool off overnight, then cut it down and rewrite it again. If it remains more than two pages long, rest assured that it's full of information no one will read, so cut it again. Follow the models and principles set out for you in this chapter. Take the resume to a friend or colleague who's good with the language and get an evaluation, but again, don't set sail on your job search with a bad resume or a resume written by someone else.

Thus far, this has been a chapter full of theory. But one of our bedrock beliefs about job search is that people shouldn't be overdosed on theory. Hands-on, real-world training works best. So let's get to that. Here's how to build the two-page, chronological resume that will get your job search moving in high gear.

Start at the top of page one by centering your name, mailing address, and phone numbers, with area codes. Include only numbers for which you have a voice mail system: Your home number, an office number if appropriate, and your cell phone. Your e-mail address should be included when available. Some job seekers elect to set up a special email account for their job search to ensure no contact is overlooked.

YOUR PHONE MUST BE ANSWERED

Be certain that your phone will be answered at all times, especially during business hours. Having a cell phone is an ideal way to minimize the chances of missing an important call.

Let's assume that a company has selected your resume as one of five out of 350 to follow up on for interviews. How many times do you think they will call back if there is no answer? Your best bet is to answer the first call. When you're out interviewing or unavailable, don't allow even one caller to miss you. To that end, use a cell phone and check your voice mail when you have been out of pocket for awhile.

A SAMPLE RESUME

Look at Exhibit 3, Sample Resume A (Paul Lee). Lee's resume identifies the applicant, tells where the company can reach him, and then moves immediately into professional qualifications. Never include your height, weight, marital status, or any other personal information in a resume. Remarkably, some people walk around carrying an occupational death wish—Height: 4'9"; Weight: 210; Marital Status: Divorced mother of eight children. Incredible, but it happens every day. You might just as well walk into an interview with a scarlet letter on your chest. The point is that none of that information has any bearing whatsoever on your ability to do a job. If information isn't job-related, it doesn't belong in your resume. Another favorite trivial redundancy is the phrase at the top of many resumes: "Resume of Qualifications." Now that's a revelation! You can be certain that an employer isn't going to mistake a resume for your last will and testament, so it's not necessary to label it. Your cover letter will introduce the resume anyway.

Moving along to the meat of the resume, the Objective tells what job Paul Lee wants to get. Period. Don't include a lot of extraneous nonsense about a "challenging career position with a dynamic, growth-oriented company." Similarly, the Summary is direct and to-the-point. It doesn't drag the reader through every detail of Lee's life; it simply states what he's done to qualify for the job objective stated above. It's brief, well-organized, and complete. Again, there are no extraneous words cluttering up the page and stealing time from the 15 to 20 seconds Lee has in which to grab the reader's interest.

ANALYZING THE SAMPLE

In the Lee sample resume, within 5 to 7 seconds the employer can learn the applicant's name, that he wants a job in senior executive management and that he has over twenty years' experience in engineering and construction. Always remember that the people who read resumes are busy and that yours is competing with hundreds of others for their attention. Almost every other resume either will be abysmally unprofessional or will consume all 15 to 20 seconds of reading time just to discover who the applicant is. Instantaneously, you've achieved a competitive advantage.

That advantage isn't confined to just reading time required, however. Don't you agree that the sample resume is a high-impact, professional piece of work? We're not claiming originality. Our resume format is nothing but a compendium of effective features we've encountered throughout many years of human resources counseling. Still, one of the hardest lessons to get across to applicants is that no one but their mothers enjoys reading their resumes.

In this sample, the professional look with ample white spaces, brief statements, plus right and left margin justification is excellent. If you are not proficient with computer software, enlist the help of a family member or friend or go to the expense of hiring someone to process your resume professionally, but *write* your own! That's the only way to get a professionally organized appearance. Electronic software also gives the flexibility you must have for customizing the top of a resume. The following commandment blows another resume platitude out of the water: *Don't Waste Time on a Completed Resume.*

> Don't Waste Time on a Completed Resume.

Although a resume should be custom-designed for each job opening, redesigning your entire resume for every job lead is a waste of time. Many misguided job hunters tailor their resumes to each job opportunity. You're supposed to be busy researching, networking, getting job leads. Wasting time on a completed resume won't accomplish anything but delay in your job search. Since time is the ultimate, finite resource for us all, don't rewrite a resume after you have arrived at the final, polished draft.

To custom-design a resume, all you need to do is change the *Objective* and possibly rephrase the *Summary,* if necessary. Your basic resume remains intact. You can quickly electronically modify the information to lead off the resume, and instantly you have a custom-tailored document ready to help you get that interview.

Good human resources professionals and hiring managers can tell all they need to know about you from your resume. That's why we stress the importance of the complete package, custom-designed. Beyond your professional qualifications, the employer can tell how well you'll fit the corporate culture just from the appearance of the resume. A real pro can gauge your professionalism, your maturity, how much effort you put into preparing the resume, and a myriad of other impressions that virtually jump off the page for a trained interviewer.

Most of all, the interviewer is looking for excuses to stop reading. That's why it's so important to ensure that your resume presents you as a solid professional. That's what complements your technical skills and experience—not some gimmick or eye-catching departure from format. For example, on the Lee resume sample, the interviewer can quickly tell that Paul Lee is a pro, just from the overall impact. Then the reader learns immediately his Objective—Senior Executive Management. If that objective doesn't fit the company's needs, the resume is culled. (See, now, the paramount importance of custom-designing the top of your resume?) If the objective fits, the reader moves along to the Summary.

Resume Selling Points:

It's not what you do in terms of duties, but what you did to help your company make or save money!

The Summary must justify Lee's desire to fill his job objective. If it does that, the reader continues. If not—if the summary of experience isn't heavy enough to qualify for the position targeted —the resume is tossed aside. The summary pushes the reader along to Professional Experience. Quickly and cleanly, Lee tells where he worked, when, and what he did. But here's the critical part of the resume—the selling statements for Lee's skills. It's not what he did in terms of duties, but what he did to help his company make or save money! Read that again, underline it, commit it to memory. That's the part of your resume that catches the employer's attention. It's what causes them to put your resume on the "good" stack rather than the "bad" one.

ANOTHER SAMPLE: SIMILARITIES AND A DIFFERENCE

Now look at Exhibit 4, Sample Resume B (Joseph Jenkins). Jenkins's Objective and Summary are presented similarly to Paul Lee's. Below that, however, the two samples differ slightly. This style variance is the only discretionary element in our system. Both resumes list the company and length of service, then break out jobs within the organization as transfers and promotions occur. (Note: Both resumes use years only, not months. Never use months on your resume. That causes the reader to focus on short-term details rather than long-range accomplishments in your career.)

The new graduate who may have a series of short-term work experiences while attending school should not be concerned, however, that these experiences are problematic. Summer jobs and internships are expected by employers and you should include these work experiences in your early career resume. See the samples of new college graduate resumes.

Here is the writer's discretion: Jenkins gets right into his accomplishments and incorporates his job duties into those statements. In contrast, Lee briefly summarizes his responsibilities before listing accomplishments: "Vice President, Business Development—Responsible for sales, marketing, and major proposals," and so forth. Either format is acceptable. Both work. Just be certain that you don't clutter up the accomplishment statements with a list of duties. Responsibility statements that summarize job duties are useful in outlining the scope of your job in regard to revenues, people supervised and breadth and areas of responsibility.

Note that both resume samples address *problems* faced in their jobs, what actions they took to solve the problems, and what *resulted* from their efforts. Refer back to Lee's resume: Led sales team to award of multiple contracts . . . resulting in $60 million of additional revenue; Initiated marketing effort . . . resulting in $750 million of new work prospects; Built sales program resulting in more than $1 billion of outstanding proposals.

Similarly, Jenkins's resume informs the company that he helped his previous employer by doubling sales volume from $4 million to $8 million in four years, increasing regional productivity by 11% or $250,000 annually, and achieving margins of 25-75% while improving divisional cash flow.

Two points in common are evident in the two resumes, and you should adapt the same idea for yours. Both Jenkins and Lee express their job performance or results in terms of numbers — either percentages or dollars or both. Those are *quantitative* accomplishment statements. If your resume doesn't have that type of forcefulness, it's not yet ready for the employer to read. There are exceptions, however. Some professions just don't lend themselves to the use of flat quantitative accomplishment statements. In such cases, use *qualitative* accomplishment statements that indicate results, such as "substantial reductions," "significant increases," "improved results," and so forth. In short, the reader should infer from your accomplishment statements that you are a walking, talking, breathing bundle of management and/or technical skills. That's what your accomplishments implicitly communicate.

If your first reaction to the accomplishment approach to resumes is "I don't have any," don't despair. Whether you are just graduating, returning to work, or transitioning from the military, you do have accomplishments and skills which, without a doubt, can be included in your resume. We have assisted hundreds of hourly workers and entry level employees to draft their resumes using this approach, so trust us, you can do it too! Read on to learn how.

WHAT'S IN IT FOR THE COMPANY?

Many people can't shake loose from the concept of what they did on the job—their duties or responsibilities. But to write solid accomplishment statements, you must think in terms of *value* to the employer. The following accomplishment statements include some of the values that will push the hot button of any company and can be expressed in either *quantitative* or *qualitative* terms:

- Contributed to profit increase, cost reduction, increased sales or market share.

- Increased productivity and quality; improved product or service.

- Improved relations with customers, consumer groups, governments.

- Improved employer/employee relations.

- Improved teamwork and resolved conflict.

- Improved communications and information flow.

- Reduced operating downtime, streamlined operations.

- Developed new technology or administrative procedures.

- Anticipated a need or problem and initiated effective remedial action.

- Planned or directed in an innovative manner.

- Implemented an important program or acted with significant benefits.

- Increased return on investment.

The common denominator isn't difficult to determine in that list of accomplishments. It is, of course, the corporate bottom line. The only reason a company wants to hire you is to solve its problems and enhance its performance and profitability or for a nonprofit organization, to achieve its goals within budget. The foregoing accomplishments illustrate that you know how to do both. Generally, a true accomplishment must meet one of the following tests to aid the company:

- Achieved more without utilizing increased resources.

- Achieved the same but reduced resource utilization.

- Achieved improved operations or relations.

- Achieved a goal for the first time under existing conditions.

- Achieved resolution of problems or conflicts with little or no negative effect.

THE RIGHT WORD IN THE RIGHT PLACE

The importance of measurable results in your accomplishment statements has already been addressed. Think of the statements as flags waving at the top of a fortress. But you need a foundation for each statement — the word that starts each phrase. Without fail, that word must be a strong, active-voice verb. Look over the following lists of suggested verbs, and use them in your resume. Again, refer to the Lee and Jenkins sample resumes. The opening word of each accomplishment statement captures the reader's attention and encourages the eye to move along toward the critically important dollar, percentage figure or result that illustrates the job hunter's potential worth to the employer. Since your resume in most cases describes previous employment experience, these verbs should be written in the past tense.

Action verbs that address your *planning* skills include:

Conceived	Innovated	Scheduled
Created	Instituted	Solved
Designed	Invented	Systematized
Developed	Justified	Transformed
Devised	Laid Out	
Engineered	Modeled	
Established	Organized	
Estimated	Originated	
Experimented	Planned	
Formed	Projected	
Formulated	Reorganized	
Initiated	Revised	

Action verbs that address your skills in *directing* employees include:

Administered	Determined	Ordered
Approved	Directed	Prescribed
Authorized	Guided	Regulated
Conducted	Headed	Specified
Controlled	Instructed	Supervised
Decided	Led	Trained
Delegated	Managed	

Action verbs that suggest that you have skills in *assuming responsibility* include:

Accepted	Described	Operated
Achieved	Doubled	Overcame
Adopted	Established	Performed
Arranged	Evaluated	Prepared
Assembled	Experienced	Produced
Assumed	Gathered	Received
Attended	Halted	Reduced
Audited	Handled	Reviewed
Authored	Implemented	Simplified
Built	Improved	Sold
Checked	Initiated	Spearheaded
Classified	Installed	Transacted
Collected	Integrated	Tripled
Compiled	Made	Used
Constructed	Maintained	Utilized

Action verbs that embody an ability to provide effective *service* include:

Carried Out	Explained	Provided
Committed	Facilitated	Purchased
Delivered	Furnished	Rewrote
Demonstrated	Generated	Sent
Earned	Inspected	Serviced
Exchanged	Installed	Submitted
Expanded	Issued	Transmitted
Expedited	Procured	Wrote

Interactive skills with people are suggested by the use of these action verbs in your accomplishment statements:

Advised	Coordinated	Negotiated
Aided	Counseled	Participated
Apprised	Helped	Promoted
Clarified	Informed	Recommended
Conferred	Inspired	Represented
Consulted	Interpreted	Resolved
Contributed	Interviewed	Suggested
Cooperated	Mediated	Unified

Finally, your *investigative* skills emerge with the use of these action verbs:

Analyzed	Evaluated	Reviewed
Assessed	Familiarized	Searched
Calculated	Investigated	Studied
Computed	Observed	Verified
Correlated	Proved	
Discovered	Researched	

That's only a sampling of the types of words you must include in your resume. Use these lists or use other verbs to communicate your skills and how they generated accomplishments. Just be sure that you use a strong action verb to open every statement.

HITTING THE BULLSEYE

Note the • symbols that precede the accomplishment statements in the following list as well as in all the Sample Resumes. They're called *bullets,* and your job is to see that each one of them hits the target — it will if it is followed by a winning accomplishment statement. The ultimate *target* is to develop a resume that will be selected by the hiring authority to be followed up for interviews, rather than discarded. To hit that target, each bullet or accomplishment statement needs an action verb followed by a result.

Your completed accomplishment statements should read like these:

- Achieved a 25% cost reduction in the amount of $500,000 by creating and installing a complete accounting system by department in a large agency. (Whenever possible, include dollar amounts)

- Created a profit and loss statement, by product, resulting in substantial increase of sales in the high-profit products. (If actual numbers cannot be given, utilize the term "substantial")

(Do you recognize the categories of those first two? The first is *quantitative;* the second is *qualitative.* But they both work.)

Examples of additional quantitative accomplishment statements include:

- Participated in core team to develop strategy to expand worldwide business to more than $1 billion per year through internal growth and acquisition.

- Developed the start-up strategy for the company's entry into the Mid-East and Far East and then led efforts in all phases of the strategy. The strategy resulted in the company's first international turnkey projects contributing $5 million revenue in the first year.

- Advised a major U.S. company on the reorganization of operations and sales resulting in an increase in annual sales of $1.5 million with a 10% reduction in operating costs.

- Managed a professional group in creating a sales organization after identifying a $300 million market.

- Conceived a new management information services procedure that made vital operations reports available to management daily resulting in a savings of $75,000.

- Developed a community acceptance campaign in San Francisco (a hostile market), resulting in the reduction of processing time by nearly 25%.

- Saved millions in possible damages, and prevented embarrassment by discovering potential bankruptcy of a supplier.

- Formulated policies and procedures for the administration of zoning petitions, resulting in the reduction of processing time by nearly 25% or $50,000 annually.

- Reduced rework by 20%, eliminated schedule delays, and doubled in-house manufacturing capability through reorganization and introduction of methods and systems resulting in savings of $150,000 annually.

- Designed supporting equipment and techniques for a new process that raised product market potential from $5 million to more than $20 million per year.

- Promoted a new concept in welding procedures that reduced labor costs by $100,000 annually.

- Discovered $190,000 overstatement of a division's inventory, enabling corrective action by management.

- Reduced turnover of personnel from 17% to 9% for a savings of $165,000 per year.

- Installed a cost system for complex fabricating process, saving $75,000 per year.

- Revised shipping procedures and introduced improvements that reduced cost and shipping time by 37% or $135,000 annually.

- Instituted a wage and salary program especially tailored to improve morale reducing payroll by $40,000 annually.

- Developed and installed a unique laboratory organization that eliminated duplication, encouraged cooperation, and reduced costs by $50,000 annually.

If you've read through these quantitative accomplishments and you're still saying, "I never did any of these things," try these qualitative accomplishments:

- Entered, edited, and revised information on computer system ensuring accurate client and case data.

- Assisted in running all office support activities resulting in smooth operations.

- Assisted students in meeting academic needs which resulted in reducing student frustration and increased retention.

- Operated cash register while providing courteous customer service.

- Resolved customer complaints resulting in increased satisfaction.

- Trained new employees on use of new computer system resulting in more efficient operations.

- Provided customers with information concerning various types of accounts and other banking services which contributed to increased business.

- Drafted for small architectural office resulting in precise and neat drawings.

- Performed deliveries and pickups for the office which ensured timely business transaction.

- Wrote executive summaries of audit findings for senior management which provided adequate information for decision making.

- Awarded corporate merit bonus for exemplary performance in the audit department.

- Established computerized standards and samples for production resulting in improved quality.

- Planned and implemented first summary energy conservation and food nutrition festival which resulted in excellent community participation and increased awareness of program goals.

- Developed a program using DBase II resulting in significantly improved tracking of manpower needs.

- Greeted potential clients providing a positive and personalized image for the organization.

- Designed and implemented in-store displays resulting in improved customer traffic and increased sales.

- Served as camp counselor, aquatic instructor, and entertainment director for exclusive summer camp, providing effective staff operations support for the administrators.

These entry-level accomplishment statements prove that whatever your work experience, the tasks you have performed and the skills you have demonstrated contribute in *some* way to an organization even if you are not able to quantify your results.

This list is intended only to get you into the right frame of mind to state your accomplishments in terms of dollars, percentages and results. Review your jobs and career and pick out your accomplishment highlights. If you're still telling yourself, "I didn't do anything like that," welcome to the crowd. That's the initial reaction of most people facing resume writing. Push beyond those initial doubts. Jot down notes and thoughts and phrases as they occur to you. This is a building process, and it takes time, reflection, and effort.

Remember, we require a couple of dozen hours of commitment as your investment in your resume for the benefit of your career. This is where you'll spend the bulk of that time. One good way to get off dead center is to go ahead and write down your duties. That's probably the only way to deal with them, because most people are so preoccupied with their responsibilities that they can't get beyond the tasks of their job to highlight their achievements. Your job or position descriptions and performance appraisals can be very useful in helping you get started.

When you have the duties down on paper, begin to think through them. Recall results and benefits to the company that your duties generated. That's what goes into your accomplishment statements. Do not attempt to translate each responsibility into an accomplishment, however. Some responsibilities may not generate any significant accomplishments, while others may produce two or three.

To help you move along with the process, divide a piece of paper into three columns. At the tops of the columns, write these headings:

Action Verb   **Action Taken**   **Benefit to Company**

In the Action Verb column, write a verb that indicates your intensity of effort, demonstrates the power required to achieve the result, or illustrates your level of responsibility. Be certain that you use a variety of verbs. Refer to our lists for ideas. They include more than 150 verbs, and of course you're not limited to those alone.

The reader will look at each entry in your resume in one of three ways:
- it improves your chance to get an interview;
- it detracts from your chance; or
- it's a push, a neutral.

On the contrary, be as creative as possible. And be aware that even a strong action verb becomes diluted if it is repeated in your resume. In the second column, under Action Taken, write what you accomplished. This should be a short, concise statement about what you did. It should not be a description of how you did it. Finally, in the column under Benefit to Company, write the result or impact of your achievement on the company's business. This is the payoff. This is where you use dollars and percentages at every opportunity. This is what makes you valuable to a prospective employer.

Throughout this process remember that the reader will look at each entry in your resume in one of three ways: it improves your chance to get an interview; it detracts from your chance; or it's a push, a neutral. Your primary job as a resume writer is to pack as many positives into the document as your memory, imagination, and the truth will allow.

THE TRUTH?

The Final Commandment of Resume Writing: They Don't Know What You Don't Tell Them.

There's that word. In your resume, you must tell the T-R-U-T-H — as in "the truth, the whole truth, and nothing but the truth." We don't agree, however— at least not in the context of "the whole" and "nothing but." You are not under oath as you develop your resume. So we present *The Final Commandment of Resume Writing: They Don't Know What You Don't Tell Them.*

Do tell the truth always as it relates to your ability to do the job. Certainly, we're not suggesting that you ever lie, cheat, or steal to get a job. Aside from the ethical and moral questions, you'll be saddled with work you're not qualified to perform if you falsify your background or experience.

We are telling you to get smart. Leaving some point out of your resume is not lying. We all make mistakes in our professional lives. We all have elements in our personal lives that we wouldn't run up and confess to a stranger. Nonetheless, people will confess to just about anything when they're looking for a job. You're not in a confessional and you're not defending your past errors of judgment. Tell the truth—fine. But don't look for a job the way a Kamikaze pilot flies an airplane. If the information will hurt you, leave it out of your resume. Period. That's not a lie.

We'll address how to respond to questions about your experience or background that may be sensitive in the interviewing chapter, but essentially our approach is to emphasize your strengths. If an interviewer should ask you, "What did you leave out of your resume?", you can honestly say, "I did not have room for all of my accomplishments, but can share more if you would like." Then be sure to have a few additional accomplishments outlined in your "tool kit." That question is what we call a hidden agenda question designed to get a "reaction" to uncover some negative that would disqualify you. By your preparation, you can avoid swallowing the bait and sharing past issues no longer relevant to your performance today.

We've already mentioned our philosophy of using years, never months, in presenting your career history. That's a good illustration. Suppose that you worked at Space Odyssey, Inc. from November 2007 to January 2008. If you put those months in your resume, you've probably made yourself into instant history as an applicant. However, if you put that you worked at Space Odyssey, Inc. from 2007 to 2008, you're not placing yourself in dire jeopardy immediately. Make no mistake, you'll have to address your brief tenure at Space Odyssey, Inc. during the interview, but at least you haven't prematurely removed yourself from consideration with one careless entry on a resume. Did you lie? Of course you didn't. You simply told the truth in terms that make you most attractive to the employer. If your mother or your old scoutmaster doesn't like that approach, that's too bad. Do some good turns and make it up to them later. First get a job.

FIRST THINGS FIRST GETS YOU WHERE YOU SHOULD BE

Now that you understand the truth as it relates to getting a job, get back to your accomplishments. Under your most recent job, you should include several entries to demonstrate your marketability. Remember, don't try to include everything you've ever achieved in that job, just the highlights that make you an attractive candidate. With proper margin alignment and white space between each element we've discussed thus far, you should be at the bottom of page one. And that's proper—that's the way we construct a resume. Your last position and your accomplishments in that job are most critical. Your other jobs will go on page two unless your most recent position was relatively short. Continue the same philosophy with accomplishment statements, but don't go back more than about ten years chronologically or two-thirds of the second page graphically. If you have thirty or thirty-five years' experience, just summarize the work experience and your accomplishments prior to the last ten years. Refer to Lee's resume for an example of this technique. Another acceptable presentation is to list the job titles and dates with brief responsibility statements.

The point is that if the information is more than ten years old, few really care about the details. Summarize information that is dated; otherwise, you'll be cluttering up your resume with entries that won't be read because they're obsolete and/or irrelevant. We recognize that you may earnestly feel that you want to include a critically important accomplishment from many years back, but believe us, it probably won't help. Summarize it, and keep your resume to two pages. On the other hand, if you have space remaining on the second page to include more detail from early experience, by all means include it to fill your two pages. (See Jenkins sample resume.)

"JUST THE FACTS, PLEASE"

Next, list your *Military* background, but only if you were an officer (this indicates leadership capabilities) or if you served in a career-related enlisted rate (this implies hands-on training and experience). For example, an MIS degree coupled with pre-baccalaureate working experience on a military data processing system can enhance your attractiveness as a candidate. These entries should be brief and concise.

Cover your *Education* similarly. If you have advanced degrees, list the highest degree attained first, then any undergraduate degrees. If you graduated with honors, include your grade point average; otherwise, leave it out. Do not list training courses or seminars under *Education*. As we mentioned earlier, if you're working in a field that requires a degree and you don't have one, put in your resume that you're working toward the required degree, and give the projected completion date of your studies. (Again, don't lie. If your profession requires a college degree and you haven't completed school yet, do something about that. You're on borrowed time — enroll. Get a degree plan in action so that your resume won't be lying.)

The next resume entry is *Professional Affiliations*. Include here any societies, institutes, or other *Professional Associations* to which you belong. This shows the employer what you are when you aren't working. It implies civic involvement. Also, any certifications and registrations you have achieved should be listed here.

Finally, wrap up your resume with any other important job-related data, especially *Technical Skills* including computer hardware and software proficiency and *Language* fluency. It's also permissible to include an entry on community involvement or *Civic Associations*. But be certain that the information enhances your impact on the employer. Did you coach Little League baseball? That's great, but it doesn't belong in a resume. If you served on a mayor's committee to study the community benefits of youth sports programs, that should be included. Do you serve on the PTA board at your child's school? Leave it off. If you're an elected member of the community's school board, put that in under community involvement. Get the idea? The employer will buy into activities that either lend prestige to the firm or illustrate skills you can transfer to the workplace. The employer doesn't want to read entries in your resume that indicate priorities that will take time and energy away from your career.

Again, omit all personal information. Marital status? *No.* Number of children. *No.* Salary? *Never* — you'll cover that in the interview and in the cover letter if necessary. Reason for leaving a job? *No.* Hobbies? *No.* So you like hunting, boating, and camping — *who cares?* What does that have to do with your ability to do the job? Health? *No.* That one is a real joke. Have you ever seen a resume on which an applicant wrote "Health: Below Average" or "Health: Poor" or "Health: Terminally Ill"? No — everyone writes "Health: Excellent." Therefore, it means nothing. And it doesn't belong on your resume, so keep it off.

WHEN YOU COME TO THE END, STOP

Finally, we come to the traditional closing statement on 98 percent of all resumes: "References available upon request." Remember, we don't want your resume cluttered up with useless information, which is just what this is. It's implied — you don't write it in a resume. There might be one or two human resources managers in the world who don't understand that references are always available upon request. But cluttering up a resume on the remote possibility that somebody might read it is not a smart approach. If the guy reviewing your resume is such a rook that he doesn't comprehend this, you probably don't want to work at that company anyway.

You are now at the end of two pages, which means that your resume is complete. "But," you say, "what about my publications and the training courses I've taken?" Don't panic! For those of you who have additional career information that you feel is relevant to your qualifications as a candidate for a position, place such data on a third page. However, as a Supplemental Information page, it should not be sent out with the resume but should be presented at the interview. Your resume should remain two pages and only two pages. (Exhibit 5 is a sample supplemental information page showing the various categories that are pertinent to career advancement.)

RESUME TRACKING DATABASES

We've explained the importance of *verbs* in building your accomplishment statements. Now a note about the importance of *nouns!* Many companies utilize computer applicant tracking systems to manage the glut of resumes they receive and to facilitate the initial selection process. These databases search for *key words* to identify candidates with the background and skills required for positions. For this reason, it is important to include the nouns and technical terms that reflect your skills and knowledge. Standard abbreviations can be included, but also spell out their meaning unless they're common buzz words in your field. Using the technical jargon for your industry and function will come naturally, but be sure not to overdo their use at the expense of strong accomplishments.

Also keep in mind that scanners "read" differently than humans so follow these tips:

- Use font size of 10 to 11 points.

- Avoid italics, script, and excessive underlining and bolding.

- Avoid graphics and shading.

- Use a high quality printer.

- Use an original or high quality copy.

- Avoid faxing your resume.

- Do not use staples.

- Use light shaded paper — we prefer white.

- Avoid columns and other complex formatting.

When sending electronic resumes:

- Consider not using the most current software version – often companies have an older version.

- If you prefer sending a PDF version, follow up to see if the company needs the WORD version for entering into their data base.

THE PERSONAL TOUCH – COVER LETTERS

Now your resume is complete, but your work has just begun. Stay with us while we help you construct an excellent cover letter to introduce your resume, or else all your work will have been in vain. As good as your two-page resume will be, by its nature it's impersonal. Your cover letter will solve that problem. With a cover letter, your resume is targeted to a specific individual in the company. Always find out the name of the hiring authority. If you're an engineer, address the letter to the engineering manager, by name. If you're in sales, send it to the sales and marketing manager, and so on. No cover letter should carry the salutation "To whom it may concern." It will concern no one if you don't personalize it. The surest way to get the information is to find the name on the company's website, in online directories, in publications or through your network. Failing all that call the company and ask for the name of the appropriate person.

Think of your cover letter in three parts, and keep it short with generally three to five short paragraphs. (Exhibits 6 through 11 provide examples of cover letters.)

The first paragraph introduces you and gives your purpose for writing. Perhaps you got the company's name from a networking contact or from a listing, or maybe you read an article in a trade journal about the firm's plans for expansion or introduction of a new product. Whatever your reason for sending a resume, this is where you state it.

In the second paragraph, briefly summarize your experience as it relates to this company's needs. In this section, you're attempting to hook the company's interest by answering the question: "What can this person do for us?" Also in this paragraph (or in a short, separate paragraph), you address salary if you're answering a listing that demands current salary or salary requirements. You must not ignore such a request since that might disqualify you from consideration. Rather than listing your actual salary, we recommend submitting your compensation range based on your research. We'll cover how you do that in Chapter 9.

In the final paragraph, close with a proactive statement. This means that you take the initiative for the next contact. Don't leave it to the company. For example, many cover letters close with the statement, "Please contact me if you think my skills would help," and so forth. No — that's the wrong approach. That's reactive. When you're proactive, you write, "I'll contact you the week of July 7 to arrange an interview." Don't ever be passive when you write a cover letter. You'll sit on your hands and wait forever. Be assertive. Be professionally persistent. Go for it. (Two exceptions to this rule are cover letters to a search firm—Exhibit 10—and in response to a listing—Exhibit 6.)

Much is made of the importance of first impressions in job search—all of it valid. Few people stop to realize, however, that the format and style, plus the opening few words of a cover letter, actually constitute the very first impression they'll make on the company.

Your cover letter should be a product of your resume and your networking efforts. We've discussed cover letters in about 300 words while you've read maybe twenty times that much about resume writing in this book. That's not to minimize the role of a cover letter—there's just not that much to say about it. However, the cover letter is of critical importance, and you should strive for excellence in creating it, just as you do with your resume.

One note of caution: The cover letter is a business letter, not a personal letter (except when written to very close contacts) or poetic creation or prosaic dissertation. Please do not use flowery language or lengthy and complicated prose. Be direct and brief if you want to get the reader's attention. Remember, busy professionals and executives have stacks of reading that just may take priority over your cover letter. If they can't find the purpose of your letter quickly, it will be quickly ignored!

HOW TO GET NOTICED

Here is an example of how an effectively targeted and well written cover letter can get you noticed by a company:

> Carol had relocated to a new city and with a number of years experience in the purchasing arena, she had targeted a major company headquartered in her new home city as an ideal company for her industry experience. She did not know anyone in the company and her network was very limited having just relocated. She did some research and identified the senior vice president of purchasing in the company and crafted a letter of introduction to him indicating that she would be following up. The senior vice president passed her letter along to his procurement vice president, and before she even had a chance to follow up, she received a call from the vice president indicating his interest in her resume. Her initial letter of introduction with resume to the senior vice president led to an interview!

In this electronic age of email and online applications, do not overlook the power of a personal letter and follow-up to your targeted companies. When you do use email, we have some important guidelines outlined in Exhibit 12.

ACCEPT THE CHALLENGE

Striving for excellence is an imperative for your entire job search (and your life, as well). Follow the standards of excellence that we've set out for you in resume preparation, and adhere to the same conceptual approach in every step of your job campaign, up to and including the acceptance of an offer. Don't be discouraged by the bombardment of negatives you'll be hit with in your search. Certainly, there are thousands of others looking for jobs. Of course the market is tough—maybe tougher than ever before. But don't hide from the competitive nature of job campaigning. Respond to it. Challenge the numbers. Most of all have confidence—both in yourself and in our principles of searching for a new job. The fundamentals are the same as they were 30 years ago and as they will be 30 years into the future.

Having lived in Texas for many years now, we can safely adopt one of the building blocks of Texan philosophy: "If it ain't broke, don't fix it." So it is with resume preparation. Personal websites and video resumes are the latest craze. Whether or not these are appropriate to your campaign, you will still need your "A+" chronological, accomplishment-based resume to implement your job search effectively and optimize your use of linkage and psychological leverage to achieve a better job for better pay.

The tried-and-true system works. The only problem is that most people don't use it correctly. Strive to do it right. Expect to win. If you can't go into a competitive endeavor (which job search certainly is) expecting to win, don't play. It's the positive expectation of success that fosters success. If you don't expect to get the job offer, that attitude will show in all that you do, including your resume—especially your resume. The principles of positive thinking work every day for our clients. They will work for you, as well. Expect to get a job—not just any job, but the right career position for you.

Stop now and absorb what we've covered. Refer to the sample resumes and cover letters. Take the next two or three days to create a winning "A+" resume. Then read on and we'll make that resume work as hard for you as you worked at writing it.

EXHIBIT 3
Sample Resume A

PAUL LEE, P.E.
Address
Cell/Office/Home Phone
Email Address

OBJECTIVE

Senior Executive Management

SUMMARY

Over twenty-three years of experience in acquisition and successful management of domestic and international project opportunities in addition to extensive operations and business development activities. Have a proven track record in managing business opportunities to achieve superior financial results. Have demonstrated ability to develop and implement strategic business initiatives, integrate acquisitions into ongoing operations, and build winning engineering, field, and sales teams which have had a significant bottom line impact on overall company operations.

PROFESSIONAL EXPERIENCE

INDEPENDENT MANAGEMENT CONSULTANT   YEAR-Present

Currently under contract to Development E&C, Inc., with areas of responsibility which include: (1) advising senior management, (2) customer relations, and (3) special tasks. Agreement is non-exclusive and cancelable upon either full time employment or a full time consulting contract.

DEVELOPMENT E&C, INC. – City, State   YEAR-YEAR

Vice President Business Development (YEAR-YEAR)
Responsible for sales, marketing, and major proposals for environmental business unit with a 19 person staff and a $5.8 million budget. Environmental business unit was formed in YEAR by combining the assets of three business units. Primary focus was to capture the synergy that potentially existed with the company customer base while pursuing major program opportunities with government agencies. Participated in the development of annual business and operating plans which resulted in a restructuring of the long term strategic plan for the business unit.

- Led sales team to award of multiple contracts from first time industrial customers resulting in $60 million of additional revenue.
- Initiated marketing effort to introduce the environmental unit to industrial/commercial customers resulting in $750 million of new work prospects.
- Built sales program using national account coverage and 8 account executives to identify more that 100 prospects totaling $6 billion of potential work resulting in more than $1 billion of outstanding proposals.
- Led team which developed standards and work processes for managing major proposals with the goal to reduce proposal costs by 25% or $1 million.
- Led development and implementation of computerized common data base for tracking and reporting all aspects of business acquisition process targeted to improve competitive position with goal to increase win rate of new work by 40%.

EXHIBIT 3 *(Continued)*

PAUL LEE, P.E.

<u>Vice President Operations, Vice President Engineering</u>   (YEAR-YEAR)
Responsible for engineering and project operations in the field offices for the petroleum and chemical business unit. Managed $150 million annual segment of business with overhead budget of $12 million. Participated in steering committee overseeing the integration of acquired company into engineering operations. Directed or served as executive sponsor of projects for $1.2 billion of contracts in Texas, Illinois, Ohio, Wisconsin, Pennsylvania, Louisiana, China, Malaysia, Oman, Syria, Abu Dhabi, Ecuador, and Mexico. Served as executive sponsor for the largest remediation project ever managed by the company in the northeast U.S. and several other major projects

- Led task force to develop standard practices for bidding lump sum projects which reduced bidding costs by 40% or $4 million.
- Instituted overhead reduction program resulting in $1.2 million savings.
- Initiated project management programs to focus on consistent execution, and standardized reporting which improved accountability, cost effectiveness and bottom line returns.
- Directed reorganization of process engineering department to provide focus for oil and gas, polymers, and specific refining capabilities. Increased department size 35% to 140 employees.

<u>General Manager Marine Engineering: U.S. Operations</u>   (YEAR-YEAR)
Responsible for Marine engineering Operations in the Houston office. Directed or served as executive sponsor of projects for $1 billion of contracts for offshore Alaska, California, Louisiana, Texas, China, Egypt, Iraq, and Canada. Managed engineering staff of 400 involved in design of offshore structures, facilities, subsea pipelines, and naval architecture. Participated in development of company's global marine strategy and five year business plan.

- Managed $35 million segment of business which contributed $2.5 million to company bottom line.
- Increased backlog to greater than 1 million man hours for first time in five years resulting in $40 million of new revenues.
- Led management team which won President's Award for innovative design in offshore structures resulting in $500 thousand savings per application.
- Led acquisition teams to successful awards of $19 million in design engineering contracts. The Mobile Bay project is the largest sour gas treating plant in shallow water in the Gulf of Mexico. The Zinc Project is the first subsea completion in Gulf of Mexico using North Sea technology.
- Renegotiated master services agreement with major customer leading to 20% increase in operating margin/hour.

<u>Various Positions</u>   (YEAR-YEAR)
Held positions of increasing responsibility in engineering, project management, and general management.

EDUCATION

B.S., Chemical Engineering, State University, City, State – YEAR
Advanced Management Institute, Top University, City, State – YEAR

PROFESSIONAL REGISTRATIONS

Registered Professional Engineer in 9 states: (list States)

PROFESSIONAL AFFILIATIONS

Texas Society of Professional Engineers
National Society of Professional Engineers

EXHIBIT 4
Sample Resume B

JOSEPH JENKINS
Address
City, State Zip Code
Cell Phone
Home Phone
Email Address

OBJECTIVE

Sales Manager

SUMMARY

Over eighteen years' of successful technical sales and management experience including thirteen with a Fortune 200 medical diagnostics company. Have developed a proven track record in domestic and international sales of medical equipment and consumables with technical after market service. Have demonstrated negotiation, creativity and problem solving skills as well as excellent interpersonal skills emphasizing the team approach which have contributed to many successful projects and accomplishments.

PROFESSIONAL EXPERIENCE

RIDELLE BAKER & CO.– City, State   YEAR-Present

Regional Sales Manager, Diagnostic Instrument Systems   (YEAR – YEAR)

- Managed one of eight regions with eight sales representatives, directing sales, technical support and customer satisfaction resulting in $10 million in annual sales.

- Directed tactical implementation of regional/divisional strategic business plan which generated capital equipment sales in excess of $2 million annually, with $8 million in after market consumables for fiscal year (insert YEAR), and doubled sales volume from $4 million to $8 million in 4 years.

- Achieved consistent market share penetration over seven years resulting in an increase in regional productivity of 11% or $250,000 annually and an increase in market share for region to 75%.

- Coordinated customer-oriented sales penetration within a very competitive marketplace by integrating desired financial acquisition methods, which resulted in consistently high gross profit margins of 25-75% and improved divisional cash flow.

- Directed an international sales, marketing and service team of ten people, to create and implement strategic business plan for new market penetration in Mexico, resulting in incremental sales of $684,700 the first year, with gross profit margins exceeding 50%.

- Recruited, supervised and developed eight sales representatives in the Southwest Region comprised of ten states. Several sales representatives were recognized for national sales achievements (Presidents Club) which was comprised of the top 20% of the sales force.

- Initiated several Corporate Multi-Divisional contracts with key teaching hospital and private reference labs supporting various company divisions creating a prime vendor focus resulting in excess of $5 million in revenue.

- Established and promoted on-going business relationships with influential opinion leaders and executives, resulting in key clinical field trial sites, successful publication of data and significantly enhanced corporate image.

EXHIBIT 4 *(continued)*

JOSEPH JENKINS

National Accounts Manager – City, State   YEAR-YEAR

- Initiated and restarted divisional national account program, designed policy and procedure manuals and account reference book for field sales force which significantly improved efficiency.
- Developed and instituted strategic market profile analysis to systematize a prime vendor focus which resulted in key marketing alliances with national reference.
- Initiated new national agreements and negotiated renewals with existing customers of 14 major purchasing groups throughout North America resulting in $9.5 million annual revenue.
- Built and developed key, long-term business relationships with top management through the technologist level in national reference laboratories throughout the United States.
- Attained 250,000-unit increase in one year which represented an increase of $395,000 in revenues.
- Streamlined all policies and procedures and developed sales data audit program which resulted in significantly increased productivity of the field sales force and regional sales managers.
- Coordinated national account strategy for the entire North American sales team promoting improved sales focus which resulted in increased customer compliance to greater than 90%.
- Developed divisional reference material for implementation of corporate National Account incentive agreements for numerous institutions which provided a significant competitive advantage to the company.
- Compiled all sales information on a monthly and quarterly basis which was presented to top management contributing to effective communications throughout the organization.

Regional Sales Coordinator – City, State   YEAR-YEAR

- Assisted Regional Sales Manager with recruiting, interviewing and in-field training. Managed active sales territory of four states with a sales volume of $1.4 million annually and growth rate of 10%.

Territory Manager – City, State   YEAR-YEAR

- Increased revenues and sales, through new product introduction of diagnostic product lines, consistently averaging 20-25% growth per year in a highly competitive Northeast territory.

ALEX, INC. – City, State   YEAR-YEAR

Sales Representative

- Sold generic pharmaceutical products throughout the Northeast.

DUTTON – BAKER PHARMACEUTICALS – City, State   YEAR-YEAR

Sales Representative

- Sold pharmaceuticals to major teaching hospitals, physicians and drugstores in New York City.

EDUCATION

The Management Program – Top University, City, State – YEAR

B. S. Degree, Hospital Management, Pharmacy Minor
St. John's University, New York, New York – YEAR

EXHIBIT 5
Examples of Headings for Supplemental Information

SUPPLEMENTAL INFORMATION

Language Fluency

Fluent in French, working knowledge of Spanish

Additional Education

In-House Technical Courses: Utilities, VMS Concepts, Datatreive, DECWrite, Six Sigma, Customer Satisfaction, DECNET,VAXMAIL, ALL-IN-ONE

Honors

Sigma Theta Tau
Y.W.C.A.—Outstanding Woman YEAR Award
Dean's List—YEAR-YEAR, three semesters
College Expenses Earned—Undergraduate: 60% Graduate: 100%

Military

Captain, Medical Service Corps, United States Army, YEAR-YEAR

Professional Affiliations

Member, Natural Gas Association of Houston

Civic Associations

Metropolitan YMCA Board of Managers, Member, YEAR-YEAR

Professional Registrations

Registered Professional Engineer in 2 states: List States

Professional Licensure

Registered Pharmacist: List States and License Numbers

Publications

"HP 41 CV Simplifies API Leak Resistance Calculations." Published in June, YEAR of World Oil.

Seminars Conducted

Emergency Ambulatory Nurse Practitioner Program YEAR —
"OB/GYN Emergencies"

Selected Presentations

"Quality Assurance Supervisor in a Pediatric Hospital", Kang, Nancy, and Hotaling, William H.;

Mid-year clinical Meeting, ASHP, City, State, DATE,

EXHIBIT 6
Sample Cover Letter
Response to Listing

NAME
Address
City, State Zip Code
Cell Phone Number
Home Phone Number
Email Address

Date

NAME
TITLE
COMPANY
ADDRESS1
ADDRESS2
CITY, STATE ZIP CODE

Dear SALUTATION:

Your advertisement in the PUBLICATION on DATE for a POSITION is very attractive to me and I am interested in learning more about the position. I have enclosed my resume for your review and consideration.

As my resume indicates, I have twenty-five years of business experience with fourteen years in administrative management and eleven years in human resources. I have managed the Engineering Office Services Department of nearly 200 employees and was responsible for the overall management of a $3 million budget. I conferred with management and employee workforce on benefits, salary administration, worker's compensation, performance/disciplinary matters, and the company policies and procedures.

My compensation requirements are in the $100,000+ range.

I welcome the opportunity to discuss this position and my qualifications with you in person. If you have any questions or would like to schedule a meeting, please call me at the above listed number.

Sincerely,

Name

enclosure

EXHIBIT 7
Sample Cover Letter
Network Referral

NAME
Address
City, State Zip Code
Cell Phone Number
Home Phone Number
Email Address

Date

NAME
TITLE
COMPANY
ADDRESS1
ADDRESS2
CITY, STATE ZIP CODE

Dear SALUTATION:

REFERRAL suggested that I contact you concerning how my skills and abilities might serve the present or future needs of COMPANY, or other organizations and industries of which you are aware. Enclosed is a copy of my resume for your review and consideration.

As my resume indicates, I am results oriented with twenty-six years of professional broad-based worldwide purchasing and materials management experience. My ability to work with people, to find and implement innovative approaches has resulted in millions of dollars of savings during my career. Recent experience includes ISO 9002 registration and development of a formal supplier improvement process.

I will telephone you shortly to discuss our mutual interests and arrange a convenient time for us to meet. If you have questions or need additional information, please do not hesitate to contact me at the phone numbers listed above.

Sincerely,

Name

enclosure

EXHIBIT 8
Sample Cover Letter
Telephone Call Follow-Up

NAME
Address
City, State Zip Code
Cell Phone Number
Home Phone Number
Email Address

Date

NAME
TITLE
COMPANY
ADDRESS1
ADDRESS2
CITY, STATE ZIP CODE

Dear SALUTATION:

Thank you for taking time out of your busy schedule to speak with me today and, as you requested I have enclosed a copy of my current resume for your information. While you do not have any openings within your fine organization at this time, I appreciate your willingness to assist me in my job search.

As my resume indicates, I have more than 30 years of experience in the field of Information Systems and Management in several different industries. My background includes design, development, implementation and support of business applications such as financial, banking, administrative, manufacturing and distribution. I have also been functionally responsible for hardware and software evaluation and acquisition, vendor negotiations, short term and long range planning, as well as computer operations and control.

I successfully managed mainframes, mini-computers and micro-computers, as well as their integration with local area, wide area and public and private networks. In addition, I have been directly responsible for developing training curricula and conducting classes for technical and user personnel.

If you become aware of a position that matches my experience, please share my resume appropriately. I will be calling you periodically to bring you up to date on my progress. Thank you again for your help and consideration. If you have any questions or I can assist in any way, you can reach me at the above telephone numbers.

Sincerely,

Name

enclosure

EXHIBIT 9
Sample Cover Letter
Cold Contact

NAME
Address
City, State Zip Code
Cell Phone Number
Home Phone Number
Email Address

Date

NAME
TITLE
COMPANY
ADDRESS1
ADDRESS2
CITY, STATE ZIP CODE

Dear SALUTATION:

My research indicates that your company may provide me the opportunity to utilize my information management skills to make a contribution to your continued success, while achieving personal career growth.

As my enclosed resume indicates, I have over seventeen years of experience in information management relating to financial and administrative functions. In addition to providing application support and training, my background includes the ability to successfully work and communicate with all levels of an organization. Some of the highlights of my career include:

- Field tested an order processing software, which became the first fully successful field test of this application. Implementation enabled digital to shut down outdated systems country wide with an estimated savings of $100,000+.

- Assisted in the implementation of four US Expertise Centers which resulted in more effective support of in-house information systems.

- Managed software installations and upgrades by conducting project review meetings.

- Installed a procedure manual for the data center to use during evening work, which reduced the number of calls to analyst for assistance by at least 25%.

I am confident that I can achieve similar accomplishments to contribute to your organization, and would appreciate the opportunity to meet with you personally. I will contact you soon to set an appointment at your convenience. Thank you for your consideration.

Sincerely,

Name

enclosure

EXHIBIT 10
Sample Cover Letter
Search Firm

NAME
Address
City, State Zip Code
Cell Phone Number
Home Phone Number
Email Address

Date

NAME
TITLE
COMPANY
ADDRESS1
ADDRESS2
CITY, STATE ZIP CODE

Dear SALUTATION:

I am currently seeking opportunities as an Environmental Engineer. I have enclosed a copy of my confidential resume for your review and consideration.

With over six years of experience in detail engineering design and in the regulatory
and compliance field in the refining and chemical industries, I am looking for
new and challenging responsibilities in order to continue my career path. As my
resume indicates, I have a strong background in detail engineering design and
procurement, with excellent working knowledge of Federal and State codes in the
regulatory and compliance field. In addition, I have demonstrated capabilities in
quality engineering, team work, interpersonal skills, client satisfaction, and problem
solving techniques. My compensation requirements are in the range of $100,000+,
and I prefer to remain in the (City/Region) area.

If you have a client assignment matching my background, or would like to set up
an appointment, please contact me at the above phone number.

Sincerely,

Name

enclosure

EXHIBIT 11
Sample Cover Letter
Association Letter

NAME
Address
City, State Zip Code
Cell Phone Number
Home Phone Number
Email Address

Date

NAME
TITLE
COMPANY
ADDRESS1
ADDRESS2
CITY, STATE ZIP CODE

Dear SALUTATION:

You may be aware that I am currently involved in a job search. Through the years my friends and associates have been my strongest supporters and greatest asset. It is in that vein that I enclose my professional resume.

In my last position I took a diverse, discouraged, multi-cultural employee population through a difficult transition period and ownership change. This required strong communications skills at all levels, the ability to develop and lead a team and an understanding of conceptual change and appropriate actions needed to make those changes. I also have a strong background in marketing, public relations, problem-solving, organizational development, consulting and training.

In talking with a wide range of companies in the past few weeks, the most pressing need today seems to be for people who have personal integrity and a professional pride in their work. I offer those qualities to a progressive, quality-oriented organization.

Please feel free to call me at either of the numbers listed above if you should need any additional information. I will be following up with you and thank you in advance for your support.

Sincerely,

Name

enclosure

EXHIBIT 12
Email Recommendations

Some Principles:	• Send e-mail that is clear, concise, and considerate of recipients' needs. • Use correct spelling and grammar. • Respect reader's time. • Treat e-mail you receive as private. • Never assume e-mail you send will remain private. • Be very careful with forwarding e-mail messages from others. • E-mail isn't necessarily the right medium for every message. • Be very careful with attachments. • Be careful in the use of humor (never know how this might be received – consider — is it professional?). • Do not send email on weekends since they will likely be lost in the Monday morning spam mail.
Check List:	• Correct address? • Useful, descriptive subject line? • Format easy to read? • Purpose clear? • Message's tone appropriate? • Could any statement be misinterpreted? • Is e-mail the right medium to use?
The Subject Line:	• Always use one, be descriptive and to the point. • Keep it short. • Be sure it can easily be recognized in the recipient's in box. • Don't use wacky punctuation (Goes for everywhere in the e-mail).
Salutations:	• Use complete, formal address. • Use standard – Dear. • Determine if you feel comfortable with first name, or if using last name is more appropriate.
Body of Message:	• Follow suggestions for writing letters. • Clean, easy to read. • Short, double space between paragraphs. • Do not type in all capitals – some interpret this as "shouting". • Do not use italics, boldfacing, underlining, or multiple colors, fonts or backgrounds. • Do not use e-mail jargon (aamof – as a matter of fact; ASAP – as soon as possible; etc.).

EXHIBIT 12
(continued)

Sign Offs:	• Use complete sign off information, "Sincerely", or "Regards". • Full name, address, phone number, fax number, e-mail address, cell phone number. Remember, being contacted must be made as easy as possible for the reader.
E-mail Addresses:	• Keep simple and short, for ease of use by the recipient. • Consider establishing a separate e-mail address for your job search, which may help in tracking and saving information. • Design e-mail addresses without underscores – easier to read and communicate.

The Art of Preparing References: It's Not Just a List of Names

If you are tempted to skip this chapter as a non-essential step, think again. Not surprisingly, our view of gathering references links with every other facet of our job campaigning advice — that is, plan and prepare for each step of the process. Coach your references on what you'll be telling interviewers, and elicit their assistance in supporting those statements. Then carry your detailed preparation work a step further. The critical part in the entire reference-gathering process comes when you write the reference letter about your own professional background. Sounds strange, doesn't it? It's not at all strange, but it is a unique approach.

Most often references are barely mentioned in job search advice, except to verify that they are needed and to suggest that you write at the bottom of your resume: "References Available Upon Request." Having written your resume our way, you already know that statement is for use by amateurs only. In contrast, we rate the gathering of references as an imperative in successful job campaigning. Make no mistake about it, if an employer does nothing else in the way of a background check, they will usually verify your education and check your references. Therefore, you must effectively manage the flow of information from your references to potential employers. That's how you make references work for you rather than for the employer.

This step is tough, complex, and subtle. If your relationship with a former boss ranged somewhere between quiet resentment and open hostility, the process becomes even more difficult. But make it happen — there is no alternative. Even if the resume you've just created jumps off the desk into the employer's hands, and even if the interviewing techniques you'll learn in Chapter 8 convince the company that you're their last hope, the job offer you were riding high on could crash and burn if your former boss indicates that your personal interactive skills more closely resemble Saddam Hussein's rather than Mother Teresa's.

That's why we consider references an art, not just a list of names. Since for most job hunters our reference process is an untapped resource, successfully managing the complete scenario can position you for a huge advantage over the competition in the job market. For example, studies indicate that when job hunters endure a long, unproductive search, poor references are the root of the problem in about 40 percent of the cases.

Knowing that, why leave such a critical step to chance? Commit the extra effort and time to ensure that you get a reference letter, along with oral confirmation of the information, which will serve as a powerful complement to your winning resume and interview responses.

The only foolproof way to accomplish that is to write the reference letter yourself. The sequence is as follows:

- Call your potential reference to request a letter.

- Prepare a draft.

- Send it to your former associate with a cover letter inviting him or her to review and edit the draft and asking that the final draft be signed undated and returned on company letterhead.

- Put the resulting document in your job hunting tool kit, and you're beginning to stack some odds in your favor.

If you have any remaining doubts about the validity of this process, consider the case of one "Doubting Thomas."

> Tom had developed an A+ resume, which reflected outstanding accomplishments as a Vice President, Operations. When we suggested that his next step was to draft his reference letters, he looked at us like we were crazy. After considerable arm twisting, he proceeded to develop over a dozen top notch references. As his offers began to develop, he presented his references to the potential employers. He was astounded at the impression they made. As a result, he was able to negotiate a Senior Vice President title and a significant increase in compensation. He later used his new-found negotiating leverage to achieve a CEO position with another company.

References not only enhance the marketability of candidates with spotless records, but can salvage the careers of candidates who were terminated under difficult circumstances.

MEND YOUR FENCES, NO MATTER HOW BROKEN DOWN THEY ARE

Most employer-employee relationships can be patched up. Most bosses will cooperate. Most companies are as anxious for terminated employees to find a new position as the individuals are. When you run into an exception to that, you must bear part of the responsibility. And you'd better accept that responsibility now if you're in that situation, because — like it or not — your next potential employer will certainly assign you guilt. If you do have a bad relationship with your ex-boss — if you parted on difficult terms — this is an area where you must use psychological leverage to your advantage. There's nothing to be gained from maintaining a negative relationship with anyone. Our suggestion is that whenever you have a rift with someone in a job setting, bridge the gap immediately. The best way to bridge that gap is to ask for a letter of reference. Psychologically, this causes you to eat a slice of humble pie — which is good for anyone. Also, it causes your boss to rethink your work experience and, usually, to accept his or her share of the blame for the negative results of your previous relationship. Usually, the conclusion to the process is, "The least I can do now is write Tom a letter of reference."

We concede that there are impossible cases in which the resentment and anger simply can't be neutralized. But you can be sure that such a situation will hurt you in your job search. You'll be admitting that you don't have sufficient interpersonal skills to establish, maintain, or repair a key working relationship, and you'll be judged on that. You'll be in danger of joining that 40 percent of the job hunting population whose search keeps tripping over reference problems.

Never write off your relationship with your ex-boss, however, until you've given your best shot at getting a reference. And note that your best shot doesn't mean one phone call or a perfunctory inquiry through his secretary. It means professional persistence and courteous insistence that you expect nothing less. This is another example of what we call psychological leverage. In today's corporate legal environment, however, the reality is that companies are increasingly leery of providing references for terminated former employees. This is very unfortunate since excellent references are an important link in our job search system and are invaluable to your campaign.

Most of the time, however, the difficulty revolves more around pride and wounded feelings than it does around substantive or irresolvable differences between two people. The following illustrates this most clearly:

> Pete Smith, a terminated, angry former Vice President of Administration, entered our program. He did not have a reference from his former boss. We told Pete that he was making a mistake by not attempting to get one. He replied that he couldn't ask for one and, moreover, that he would never ask "that [expletive deleted]" for anything. Our reasoning fell on deaf ears, and Pete lost three straight potential jobs. When he learned that a poor reference was the cause, he came to us and asked for help in getting a reference from that most recent boss. Resisting the temptation to say "We told you so," we constructed a letter of reference, laid the groundwork with a diplomatic phone call, and forwarded the material to his former boss. Without the slightest delay or protest, the reference letter was routed back to us on the company letterhead. Pete got the next job for which he interviewed.

Your references validate your accomplishments. For each accomplishment on your resume, identify which of your references can support and vouch for your achievements.

Almost everyone underestimates the importance of a letter of reference. It can kill a job offer to not have one or to have a negative one. As we have indicated, there are situations in which corporate policy prohibits your former boss from writing in support of your job search. Often, former employers will do nothing except confirm employment, with starting and stopping dates of service. But before you give up and accept that policy, try to work around it — in a professional manner. For example, you might be able to convince your ex-boss to sign a personal letter vouching for your performance record; the letter can be on plain bond paper or on his or her own letterhead, rather than the corporation's. This would not have the impact of a corporate letterhead reference, but it's better than no reference at all. And take heart, even when your former boss cannot or will not violate a corporate regulation, at least you emerge even on the scale. Your lack of a reference is a result of corporate policy. Your new employer will get dates only, with no comments on personality or motivation and no confirmation of your accomplishments. Although this certainly won't help you convince the potential employer that you're the person for the job, neither will it detract from your campaign. When done correctly, writing your references yourself can be as difficult, or even more difficult, than writing your resume. First of all, you must write from the perspective and in the style of each reference, otherwise, they may all sound alike — a dead giveaway as to who wrote them! Secondly, they must validate your accomplishments. Once again, linkage is at work as you return to your resume. For each accomplishment on your resume, identify which of your references can support and vouch for your achievements. Then include them in the appropriate letters. You may also use performance appraisals or job evaluations written by specific references to help you create each letter. Here is one example:

> Karen left her former company under difficult circumstances related to performance issues. Her boss was reticent to discuss performance for this reason. To develop an excellent letter without compromising the reference's need for accuracy, Karen selected positive phrases directly from his performance review of her, leaving questionable areas unaddressed. The reference signed without objection and Karen avoided a potentially dangerous reference check.

Another excellent source of information for reference letters is your assessment. Selecting skills and qualities from your self-assessment or other assessment instruments helps to round out the reference letter on some of the personality and style issues in which companies are interested.

Most of our discussion has centered on a reference from your ex-boss, because that's typically the one that is toughest to get and hardest to control in terms of content. Getting it can be fraught with potential for conflict or at least uncertainty. That's not the only reference you'll need, however. We suggest a minimum of three — your boss, your boss's boss, and a peer. If you go beyond three, we suggest getting a letter from a subordinate next. That's extremely valuable to some employers. Conversely, you might want to go as high up in the company as possible for another reference. The higher the title — the more influence — the better. But remember, this is not just a list of names; your top executive reference must know who you are and what you did. If he or she is called, it's imperative that the responses given to a prospective employer will be consistent with what you said in the interview as well as with what your other references said about you.

Consistency becomes the key word here. It's not so much that the prospective employer will perform a cartwheel every time a positive statement is made about you. Nor will one negative comment hurt you that much. Everyone recognizes that personality conflicts exist in all workplaces. What's critical to the process is that, on balance, the employer expects to hear a common thread emerging when your personality, duties, accomplishments, and skills are discussed. That consistency drives this entire process. And of course it is an integral part of our linkage concept, which touches every element of your job search.

SPECIAL SITUATION REFERENCES

Beyond the traditional references, if you are a new graduate you may seek references from college faculty, staff, and organizational advisors. If you are involved in internships, these also may serve as excellent sources for references. For military personnel transitioning to the civilian workforce, seek references from your commanding officer, other personnel with whom you served but who also have transitioned out of the military and civilian personnel on base with whom you worked. For the return-to-workforce situation, references may come from volunteer organizations in which you were involved. A paid staffer can be especially helpful, since their credibility in evaluating skills and contributions would be significant.

Professional organizations can also serve as excellent references for regular employment roles, especially when involvement was extensive and resulted in significant contributions to your industry.

Finally, for the entrepreneur or consultant, references from clients and customers can be very valuable in soliciting new business. Do not hesitate to ask for these references to validate your contributions.

HOW MANY?

Six references are usually sufficient — and they all must be professional contacts. They all must be people who are familiar with your work experience. What your minister thinks, or your tennis partner, or your neighbor will have absolutely no impact on a prospective employer. Why should it? When do you suppose was the last time your minister gave someone a poor reference? Personal references are a waste of time and do not belong in your job campaigning tool kit.

Usually, references from your most recent employer are of greatest value. However, there are many situations when going back to earlier employers is important — for instance, when you have been with your latest employer only a short time or are still employed; when you are leaving a company that's in trouble or an industry that's in decline; or when your previous experience is of particular value to the new position you are seeking.

In addition, when you prepare your draft letter of reference, don't get too flowery. Keep the statements job-related. Don't try to convince a reader that you are without fault or that Michener could have chronicled your adventures in the office. Keep it simple, straightforward, professional. Obviously, your former boss is not suicidal simply because you no longer work there, so don't try to make it sound as if the company can't stay in business without you.

Specifically, think of a three-phase approach to reference gathering:

1. Get the letter.

2. Put your resume, a copy of the letter, and a brief worksheet outlining your responses to typical, tough interview questions into the hands of all of your references.

3. Immediately upon completion of an interview that has gone well, notify your references that you believe the company is considering making you an offer and that reference-checking calls likely are forthcoming. Then highlight what was discussed in the interview and tell your references briefly about the company and the person who interviewed you, what job you're pursuing, and what qualifications from your background you highlighted during the discussions.

THE REFERENCE INTERVIEW WORKSHEET

The brief interview worksheet can be informal. You simply want to cover some of the key questions to which you'll respond in the interview and determine that your former associate can and will support your statements. Remember, don't try to tell your former boss to do this and do that. The entire process involves negotiation, communication, and flexibility. State what you will be saying regarding your accomplishments and ask if there is any problem with that. If so, discuss it and make your points. Walk step-by-step through your accomplishments at the company, reminding your former boss why you are claiming the accomplishments listed on your resume.

This process links with our earlier discussion of truth in preparing your resume. Many of our clients initially think that we encourage people to play fast and loose with the truth, to say whatever looks good in a resume. But that is absolutely not the case. You state what you accomplished in terms that make you appear as attractive as possible to the prospective employer, but you never go outside the limits of truthfulness. If you do, the negotiation step with your former boss will roadblock you.

PREP YOUR REFERENCES

On your worksheet, jot down typical interview questions and what your responses will be. (You'll learn later, in our interviewing chapter, that your answers to these questions will be identical from one interview to the next, so it's perfectly logical to commit them to paper.) For example, prep your reference with your responses to these questions:

- How do you know me?

- How long have you known me?

- What specific results or accomplishments have I provided for the company?

- What are my strengths and weaknesses?

- Under what circumstances did I leave?

- Would you rehire me?

- How did I get along with people?

- Did I meet deadlines?

- Do you know of anything that would disqualify me from performing the job in question?

- Is there any other information you can share?

- Is there any other person in the company who can discuss my work performance?

Remember, your references must have your resume, preferably the worksheet, and a copy of the reference letters they have agreed to sign in their possession. Moreover, they should be on the person's desk when the reference checker calls. That's the purpose of your last-minute, post-interview phone conversation with each reference. It gets you fresh in his or her mind, and you can encourage the reference to pull out your file and be ready to confirm the responses to which both of you have already agreed.

Exhibits 13 and 14 provide examples of the cover letter and the draft of the letter of reference. Notice how the reference letter validates the accomplishments of Paul Lee from Chapter 3.

One more key point — along with your letters, carry a list of references in your job search tool kit everywhere you go. Your four, five, or six names should be listed as shown in Exhibit 15.

PREPARATION IS THE KEY

Put all the information in your tool kit, and you're ready to face any job search scenario with a high-impact, impeccably professional stack of assets in your corner — your resume, letters of reference, and a list of references. Be certain that you have multiple copies of each, and present them to each interviewer you meet at a company. Preparation is what job search is all about. Most often, landing a job will require multiple interviews over an extended period of time. On occasion, however, a window of opportunity will open, perhaps only for hours. That's the eventuality for which you always want to be prepared. By arriving for your interview with a tool kit full of information, you're ready for multiple interviews, you're ready for a reference check, and you're ready to entertain a job offer today. Whether or not you accept it depends on other varied factors that we'll address in subsequent chapters. In every case, however, whether it takes two hours or six weeks to draw an offer from the employer, you want to be ready. Have your references coached and prepped, with the appropriate papers on their desks — ready to support your statements and your career future.

Put linkage into action in gathering your references, and enjoy the fruits of your extra effort as your job search builds momentum.

Do you see how our professional approach to job search unfolds—each step linked to the one before and the one to come next? You take a proactive posture to touch every base, to cover any eventuality. And you anticipate events—you don't react to them. The numbers for an employer's search work like this: start with 100 - 250 resumes in response to an opening; screen out 75% on the first reading. Forward the remaining resumes to the hiring authority; screen out all but eight. Interview those eight and invite five back for follow-up sessions. Cut it to two candidates, and finally pick the winner. Except for the first cut, this screening process is seldom cut and dried. By the way, when companies utilize online resume portals, they often select the first 100 or so resumes to review and if they do not provide sufficient candidates for interviews, they will select another 100, and so on.

So timing is often very critical to being in the cut. This is why utilizing your network is so important to ensure that you are among those interviewed!   In each step of the process, there are small distinctions between winners and losers.

> Martha was interviewing for a director-level position for the first time. After considerable negotiation, she accepted the position. Later her new boss shared with her that while she was not initially the number one candidate, her strong references pushed her ahead of her competitor, whose references were poorly prepared and failed to validate his accomplishment/capability claims.

That's what our philosophy of psychological leverage is all about. We want you to be a half-step ahead of the competition, just as Martha was.

That doesn't come easily, however. It's an outgrowth of your time and effort, hard work, consistency, preparation, and discipline. Always, the winners in any endeavor will tell you that there's a direct correlation between hard work and good fortune. And nowhere is that "hard work/good luck" scenario more evident than in a job search. So put linkage into action in gathering your references, and enjoy the fruits of your extra effort as your job search builds momentum.

EXHIBIT 13
Cover Letter Requesting a Reference

PAUL LEE
Address
City, State Zip Code
Cell Phone
Home Phone
Email Address

DATE

Mr. Brandon Smith
President
Bayou Development Co., Inc.
PO Box 334
Houston, Texas 77002

Dear Brandon:

I appreciated the opportunity to speak with you last week and would like to thank you for agreeing to write a letter of reference on my behalf. To date, I have initiated a very aggressive job search campaign and am confident that letters of reference will play an important part in obtaining a new and challenging opportunity in a timely manner.

As we discussed, in order to assist you I have enclosed a draft letter for your review and consideration. I would encourage you to make any changes you feel necessary and then ask you to return the final letter to me on company letterhead, undated. Also enclosed is a copy of my resume for your information.

Brandon, I appreciate your assistance very much in this matter. Please let me know if you have any questions or if I can be of assistance to you in any way.

Sincerely,

Paul Lee

PL:ccr
enclosure

EXHIBIT 14
Draft of a Letter of Reference

COMPANY LETTERHEAD

(DRAFT)

Re: Paul Lee

To Whom It May Concern:

It gives me great pleasure to introduce Paul Lee. For two important assignments at Development E&C—General Manager, Marine Engineering and Manager of the Mobile Office—I was his direct supervisor.

The Mobile Office was opened to provide design engineering to the local plants of Development E&C's Gulf Coast customer base. Paul started the office and served as the first manager. During the start-up phase, his management duties included site selection, staff development, strategy implementation and business development. Most of the work was obtained by calling at the local level in the engineering and maintenance departments or the purchasing department of the plants and mills in the surrounding area. The ability to become competitive against local competition quickly required a thorough understanding of the local conditions and the overall engineering business, careful planning, cost control and prudent management. The action plan successfully implemented for Mobile is an example of Paul's organized logical approach to solving complex tasks. The office has grown rapidly both in reputation and size of staff. Today it is one of Development E&C's major domestic resource centers. Again, much of the success the office has earned is the result of the efforts of and traditions established by the original management team assembled by Paul and the dynamic leadership he provided.

I was particularly pleased when the $1 million investment to start the office was recovered one year ahead of plan despite very difficult market conditions and a general downturn in the economy. This achievement further demonstrates Paul's unique business skills and ability to impact the bottom line.

As General Manager, Marine Engineering, Paul was responsible for maintaining Development E&C's offshore engineering capabilities in the Houston office. His energy, strong technical background and overall management skills made him ideally suited for the assignment. In a very competitive market his group was able to translate the value of our marine engineering credentials for technical excellence and innovation into awards of more that $19 million of high margin design work from Exxon. Paul's creative approach, leadership and organizational skills were instrumental in our winning acquisition strategies for these projects.

As a final point I would like to comment on Paul's integrity and character. In many challenging assignments, he has always maintained the highest standards of quality. His work ethic and commitment to excellence are outstanding personal traits.

It would be a pleasure to assist Paul in any way that I can. As an executive, he would make an excellent addition to any organization. Please call me if you have questions or desire additional information.

Sincerely,

Tommy E. Carlin
Vice President, International Development

EXHIBIT 15
Sample Reference List

PROFESSIONAL REFERENCES FOR PAUL LEE

Mr. Edwin Galworthy
President
Development E&C, Inc.
Street
City, State, Zip
Phone
Email

Mr. Tommy E. Carlin
Vice President, International Development
Development E&C, Inc.
Street
City, State, Zip
Phone
Email

Mr. Brandon Smith
President
Bayou Development Co., Inc.
Street
City, State, Zip
Phone
Email

Mr. Perry Winstead III
President & CEO
Melanesia Exploration, Ltd.
Street
City, State, Zip
Phone
Email

Build Your Network: Eighty Percent of Successful Job Hunters Can't Be Wrong

As you no doubt have already noticed, we are not at all shy about telling you what *won't* work in job search. With the same degree of confidence, when we find a technique that does work—such as a two-page, chronological resume or networking—we'll tell you straightaway. You now know that a two-page, chronological resume should serve as the drive wheel for your job search. But the fuel for your search engine is networking.

We're well aware that networking has fallen into disfavor among so-called "savvy" job hunters. Many self-anointed "experts" now claim that networking is passé, that the American job market has been just about networked to death. Well, we dismiss that nonsense out of hand. Successful job hunters are like salmon swimming upstream. The one percent courageous enough to go against the current instinctively struggle to reach the river's source. Although the majority of job searchers looking for an easy placement float downstream, the one percenters who take control of their campaigns know that they must go against the

One Percenters Club
Successful job hunters are like salmon swimming upstream. The one percent courageous enough to battle the current achieve success.

current to get to where the jobs are. The truth is that if you wish to join our *One Percenters Club* of successful job hunters, you must unequivocally accept the concept of networking. Further, you must study it until you're a master. When you can make the telephone sing as though Chopin had scored a networking concerto for it, you will begin to break loose from the masses out there who are failing at job search. In our view, those who bad-mouth networking are selling you a rotten bill of goods—suggesting that networking is nothing more than another transitory fad in our disposable society. This reveals their purely commercial intent: Peddle it, use it, and then discard it like an empty plastic soft drink container. Then search for a new fad—another hot-button that will sell a few more books or CDs, or schedule a few more talk shows.

Job hunters, if you swallow that—if you accept the flawed logic that networking is old and cold—you're practically guaranteeing failure in your campaign. Networking is not and never has been simply a manifestation of pop culture. Rather, it is one of three key strategies to a winning game plan in job search. For strategy A, we created the resume (yours should be complete by now). For strategy C, you will put on an interviewing performance that ensures that the employer will want to put your name in lights, to say nothing of offering you a job (you'll learn all that in Chapter 8). As important as these two strategies are, however, without networking you're trying to skip a step, a very difficult proposition indeed.

When you utilize networking, strategy B is in place. This assures proper use of linkage in your job search, and it practically guarantees that you'll be a step ahead of the rest of the world in locating and accessing job openings. Even beyond specified openings, truly excellent networkers create their own positions by identifying an employer's need, and then selling their skills and background as the solution. So take our word for it; we've learned from many long, difficult counseling sessions with clients trying to make the tortuous journey from A to C without networking. Use our A, B, C strategy in your search, and let linkage build your momentum.

This is not meant to minimize the difficulties of networking. The reason this concept has slipped from its favored status among job search "experts" who are always looking for a hot fad is simply because too many people use it unprofessionally. Each time some unprepared person calls a company executive without a conversational agenda, without direction, and without goals, he or she wastes everyone's time. As a consequence, the road is that much rougher for everyone who follows. Your task will be that much more challenging.

Don't confuse the issues here, however. Just because networking is misused, abused, and trivialized by amateurs doesn't mean that you must choose an alternative. Quite simply, there are none. U.S. Department of Labor statistics prove that 80 percent of people who find jobs do so by networking. Even when you factor in the impact of the internet on job search, networking is still integral to success. In fact, the internet has actually accelerated the value, efficiency and popularity of networking! Effective networking gets jobs. The more you do it and the better you do it, the sooner you'll be selecting the best position from among several offers.

HANDLING THE "NO" IN NETWORKING

So much negativity permeates job search that people despair easily during the journey. "No'" is a major part of the process. We mentioned earlier the juvenile system of working through the no's and rejoicing because each no means that you're getting closer to the ultimate yes. Although this is an attempt to instill positive thinking, it overlooks the more proactive approach. Our promise to you is that when you network effectively, you do more than move toward the final yes. In fact, you modify, or even circumvent, the no's. Rather than receiving a rejection, a good networker can transform an unproductive conversation into a lead at another company, with another person—another potential job opportunity, another potential *yes.*

With effective networking, you take command of your job search. Certainly, there will be no's. Rest assured that you will run into people who won't even give you the time of day. But remember, you can make the numbers work for you. When you're making twenty-five, forty, or fifty phone calls a day, it is not so depressing to get a no, even if it is from someone who is rude. The trick is to distill out nonproductive calls after about ten seconds and move along to your next call. You'll learn the fundamentals of using the phone to generate leads—what to say, what not to say, how to set goals for each day and each phone call—in Chapter 7. Our point here is that you must commit now to the philosophy of building and using a network in job search. If you're swayed by any advice to the contrary, you're only postponing success and complicating your job search.

We've counseled with thousands of clients, and we can attest to the fact that good networkers never sit idle—wallowing in self-pity, drowning in rejections. They stay up, active, and positive. They don't have time to be depressed, because they're so active on the phone. Moreover, results sustain that positive momentum. When you do networking the right way— when you fully commit to it—the constant leads and new information you obtain will guarantee that you won't be defeated by rejection. Although there are many negatives to overcome in job search, they should never dominate your life. The people who sit by the phone, depressed, are typically those who rely on search firms and internet listings or resume postings to do the work for them. We agree that the situation is tough to go through, but at the risk of sounding unsympathetic, those people are getting out of job search just about what they put into it—nothing. That's the nature of job search when you abandon the tried-and-true principles set forth on these pages—when you won't put in the time, effort, and dedication necessary to take charge of your own campaign.

NETWORKING GIVES YOU A MARKET ADVANTAGE

The statistics from the U.S. Labor Department cited earlier—that 80 percent of jobs come from networking—become even more dramatic when you consider the following ironic pattern. Even when you consider the dramatic impact of the internet on connecting candidates and companies, networking is critical to ultimately obtaining an interview and an offer leading to placement. Even if you may find a listing online and a company requires an online application or submittal of your resume, it is often your follow-up through your network or cold calling to the hiring authority that gets your resume and credentials considered.

Although only 10 to 30 percent of jobs are found through listings and search firms, our informal surveys indicate that about 80 percent of job searchers concentrate their searches there. These are, of course, the simplest ways to look for a job—that's what draws the majority to them. By contrast, only 20 percent of job searchers concentrate full-bore on networking. When you realize that most job seekers, perhaps as many as 80% concentrate their efforts online or through agencies, than you begin to see the advantage of going a step further and integrating your online leads with networking. While 80% of seekers sit back and wait for a response, only 20% of job seekers aggressively network into the interview. Another way to put the statistics into perspective is to consider that 80% of job seekers are concentrating on 20% of the potential!

> Networking is like shopping in an area where 80% of the merchandise is located, but only 20% of the shoppers!

Which side of the equation do you want to be on? With the 80% who are passive seekers, or with the 20% who are in control of their destiny through proactive networking? Imagine it! If you follow our approach, you will be shopping in an area where 80% of the merchandise is located, but only 20% of the shoppers! If that supply/demand market advantage doesn't convert you to networking, perhaps you are not really that serious about your search.

Our feeling is that many people who fail to buy into the concept of networking misunderstand what it is and what it isn't. The statement "Network your way into the hidden job market" can be intimidating to a novice, even if you're a novice with twenty-five years' experience in health care, in general management, or in any other field. So let's dissect that statement:

- *Networking:* If you can talk, you can do it. Cold-calling on the phone is very difficult initially, but it's a learnable, doable skill. If you think, "I'm an analyst, not a salesman; we don't do that" or "I'm a Senior Vice President and Chief Counsel; we don't do that at this level" think again. If you want a job, you'll do it. Does networking mean talking to important people who can offer you a position? Yes, it does, but that's only one very limited fraction of the whole equation. In total, networking means talking to everyone—personal and professional acquaintances and friends as well as brand-new contacts—telling them your situation, and asking if they can assist or refer you.

- *The hidden job market:* This one throws a lot of people, and it's probably somewhat misleading. Our view is that too many people think that the hidden job market means a closed market, with all the jobs reserved for insiders or the sons-in-law of the Chairman. Without dwelling on family relationships, trust us—many Board Chairmen would much rather hire you than their sons-in-law. So, in fact, that job isn't hidden; it's just not public knowledge. It will come open and be filled before most people know about the vacancy. Frequently, that includes the corporate human resources department—to say nothing about search firms or readers of newspaper ads. Your challenge is to make a networking contact at the right place and the right time to learn about that "hidden" job.

LUCK HAPPENS WHEN OPPORTUNITY MEETS PREPARATION

Is all this luck? You'd better believe it. We guarantee that networkers who place at least 25 phone calls a day will experience the same sort of luck generally believed to be reserved for successful or famous people. Strive toward becoming a one percenter. The hidden job market is really analogous to an iceberg, 90 percent of which is out of sight. Just go below the surface and you'll find out how big it really is. That's precisely how the job market operates—not so much hidden as undiscovered by the superficial job seeker.

The elements of success in networking center on confidence in what you're doing, coupled with the requirement that you make each networking contact a true exchange of information. People who use a networking contact to get what they want but give nothing in return are the people who are contaminating the networking landscape for the rest of us. For example, we can't stand the phrase, "I'd like to pick your brain." That's an insult to us; we infer from that statement that someone wants for free what it took us years of hard work to build.

> The hidden job market is really analogous to an iceberg...90% of it is out of sight.

As part of your job search, you'll be researching companies and industries, so be prepared to share that information if it's useful to your contact. Also, offer to help with a problem if you can. And don't forget, for your hottest contacts, The Number One Rule of Networking: Everyone Likes to Eat. The corollary to that is Rule One-A: Everyone Really Likes to Eat When Someone Else Pays for It!

Our point is that you must be prepared to give back while you receive. And commit to certain fundamentals—such as asking for one minute of the contact's time (generally, that gives you license to take three minutes). Just be certain that you don't waste anyone's time — yours or the contact's. Get in and out quickly. (We'll cover all the do's and don'ts in Chapter 7, under lead generation.)

If you're like most people, you've probably listed five to ten people that you think can help you find a job. Our network includes over 5,000 names. We're not insisting that yours be that extensive, but five or ten just won't get it done. If you don't have at least 100 names listed, you're not thinking creatively. Consider these sources:

- Family members
- Colleagues, present and past, and executives for whom you've worked
- Classmates, teachers, campus placement officials, and alumni
- Fellow members and alumni of organizations, fraternities or sororities to which you belong
- Professional acquaintances: lawyers, stockbrokers, accountants, bankers, real estate brokers, insurance agents, elected officials, industry leaders, consultants, doctors, dentists, salespeople, and so forth
- Community members in clubs or associations to which you belong, neighbors, church members, local merchants, fund raisers, sponsors of performing arts, and wealthy people
- Officials of professional organizations, whether or not you are a member, as well as speakers at any of their meetings
- Suppliers, previous customers, even creditors
- Editors and writers for trade journals
- Internal and external recruiters — retired or active
- The local Chamber of Commerce
- Anyone and everyone on your Christmas card list
- Internet forum and social network contacts

Finally, don't forget your checkbook as another source. Anyone to whom you've written a check within the past year can be considered a possible network contact.

Remember, build your contact list on the strength of your acquaintance or friendship with each person. Do not, at this time, attempt to evaluate whether or not these people will be able to help you. That is a subjective process which wastes time and is inherently self-defeating.

One of our clients recently obtained exactly the position he sought with the help of his former boss, an obvious contact frequently overlooked.

Henry Little wanted to move from a huge, billion-dollar company to a small, growing organization where he could utilize his entrepreneurial skills. Among the primary contacts he made was Joe Stratton, his former boss. Joe suggested a company that, as a subsidiary of a major U.S. firm, could offer him a ground-floor opportunity in a dynamic entrepreneurial environment—and one with significant financial backing. After four rounds of interviews, Henry got the job he wanted. Had he not contacted his former boss, he never would have discovered this opportunity.

Don't judge your contacts: list them and use them. In your personal organizer record each name, phone number, title, address, the initial contact and when and how you will follow up, plus that follow-up contact and what happened in the follow-up. Let's stop here for a key point. Job hunters and those who offer advice on the subject wrestle interminably with the question of timing follow-ups to contacts: "How long should I wait?" Stop all that nonsense and think. Communicate. The quickest, simplest, and most direct way to resolve the question is to ask your contact. There is no set formula, no right or wrong answer. Simply ask your contact when he would be agreeable to a re-contact, and note that in your record book. (Exhibit 16 provides a form for listing personal/professional contacts.) Chapter 7 discusses record keeping further.

THE NEXT STEP

Now for the critical part of networking—going beyond the initial contacts. Seldom will the 100 people on your list of primary contacts actually provide you with a job lead. What they can do is provide you with another level of contacts. So you must develop techniques for expanding your network. Even the second level of contacts usually doesn't ring the bell. But when you broaden and deepen your network to the third tier—your tertiary network—you will begin to access viable job leads. To that end, part of every networking contact should include questions such as "Do you know who your counterpart is in XYZ company?" Again, we'll cover all the techniques of lead generation in Chapter 7. But rest assured that you must push each contact to the limit if you're to succeed at networking. Your goal should be to get at least two or three additional names from each contact. Assuming that you start with 100, do you begin to see the impact you're about to make on your job search?

Remember, you must, *without fail,* send a thank-you letter or email to each productive contact. If a person takes the time to try to help, acknowledge that with a thank-you note and resume. Of course, if you arranged a follow-up contact with the same person, confirm that in the letter or email as well. The thank-you letter should be very brief, but it's essential. It confirms to the network contact that he or she is dealing with a pro when talking to you.

WHAT ABOUT HUMAN RESOURCES?

You're probably wondering why we haven't mentioned human resources as a contact. It's not that we don't like human resources, or that they are unimportant to the hiring process. But when it comes to networking, they are not usually your best starting point. As you network within a company in regard to a specific opening, you will probably make contact with human resources at some point, and they may even conduct your first interview. However, your initial networking target should be the *hiring authority,* who is usually the top person in your functional area or the person to whom this position reports. In addition, your initial networking contact may be someone you already know either within or outside the target company, who has some association with the hiring authority. If you have no "warm" contact to help you get to the hiring authority, then target him/her directly with a "cold" contact. Here's a classic example of why this strategy is necessary:

> Deborah had networked within a company from several directions; leaving no stone unturned, she included human resources, sending them a letter and resume. She also contacted the hiring authority, as well as Linda, a former associate in another department. When she followed up with a phone call to the hiring authority, he indicated that he had received her letter with resume, and had also received Deborah's resume from Linda along with her recommendation. Impressed, he suggested an interview, which led to a series of interviews, an offer, negotiations, and Deborah's acceptance of the final offer. Later Deborah received a post card from human resources thanking her for her resume but indicating that there were currently no openings!

OTHER NETWORKING LEADS

Theoretically, the networking process should never end, but inevitably you'll hit a few days when your contact potentials seem to have dwindled. What then? Do you go into withdrawal and begin to hallucinate that you'll never find a job? Not if you use your head and develop a list of target companies besides those your personal/professional referral network helped turn up. Potentially, this is where cold-calling can really turn frigid. But don't panic—your research on the companies and industries you target will provide you with the knowledge and confidence to warm up your calls and produce new leads.

The internet has dramatically improved the access to information, however there are five major reference sources for researching target companies and industries, most of which can be accessed through the internet:

- Directories and databases.

- Annual reports/10K reports.

- Newspapers and other current periodicals.

- Professional associations.

- People in general.

Exhibit 17 provides a listing of suggested resources that are invaluable to your research. If you use them, you will never deplete your list of cold-calling prospects. When you first begin to review the directories and databases, you'll likely be overwhelmed with the sinking feeling that you're about to look for the proverbial needle in the haystack. Obviously, you must narrow down the target area on the basis of your preferences as well as market realities. The following are some of the criteria to consider in targeting companies:

- Type of industry.
- Products/services.
- Growth/decline industry.
- Geography/locality.
- Job availability.
- Company size.
- Corporate culture/management style.
- Employment policies.
- Compensation/benefit policies.

Research as much information as you possibly can about a company and its requirements.

- Read materials about the company and check the online forums and blogs.

- Arrange a tour of the company if possible.

- Inquire about the nature of the work.

- Learn about possible job functions.

- Study job requirements.

- Ask about recruitment policies.

- Find out why management hires the people they do.

- Ask about the potential for advancement.

- Learn what you can about compensation, benefits, perks.

- Keep notes on each company you explore.

Exhibits 18 and 19 provide forms on which to list your target companies by high, medium, or low priority and to record your research notes.

INTERNET DATABASES

Developing target lists of companies is facilitated by the use of internet databases of companies. There are a number of databases available and the range and ability to manipulate data varies widely, affecting their usefulness. For public companies, access to SEC data including annual, 10K, and quarterly reports is ideal. To target companies in specific geographical areas and industries efficiently, the database must be designed to search by multiple variables including industry segment, product, key words, geographical location, and size. Databases which are particularly useful for identifying target companies include private as well as public companies, and provide access to divisions and subsidiaries of larger companies. Effective databases can reduce research time significantly and expand your list of target companies beyond your personal and professional contacts—a real boost to the networking process. Beyond public data bases, check with your public and university libraries to enhance your research capabilities. Many of these data bases are free, but some are fee based.

OTHER ON-LINE INFORMATION SERVICES

In our technologically driven marketplace, the on-line information boom has provided new ways of networking. Resume databases, on-line job postings, specialized forums and blogs, and job and career resources can be useful tools, but be cautious in their use. Similar to ads and agencies, these "listings," while electronic, can still be dangerous! When it comes to resume databases, ask first who has access to them. If searches are included without your control of your resume, steer clear. With job postings, keep in mind that all other users have access to the same listings—remember the 80-20 odds! Beware too of listings by search agencies—know to whom you are sending your resume. (See Chapter 6 for cautions on the use of search firms.)

Universities and associations are using on-line services to meet student and member needs. These forums can give you access to a "warm" network of contacts. While the information super highway and these high-tech methods of networking can provide access to vast numbers of contacts, the traditional methods of calling and following up are still essential to getting in front of the hiring authority to get the offer.

FACE-TO-FACE NETWORKING

While research and lead generation are essential to effective networking, nothing energizes your network more than face-to-face contacts. Getting in front of people, shaking hands, smiling, conversing, and sharing information may sound like socializing, but when it comes to your job search, these encounters are networking at its best. Wherever you meet people, make it an opportunity to network:

- Association meetings—civic and professional.

- Club meetings and activities.

- Church gatherings.

- Luncheons.

- Shopping, banking, appointments of any kind.

- Conventions.

Following are some typical examples:

> Craig went to the club to exercise three times a week. After a particularly hard workout, he decided to take a whirlpool bath. As he chatted with a fellow club member whom he had never met, they started to discuss his job status. The result was a lead which ultimately led to an offer!

> Beth was doing some grocery shopping and as she waited in line, she began conversing with another shopper. She mentioned her job search—one thing led to another until the shopper asked for her resume which Beth just happened to have in her car. She obtained the shopper's name and number to follow up.

> Cliff was on a flight and began a conversation with another passenger, who he learned was an attorney. As they shared information, Cliff realized that the attorney could be a source of clients for his expert witness consultancy. They exchanged business cards. Cliff later followed up with a resume and a phone call which resulted in additional business.

Wherever two or three are gathered together, it is an opportunity to network. If you are an introvert, this is no time to be shy. Take the initiative and practice being an extrovert! To help you develop opportunities for interaction, follow these tips:

- Structure networking opportunities by attending scheduled activities.

- Follow-up your letters by suggesting one-on-one get togethers.

- Offer to assume formal roles in associations or other clubs in which you have a greater chance of developing contacts.

- Offer to help at the registration table for conferences or other formal meetings.

Here are additional tips on how to "work the room" at association meetings and other gatherings:

- Keep a positive attitude and be friendly.

- Read name tags and use names frequently.

- Have business cards available, even if you are currently unemployed; be sure to collect business cards and follow up with those you meet.

- Similar to your two-minute response to the interview question, "tell me about yourself," prepare a self-introduction.

- Prepare several conversation topics that would be of interest to attendees as well as questions to ask.

- Look for loners—they are probably introverts who would just love to be approached!

- Set a goal for number of contacts you would like to make for the meeting.

- Circulate and have fun.

- Follow up with contacts and expand your network and your leads!

THE PROCESS

In summary, think of networking as a five-step process:

1. Prepare your contact list. Include not just important decision-makers but everyone who may be able to help you. Also include your list of target companies.

2. Send a resume and cover letter to each of your primary contacts. Just because a contact happens to be your brother, you're making a serious mistake if you assume that he knows all there is to know about you and your career.

3. Use your contacts properly. Be aware that your network will usually think more in terms of jobs open or not open than in terms of your individual skills and background. Help keep each contact focused on you—on what you've done before and can do in the future as well as on how potential employers might use your skills and experience. Remember to offer your assistance to your contacts in any way possible.

4. Always ask permission to use the name of your contact. Then do just that, both in phone conversations and in correspondence. Nothing drives the networking process more quickly and more effectively than a personal reference. That's how you break through into secondary and tertiary contacts. Always open the conversation or letter with a phrase such as "A mutual acquaintance, John Robertson, suggested that I contact you." The body of the letter (or phone conversation) should very briefly summarize

who you are and why you're making contact. Then close with a proactive statement about calling or visiting soon to discuss mutually beneficial ideas.

5. Follow up. Again, let your contact set the schedule. Just be certain that you adhere to it and re-contact each person within the agreed-upon time. Report back to your contact when a lead pans out. It's not only professional to do this, but it keeps that person aware of and interested in what you're doing and where you're going. Even if a secondary contact doesn't develop into a job lead, when you keep your primary contacts advised, you're inevitably drawing them closer to your corner for future contacts and assistance. This is how psychological leverage works in networking. In your initial contact, you've offered to help them in any way possible. You've been thorough, courteous, and professional in following up each time, and now you're reporting back with a progress update and another thank-you.

Always keep your goals foremost in your mind for each contact. First, you want leads about openings. Failing that, you want the names of other people in the firm or elsewhere with whom you might talk. Keep pushing, deepening and broadening your network. Here's an example:

> Todd Moore, a senior executive with an extensive network, has a base of contacts that requires tremendous organization and persistence to work. Todd was getting a bit discouraged after a few months and was beginning to wonder whether he would ever find the right position. To take a new tack, we suggested approaching a couple of the firms with which he was carrying on discussions about consulting proposals. This would get his foot in the door until a permanent position could be found or created in the organization. The approach worked. Todd's aggressive networking paid off.

The realities of a transitory economy with so many people displaced can work to your advantage if you are currently unemployed. While being unemployed might once have labeled you as an undesirable or a chronic problem case, unemployed people now are generally viewed as first-rate employees who are victims of the economy. Members of your network usually have been recently unemployed, know they're about to be, or are scared to death that they might be in the immediate future. As a consequence, most people are more willing than ever to help you.

This is another example of how important positive thinking is. Don't dwell on the negatives when faced with a difficult economy. Think of how you can transform the negatives into positives. Make the situation work for you, rather than against you. Very often, this requires nothing more than an attitude change. Never underestimate the critical importance of a positive attitude. Like your resume and interview, your networking contacts will live or die on the strength of your attitude. If you expect a networking contact to be unsuccessful, we can just about guarantee that it will turn out that way. So pump up your mental state, and put your networking skills into action.

One of the hardest things to do in a job search is to continue even though you have a really hot offer in the works. Remember that no job offer is official until you're sitting in your new office on your first day!

> Janice Schultz was made an offer and accepted it. She immediately abandoned her efforts elsewhere, only to discover later that the person who had made the offer did not have clearance to do so. The offer was rescinded, and Janice had a lot of catch-up networking to do.

If you internalize the principles outlined here, coupled with the lead generation skills you'll learn in Chapter 7, you will be headed in the right direction — swimming upstream. Remember not to pay any attention to the doom-and-gloom preachers, who are floating downstream with all the search firms and internet listings as flotsam and jetsam. Your route will be more difficult in the short term. It will require large measures of courage, confidence, perseverance, and dedication. But your upstream direction will lead to what smart campaigners are looking for — the best jobs.

EXHIBIT16
Personal Marketing Plan: Personal/Professional Contacts

DATE: _____

NAME/AFFILIATION PHONE NUMBER	RESULT OF CALL		
	CALL BACK	WILL RETURN	SEE RECORD

Electronic Forms are available in *The Total System Organizer*

EXHIBIT 17
Sources of Company Information

LOCAL DIRECTORIES

The following are examples of local and state directories. Check with your local library and chamber of commerce for similar directories of businesses in your locality.

> Chamber of Commerce Directories
> Directory of State Manufacturers (Volumes I & II)
> County Business Guide
> City International Business Directory
> State Top 250

NATIONAL/INTERNATIONAL DIRECTORIES

Directory of Corporate Affiliations (National & International; Public & Private)
Dun & Bradstreet Million Dollar Directory
Hoovers Handbook
Standard & Poor's Register
Thomas Register of American Manufacturers

ADDITIONAL SOURCES OF INFORMATION

Almanac of American Employers
Alumni Directories
American Almanac of Jobs and Salaries
Association Directories
Associations Yellow Book
Business Periodicals Index
Business Week: Scoreboard
Company Reports – Annual, 10K, Proxy
Directory of Occupational Titles
F & S Index of Corporations and Industries
Forbes: Annual Report of American Business
Forbes 500
Fortune 500
Inc. 500
Industry Specific Directories
Industry Specific Publications
Moody's Investors Services
Newspaper and Business Publications
Special Issues Index
Standard & Poor's Corporation Records
Standard & Poor's Industry Surveys
U.S. Bureau of Labor Statistics: Area Wage Surveys
Valueline
Wall Street Journal Index
100 Best Companies to Work for in America

Many directories are available on the internet. See the Technology Update for some of them.

EXHIBIT 18
Personal Marketing Plan: Target Companies

	DATE: _____		
Circle to indicate priority:	**A (high)**	**B (medium)**	**C (low)**
	RESULT OF CALL		
TARGET COMPANY DECISION MAKER (Name & Title)	CALL BACK	WILL RETURN	SEE RECORD

Electronic Forms are available in *The Total System Organizer*

EXHIBIT 19
Personal Marketing Plan: Target Company Research

PROSPECTIVE JOB TITLE	
HIRING AUTHORITY	TITLE
OTHER CONTACT	TITLE
COMPANY	TELEPHONE #
ADDRESS	
RESEARCH SOURCE (person, directory, etc.)	
SIZE (employees, sales, income)	
INDUSTRY	
PRODUCTS/SERVICES	
GROWTH	
ORGANIZATIONS/SUBSIDIARY OF	
EMPLOYMENT POLICIES:	
COMPENSATION/BENEFIT POLICIES:	
CURRENT INDUSTRY INFORMATION:	
CURRENT COMPANY INFORMATION:	

Electronic Forms are available in *The Total System Organizer*

Search Firms: How to Distinguish the Pros from the Peddlers

When we say that you, and only you, can get yourself a new job, does that give you a clue about how search firms fit into the picture? Certainly, that statement does not minimize the importance of the assistance others can give you in some of the key segments of job search, especially networking. Obviously, the essence of networking is help from other people. You draw upon every person with whom you've had contact to help you locate job openings a step ahead of anyone else. But your networking contacts, vital as they are, can only help you. They can alert you to openings, give you leads, or at best, provide introductions—but they won't get you a job. Think of search firms as just another networking source and remember the statistics of placement – only about 10% of jobs are sourced through agencies.

Keep in mind that you should not count on headhunters, search firms, or employment agencies to always act in the best interest of your career and your future. In most situations, their client is the company who is paying the fee! Certainly, a high-quality, professional search organization can assist you effectively, but be sure that you don't assign too much responsibility to the search firm. They can assist with leads, help you understand the corporate culture, and prep you about the person with whom you'll be meeting. But never lose sight of the fact that you get a job through a winning resume and excellent references, coupled with a powerful interviewing presentation.

Equally important, you must then negotiate the best deal you can get. Again, you alone can accomplish that. Negotiation is when the money's on the table, when you apply all the skills you'll learn in Chapter 9 to secure the best deal possible without jeopardizing the job offer. Your skill in this vital step will ultimately be reflected on the bottom line every day you work for that company. Search consultants are usually very knowledgeable about the market and the going rate for the job under consideration. However, it is not their primary function to guide you through the negotiation process. You should solicit their input and recommendations but should be prepared to analyze the data against your market research. Ultimately, the search firm represents the company and its interests, not yours. Inevitably, the bottom line they're protecting is the employer's and their own, not yours.

Associate with a top-quality, professional organization—a real pro at the business.

If you elect to use any search firm, do your homework by checking credentials and reputation. You want to associate with a top-quality, professional organization—a real pro at the business. Firms that typically work on a retainer arrangement with corporations tend to have assignments for higher paid and executive level candidates. Many professional firms work on a contingency basis and receive a fee upon placement of a candidate.

We caution that there are some firms who may seek to take advantage of you; for instance, beware of agencies that may present your resume without your permission or who may attempt to "offer" help to access companies with whom you already have contact. They are seeking to benefit from your contacts without real knowledge of the position or adding any value to the relationship. Then there are the retail agencies who charge you a fee for placement, sometimes upfront. We have seen people disappointed—losing job opportunities or, worst of all, paying large sums of money when they can least afford to lose it—all because they signed the wrong piece of paper at the wrong time in the wrong place so that some peddler posing as a search consultant can line his or her pockets without doing anything to place the job seeker.

DON'T STACK THE ODDS AGAINST YOURSELF

Having briefly reviewed both ends of the contingency spectrum, consider the cold, hard statistics from the U.S. Department of Labor which are consistent with the results of our own client base. How do people find jobs? About 5 to 10 percent find them through search firms and agencies, while 80 percent locate them through networking. We've already illustrated, in the chapter on networking, how the numbers work against you when you concentrate on job listings and search firms alone. At best, 10 - 20 percent of jobs are filled from those sources, yet that's where 80 percent of job hunters look. As we have pointed out several times, even considering the increasing access to internet listings, networking is still an essential technique to optimize these online sources. The greatest numbers of people are chasing the smallest percentage of jobs when they search this way. Those are incredible odds to bet on, yet many job hunters do—day after day, year after year.

FINDING THE LEADERS

Briefly, here's how the search business works. At the top of the industry are the retainer firms. Associating your name with these reputable firms in most cases will create a positive impression on an employer. A source for identifying

The retainer firm submits only top-flight, qualified executives on an exclusive and confidential basis.

executive search firms is the Association of Executive Search Firms which has a directory on their website. Typically, a retainer firm operates with candidates who earn higher than an established minimum salary typically in the six digit range. If you don't earn more than their minimum, they usually won't accept your resume. Their retainer arrangement with companies is for exclusive assignments for which a typical fee of 30% of base salary paid out on a one-third / one-third / one-third structure. Usually, they are paid a third of the fee when they take an assignment, another third when interviews are conducted, and another third when placement is accomplished.

The retainer firm submits only top-flight, qualified executives on a confidential basis. There is implicit trust between the search firm and the potential employer. Obviously, you benefit from that professional association. To illustrate, a really upper-echelon retainer search firm will spend extensive time with a company performing a needs analysis to discover what the company really requires in an applicant for the available position. Such firms operate with subtlety, discretion, and professionalism. They are paid for their time and professional services, many times even if they are not successful in submitting a winning candidate. Finally these types of firms usually are more difficult to access, since they seek highly qualified and experienced executives.

In contrast, contingency search firms operate quite differently, receiving a fee only upon placement of a candidate. The search agency hires recruiters with back ground and contacts in the fields for which they are seeking candidates. What drives their business is acquiring new job listings from employers and finding the candidates to fill openings. Contingency firms' specifications are more generally based on the client's brand and stated requirements. If you fit a position for which they have an opening, you will acquire a new friend! However, the company is the customer and you are the "hot commodity" the search firm needs to gain revenue. Your particular goals and aspirations are not foremost on the recruiter's mind beyond whether they fit the client's need.

> Contingency search firms operate quite differently. They receive a fee only upon placement of a candidate.

Typically, when a contingency search firm gets job listings, it will be one of several such agencies with identical marching orders, hustling to get there first with the most—to get the right person hired so that they can receive their commission. It's a dash to the finish line, and the first firm that shows up with the right candidate gets the prize. That may sound a bit callous and cynical. So, what do you do? You get busy networking, and if a search agency contacts you with an opening for which you were unaware, check it out. But maintain control of your search and keep in perspective the odds of placing via a contingency firm.

CAUTIONS FOR WORKING WITH SEARCH FIRMS AND AGENCIES

You can do a better job working in your own interest than any agency will ever do for you. If you follow our guidelines on networking, time management, positive thinking, and self-discipline, you'll represent yourself better than anyone else can possibly do. How does a search firm develop job listings? On the phone—cold-calling. How do you network your way into job openings? The very same way. The difference, of course, is that when you get a hot lead, you'll jump on it one step ahead of the rest of the world. But when a contingency search agency generates a lead, they'll send you and others whose qualifications match the job order. So it is that many people complain bitterly that job hunting is a numbers game at which you can't win. It may be—but only if you play passively, expecting someone else to do your work.

When you work through agencies, beware of some of the claims that agencies will make to sell their services:

• *Job leads:* An agency may claim to network into job leads by the hundreds. Incredibly, once an unethical agency or recruiter gets your resume they may send an unauthorized copy to companies without your knowledge or permission. If you have networked your way into a job interview, in this scenario your resume may have hit that company from another direction without your knowledge. Not only is this unprofessional and damaging to your interests, it can lead to a fee dispute. The company may believe that the hire was accomplished directly by you, but the agency may send an invoice on the strength of the resume it had sent. Here is one example:

> Jerry had networked into an organization and was promised an interview upon the return of the hiring authority. When he followed up with the company recruiter, he learned a search firm also had submitted his resume for the position and the company was not willing to pay their fee. Jerry was shocked since he had not given the firm permission to present his resume. The company would not interview Jerry until he got a letter from the agency retracting their fee claim. While it was a time-consuming and frustrating process, Jerry finally got the letter and was interviewed for the position. After that experience, Jerry understood the importance of controlling his own campaign.

Many human resources departments will not accept unsolicited resumes from agencies for just this reason. If you think such unethical agencies are looking out for your best interests, just get caught in the middle of a fee dispute between an agency and your new employer. The battle can get nasty — and you are the ultimate loser, no matter how the problem is resolved. The company wants to hire you to solve a problem it is facing. But when you walk in with a fee dispute trailing in your wake, you become a new problem, not a solution. This can ultimately eliminate you from contention for the position.

• *Coordinating your search for more efficiency:* This is another unethical agency tactic that can lead to a fee dispute. A search counselor will say something like "Keep me posted. We're working together on your search, and we don't want to duplicate our efforts. So if you have a contact working, let me know about it." Although this may sound logical and in your best interests, it most assuredly is not. When you're told, "Keep me posted—let me know where you're interviewing," the search firm is, once again, doing nothing and hoping to profit by it. The agent is fishing for an easy commission, looking to capitalize on your hard work. You notify the agency that a contact looks good, and what happens next? The search agent shoots in your resume and calls the company, claiming that he represents you in your search. That gives him the right to invoice the company if you get the job.

Obviously, that can lead to the unfortunate fee dispute scenario we just described. But there are other more immediate problems. Despite the fact that you've done the work, the search agent's claim to represent you means, in effect, that you've just acquired a price tag on your head. How much does that assist your job search? Not much, we bet. What if, for example, you're one of three very close finalists for a position that pays $80,000 annually? By your call to the search firm to keep them posted, their fee gets added to that; you now carry a first-year price tag of $100,000, while your competition, not represented by a search firm, will come in for $80,000. What do you think of your chances now? Moreover, the worst part of this situation is that the effort was all yours. The contingency firm did nothing for you, only for itself.

• *Salary information:* They'll tell you that they can help you grasp the dynamics of the marketplace—what your skills are worth under current conditions. Moreover, they'll offer to help you negotiate compensation. To a certain extent, this may be true; however, you can also research the market through internet sources and your network. You may bring skills and experience worth $75,000 to the marketplace. But if an unethical agency can manipulate you into accepting a lower offer, they'll do it without regard to your income potential or needs. They may attempt to talk you into accepting the lower offer by down playing your experience and background. Quite naturally, your $75,000 skills will blow out of the water the competition with fewer skills, and you'll get the offer. The result is that you're saddled with lower compensation than it was necessary for you to take, with a corresponding setback for your future income potential. The agency gets what it wants most, of course—a placement and payday.

TEMPORARY AND CONTRACT AGENCIES

Another category of agencies is temporary employment and contract agencies. The growing trend in companies to use temporary and contract employees at all levels has caused tremendous growth in these agencies. While once the domain of clerical and secretarial workers, there are now hundreds of agencies who serve companies' needs for technical, professional, and even executive talent. Often referred to as contingency workers, this growing segment of the job market has created many opportunities for part-time and short-term as well as long-term assignments. Outsourcing of various company functions has also contributed to this trend. The need for recruiting internationally also has increased the use of firms who specialize in recruiting talent in various industries and countries. Rather than hiring candidates as employees, companies may sub-contract to these agencies.

When considering the use of temporary and contract agencies bear in mind the following positive and negative factors:

Positives	*Negatives*
Provides cash flow while seeking full time employment.	Detracts from the job search effort.
Provides opportunity to experience what a job or company is like before committing long-term.	Often pays lower compensation and no benefits.
Can lead to full-time employment.	Multiple short-term assignments may limit breadth of your experience and accomplishments.
Meets the needs for a flexible work schedule for students, retirees or young mothers	Limits involvement and commitment both to and from the organization—you may feel like a second class citizen.

Whether you obtain a contract or temporary assignment through an agency or your own networking efforts, these pluses and minuses can apply. If you prefer contingency work, however, we encourage you to first seek to market yourself rather than going through an agency. Why? Rather than the agency taking their percentage off your rate, you will gain the entire fee, in which case, the chances of experiencing the negative side of contingency work are reduced. In some cases, you may actually be able to make more money by marketing yourself for temporary or contract work than you could make in a full time position. Similar to the consultant role discussed in Chapter 2, you may discover that the independence of contract work is right for you.

AVOID THE PEDDLERS

Don't for a moment confuse the different segments of the industry. At the top are the retainer firms; on the bottom are the unprofessional and unethical up-front fee operators. They may call themselves "executive job search consulting services" or "retail outplacement consultants." Whatever they call themselves, it's easy to iden-tify them by their method of collecting money and the lack of services they provide. Their sales tactics are also a good barometer of their ineffectiveness—their strat-egy is to make you feel inadequate and attempt to get you to sign their agreement in exchange for their "access" to company contacts and job openings. In short, if someone wants your money up front for lots of promises, but very little tangible results to back them up, get out while the getting is good!

We don't have any problem with paying for excellent services. Legitimate companies may bill an individual job hunter for writing a resume or coaching. But the up-front fee collectors who take your money and give you nothing in return are a plague on the job marketplace. Job hunters who are emotionally vulnerable will pay upward of $5,000, $10,000, or more and get nothing but a resume and a list of target companies that hasn't been updated since your grandfather looked for a job. The best advice we can give you is, if someone wants your money for providing excellent services, that's fine—that's free enterprise. But if some peddler tries to get your money in return for nothing but a lot of fast talk, fancy acronyms, and stacks of printouts, get out of there as quickly as you can and avoid falling into the pits of job search—turning your job search over to someone else to manage.

In short, keep your money in your pocket, and don't think that anyone else can do your work for you—even a reputable search organization. If you conduct your job search in accordance with every one of our tough rules, you will discover that rejection is part of the process. We know from experience that's one psychological motivation that drives people to rely on search firms and agencies. They think that someone else will bite the bullet, make that tough cold call, soften the ground to make the interview less stressful, and exercise that delicate, subtle pressure to negotiate the best deal possible. Meanwhile, they sit on the sidelines, hoping to enjoy the fruit of someone else's labor. And we believe it's not necessarily because they are lazy, but rather out of fear of rejection. Whatever the motivation, such expectations are nothing but wishful thinking.

SOME GUIDELINES

The most important guideline in using search agencies is to adapt the way you allocate your time to the statistics we mentioned earlier. If you use search organizations, devote no more than 5 to 10 percent of your time to them. That's effective time management in your job search. This means that if you are currently unemployed and work a fifty-hour week on job search—which we classify as "full time"—you will spend no more than two to five hours a week on agency contacts. When you are with a company and looking for a job outside of your current company, it is especially tempting to rely strictly on search firms to conduct your search. Although the time to spend on your search is obviously limited, our cautions about allowing the search firm to control your search still apply. Use evening hours for researching target companies and early, late, and lunch hours for networking.

> When dealing with agencies, request that they never send your resume anywhere without first getting your permission.

Conducting a job campaign while you're still working requires expert time management, but it can be done; using the internet in applying for positions and email for communicating with potential employers can be especially helpful in a search limited by time constraints. Be careful, however, in the use of company time and email for your personal search – you certainly do not want to violate company policy or misuse company time.

If you elect to use agencies, be certain that you control the relationship. Be assertive. Watch out for your own interests, because it's likely that no one else will. Here's an illustration:

> For personal reasons, Joe Smith, a former client of ours, was anxious to relocate from his home in Houston to Chicago. Before he came into our program, Joe's first instinct was to go to a search firm. Then he thought, "If only one search firm is trying to find a spot for me, wouldn't I have more of a chance if 50 firms were?" So he prepared a letter of introduction and was planning to send them to fifty firms. Then his former company enrolled him in our transition program. In our first meeting with Joe, we learned of Joe's intentions and pointed out to him the folly of that strategy. "Your resume could end up coming to potential employers from multiple directions," we explained. "They aren't going to know which search firm is entitled to the fee, and as a consequence, not one of them will consider you." Joe was shocked by the risk his seemingly logical plan involved. He took our advice and ultimately found a position with an excellent firm in Chicago through his own networking efforts.

Exhibit 20 provides a form to list your search firm contacts. Follow these additional guidelines: Remember that the consultant, not the agency, will be responsible for your satisfaction in dealing with that firm, as well as for your success in accessing job leads through the firm. With that in mind, go to the agency (once again, be careful what you tell them on the phone) and determine who the best counselors are in your functional area. Interview the counselor, and make certain that he or she is professional, competent, and knowledgeable about your function. Then find out how long he's been with the company and in the industry. Learn what companies the agency represents, so that you can strategically select an agency that will best help you cover the market and best complement your search. In other words, you're taking charge of the situation. You're making sure that the agency doesn't duplicate your efforts. In addition, request that they never send your resume anywhere without first getting your permission.

> Evaluate the search firm's reputation, get to really know your recruiter and his or her background, and keep control of your search.

Finally, never sign any agreement with a search firm unless you fully understand what the agreement obligates you to do. Substantial amounts of money are involved in recruitment of employees through search firms, and the contracts are usually designed to protect the agency's right to collect a fee, even if this means that you will ultimately be responsible under a specified set of circumstances. To be safe, do not use an agency that requires you to sign an agreement. Exhibits 21 and 22 present convenient summaries of the various types of search firms including advantages and cautions in their use.

To summarize our discussion of search firms, we recommend that unless you're in a position to utilize the services of a top-echelon retainer firm, you evaluate contingency firms carefully and maintain control of your search. Obviously, there are some benefits in using an agency. Even if the statistics indicate that only 10 percent of people get jobs through agencies, that 10 percent is enough to qualify agencies as a valid source of job information. Many search consultants are honest and dedicated, and they can help you obtain job leads, assist you in preparing for interviews and in critiquing your interviewing style. If you're dealing with a reputable firm and an experienced counselor, you can enjoy some benefits, as long as you're aware of and guard against the downside potential. Our recommended approach in the utilization of search firms is to evaluate the search firm's reputation, get to really know your recruiter and his or her background, and keep control of your search.

Yes, a search firm or agency may be able to place you—not necessarily to your best advantage, but rather to their advantage and that of their client, the employer. Even when you stick with the pros, search firms and agencies can never place you as successfully as you can place yourself, if you continue reading, learning, and putting our advice into action for your job search today and your career tomorrow.

EXHIBIT 20
Personal Marketing Plan: Search Firms

SEARCH COMPANY	RESULT OF CALL		
CONTACT (Name & Title) Phone Number	CALL BACK	WILL RETURN	SEE RECORD

Electronic Forms are available in *The Total System Organizer*

EXHIBIT 21
Employment Agencies

	EMPLOYMENT AGENCIES	
	Temp Agencies	**Personnel Agencies**
Also known as:	Temporary help services Contingency firms Contract firms	Personnel placement or retail placement services
Aim:	Help employers meet emergency and short-term needs	Bring job applicants and employers together
Focus:	Short or long-term temporary positions, for most kinds of work	Permanent jobs for most kinds of work
You are hired by:	The temp agency	The employer
Who pays?	The employer always pays. The temporary staff person never pays.	You pay upfront or after you are hired. Sometimes, you and the employer split the fee. Rarely, the employer pays the fee.
How much?	By contract between employer and agency	Usually a percentage of your new salary.
Licensed?	Some states only	Some states only
Advantages	Offers screening tests. May offer training. May offer benefits in addition to hourly rate. For administrative and entry levels, provides experience and opens a door to a company. For professional and management levels, may introduce to a new industry or new city; may open the door to a company. Contract and temp-to-perm assignments have increased for all levels of workers. Retirees may prefer contract roles or roles unlike their previous careers. International assignments.	Having to pay a fee whether upfront or upon placement is the biggest disadvantage to any job seeker. Weigh carefully the value of the services offered.

EXHIBIT 21 *(continued)*

Cautions	Know how to get benefits and training. Know who pays if a company wants to hire you directly after you do temp work for them. Visit face-to-face.	Agencies do not guarantee you a job. Don't pay a large sum up front. Know what you're signing. Check with Better Business Bureau (BBB)

EXHIBIT 22
Recruiting Firms

	RECRUITING FIRMS	
	Retainer Firms	**Contingency Firms**
Also known as:	Headhunters or Executive Search firms	Search or Recruiting firms
Aim:	Find the right person for a certain job within a company or organization	Find the best candidate for job & organization
Focus:	Higher-level, white-collar and executive jobs. A few firms recruit for mid-level jobs.	Management, professional and non professional
You are hired by:	The employer	The employer
Who pays?	The employer always pays the fee directly to the recruiting firm. The executive who is recruited never pays.	The employer The candidate may pay in some cases.
How much?	Usually a 30% or higher fee, paid by the employer.	Usually 20-30% typically paid by the employer.
Licensed?	Some states only	Some states only
Advantages	Emphasis is on matching the right candidate with the right organization and assignment. Executives/highly paid professionals are sought out by retainer firms.	In a tight labor market, more companies will seek the assistance of contingency firms.
Cautions	Work with recruiters in your field. Verify a recruiting firm's legitimacy before working with them. Retain control of your resume submissions.	Work with recruiters in your field. Verify the firm's legitimacy before working with them. Retain control of your resume submissions.

CHAPTER 7

Lead Generation:
Leveraging Networking

Whether they have earned minimum wage sweeping floors or megabucks charting the course of an international corporation, jobless people invariably ask the same questions: "Who's hiring?"

The question can be stated in several ways, but whatever sophisticated terminology the corporate quarterbacks may use to ask it, like all job hunters they gravitate toward any source of job leads. Many imagine that those leads are grouped on some master list of companies that are hiring in their particular discipline. It's amazing to us, but even senior-level human resource executives, who should know better, think that new positions will materialize on a list, like manna from heaven. Well, if you're on a first-name basis with Moses, that might happen. But if you're like the rest of us, forget it. And get to work.

Not only is the "master list" concept unrealistic, but — more important — it runs counter to our basic premise of job search. If anyone gives you a list of companies that are hiring, you immediately place yourself on the wrong side of the job search equation. About nine out of ten job hunters concentrate their search efforts in the minority slice of available jobs, diluting their possibilities for success with such lists – whether they are on the internet or from an agency.

From word one in this book, we've stressed that there's no revolutionary innovation, no easy path to finding a new position. The traditional methods work if you labor hard enough at implementing them. Nowhere is that more true than when you're contacting companies, and generating job leads.

Is there a secret, fail-safe path to success? You bet. But it's only a secret because it's been pushed back into a dusty corner in the world of job search advice, outdated by more glamorous, high-tech instruction. It's dated, but not obsolete. Our secret, it shouldn't surprise you to learn, is work, then more work — coupled with dedication, preparation, discipline, planning, learning, and positive thinking. These will drive your job search, and they will ensure success. And there's not a single shortcut in this recipe. In our view, when one is out of a job working hard at job search means working full time at your search. If you ask successful people what makes them successful, invariably they will say, hard work! Be prepared to put similar time and effort into your job search if you expect to succeed.

What is the secret, fail-safe path to success?

Hard work!

HOW DO YOU FIND THE JOBS?

You pick up the phone and call each company, each department manager, and ask if they're hiring. So who's hiring? A select few, if you follow the herd mentality. Everyone, if you learn networking and cold-calling skills. The telephone and the business letter whether sent via mail or email, are your communication tools in this stage of job search. We'll discuss networking and talking to employers in the context of telephone work. Incredibly, we still come across advice that it's fine for job searchers to visit employers to fill out applications if they're uncomfortable or inexperienced on the phone. This suggestion is so absurd that it belongs in the Guinness Book of Records as the world's worst advice. Stay out of your car until you begin to arrange interviews —or at least until you've cultivated a contact to the point that a lunch or breakfast meeting might be productive. But if you spend your day driving around filling out applications, you're not looking for a job — you're wasting time, avoiding your spouse and kids, or just plain cruising. We call it the windshield mentality. Pure and simple, if you do it, you'll still be looking for work the day the sun rises in the west.

So we're agreed, right? You'll work the telephone to find job leads. If you're a novice on the phone, before you start, go ahead and draw a sketch of a monster face and tape it to the phone. We know that's how bad it is for most people who

> Work the telephone to find job leads.

are new to the process. That little mechanical instrument becomes the enemy. But that enemy's weapon is fear, and fear grows from a lack of confidence. Accept that. It's normal to start out a little shaky, with a degree of uncertainty, on your initial calls. That's the primary reason we suggested (in Chapter 5) that you call your closest professional contacts and friends, first. Learn while you're working the warmest contacts on your list. After the first 20 or 30 phone calls, your technique will begin to develop, and you'll be ready to approach and solidify some of your contacts for your top targeted organizations and "hot" leads which will likely include people you do not know.

Like any endeavor, however, your technique won't improve if you keep repeating mistakes. You can't slop your way through twenty phone calls, learn nothing, change nothing, and expect the next call to part the sea. As you make your calls, analyze what you say and what the reply is — what works and what doesn't work. Above all, listen. Lead generation by phone is a communication technique. Whenever we use an unfamiliar technique, we tend to become preoccupied with what we're saying. It's fine to script a conversation but don't fail to listen and react to the other person's comments.

Think of your evaluation process in two tiers. First, analyze your style — how you communicate your message and how smoothly you break from your preplanned script into a free-flowing conversation with your contact. Then evaluate what you say. As an illustration, suppose that you consider as the highlight of

> Those who do not set goals are doomed to finding new positions much later than those who do.

your professional career the redesign of a tool that eliminated a $23 zerk fitting. But if each time you mention your accomplishment to cold-calling contacts it generates nothing but silence on the other end of the line, that's a good indication that elimination of zerk fittings doesn't pull a lot of weight in this year's market. Change your presentation. Be flexible, attentive, and persistent. Don't stumble through your calls. Improve.

The guideposts to a fruitful, ever-improving lead generation campaign are discipline, dedication, and goal setting. Your goal is an established number of cold calls each day. We suggest 25, but set a goal that you can attain with discipline and dedication. If you want to start at 10 or 15, fine. But commit now toward reaching that number and *improving* with each call. Never lose sight of your short-range goal with each call—an interview. Your fallback goal is to get the names of three, four, or five other people you can call.

Your command of goals and time makes this process of contacting companies work. (Exhibits 23 and 24 provide forms to help you organize your time—a daily action plan for which a daily calendar may substitute and a weekly activity summary.) Surely we don't need to justify the importance of setting goals; you undoubtedly have utilized the technique in your professional career. Just be certain that you don't abandon goal setting now that you're navigating in unfamiliar territory. You need goals now more than ever. Our favorite truism about goal setting is an often-quoted statement: "Those who do not set goals are forever doomed to work for those who do." Adapting that for job search, we can say: "Those who do not set goals are doomed to finding new positions much later than those who do."

WORK THE PHONE AND IT WILL WORK FOR YOU

This all leads to a radical departure from the ritualistic advice most job searchers revere. Everyone ventures out, forewarned and forearmed, to resist depression and to shake off rejection. But succumbing to rejection just doesn't happen to our clients if they follow our principles. Time after time, across the board of professional disciplines, they find new jobs faster than they had dreamed — and not just a job, but a better position for more money.

Many people are telling job hunters that cold-calling is so tough that it's all right to avoid it as a job search technique. That advice might make you feel better, but it won't help your job search. In fact, it's dangerous to your career, because you will miss out on many potential opportunities.

Your job search is not governed by the economy, any more than a salmon swimming upstream is driven by the river's current. It is a fact of business that companies hire people every day. Companies in bankruptcy proceedings do it; companies with absolute, worldwide hiring freezes do it. By networking and cold-calling, you can access those job leads better than your competition.

When you do, you won't have to worry about lists of jobs or lists of companies that are hiring. In fact, you won't even have time to wish for their existence. Your positive momentum will build; you'll be busy and confident. Our point is that when you work the phones properly and get a rejection in spite of your improving technique, it's only one of 25 calls. Part of your technique is to get off the line quickly — don't beat on a dead contact. You don't have time to waste. You'll hang up believing that the company lost its chance at you, and you'll move along to the next contact.

Of course, there's a fine line between confidence and arrogance. Don't be so confident that you're rude and just blow people off the phone. But believe that you have skills and background to help that company. If it's not a good match, try the next company. Always be a pro.

There's one final point to be made as we try to short-circuit every possible argument anyone can mount about why they shouldn't use the phone to generate leads. Frequently, we talk with senior executives or people in traditional professions — medicine, law, accounting — who respond, "We don't do that. It's considered beneath a lawyer's standing to get on the phone and ask for help" or "That doesn't work at my level. Companies only hire through search firms at the senior levels." All we can say is, if you think cold-calling another lawyer for help is more demeaning than going for a year without a job, then there's not much we can do to help you. Even if a position is contracted to a search firm, how do you expect to find out about it? When looking for a job, *no one* is too good or too important to utilize proven techniques to get that job. So we dismiss any protest about telephone lead generation. It's the most important technique you can use to find job leads. And it works for everyone, not just sales or marketing people who are pros on the phone. People who say that they cannot or will not use the telephone to contact potential employers are blocking themselves from their own potential. It works for everyone. And the skills are learnable.

> Pete was a Ph.D. chemical engineer who had been laid off. In addition to being an introvert and technically oriented professional, Pete was Asian and English was his second language. For the first couple of weeks that he was in our transition program, Pete walked around the facility like a "zombie." We kept prodding, encouraging, and reinforcing the importance of networking and lead generation, but Pete just didn't seem to get it. Then one day he had a big smile and was all excited. Pete explained that he had made a cold contact that resulted in an interview opportunity. We asked what made the difference for him and he said, "I tried it!"

Yes, you do have to try it for lead generation to work. By the way, as a result of Pete's success, he became one of our model clients, encouraging others and setting the example. Not only did he succeed in placing in a better job, for better pay, but he discovered a new talent that led to a business development position. He continued to apply the marketing techniques he had learned in *The Total System* to succeed in his new job.

TIME TO START

With that in mind, let's get started on just what you say and how you say it. We mean, literally, *get started.* This is the phase of job search when procrastination is more prevalent and most destructive. To be sure, generating momentum on the phone can be difficult. We are all prone to make three or four calls, then fiddle around with internet research or follow up emailing or some other "non-prime-time" pursuit. Soon, you'll have mused away the morning. Come noon, you can say with conviction, "This lead generation is tough. I'm exhausted." It's easy to get caught in that trap, so set your mind now to avoid it. Set your goals and meet them. If you don't meet your goals, work on your efficiency, or shorten your horizon slightly. But your goals and time management are the benchmarks for success. Don't fail yourself.

Let's look more closely at our daily goal of 25 calls. We're actually understating our own pace — we could place 25 calls in half a day. Initially, many calls are one-minute placement calls and the contact "will return the call." You may have to call these contacts again and again to get through. We feel that we're expert in nurturing the good calls within a couple of minutes and decapitating the bad ones in seconds. Our point is that you should set a goal you can reach, and then build upon it. Both the numbers and the quality of your cold-calling should increase. As we touched upon earlier, telephoning and interviewing are your "prime-time" events in job search. They must be done during business hours. Researching, reading, responding to listings, and writing letters/email should be done in the evening or on weekends. This is linkage in action again. Remember our equation for where the jobs are. Networking generates about 70-80 percent, internet listings and search firms only 20-30 percent. That is precisely how we suggest your allocate your time. Most of job search is phone work and networking.

> Most of job search is phone work and networking.

A SCENARIO FOR COLD-CALLING

To prepare for your cold-calling, we suggest that you create a written script. We have used scripts for years in developing our company's business, and the same principles apply to your job search. There are certain fundamentals of selling that every cold call should contain. Remember that job search is a selling situation. In compiling your cold-calling script, include the following elements:

- The full name of the person you're calling: We suggest that you use the first and last names in your initial contact with an administrative assistant. If you use Mr. or Ms., it can give the impression that you're operating out of your league. And if you use the first name only, that's too familiar and inappropriate for any initial business contact.

- The name of the person who referred you (or the source from which you got the company's name).

- Why you are calling: First, you want a job; second, you want more names.

- Why your qualifications match the needs of the company.

- What your specific occupational skills are.

- Why a personal meeting can be helpful to both you and the company: The incentive for the contact meeting may be an interest in your background, your industry or product knowledge, the people you know, or ideas you can share.

- A time limit: Frequently, you'll be cautioned that you should not waste the employer's time; that you should hurry and get off the phone; that two minutes is plenty, and the employer's been gracious to give you that much. All these points are valid, but the motivation's all wrong. Certainly, get off the phone quickly, and don't waste time. But it's *your* time that must not be wasted as well as the employer's time. When you accept that concept, you will have taken a major step toward understanding and implementing a lead generation program.

- The three R's: Read, Reread, and then Role-play your script with another person. That's the only way to succeed when you call the hiring authority.

Keeping accurate records of your lead generation efforts is as important as having a script. You may have had administrative assistants to handle all your organizational work in the past. Well, welcome to life in job search (or in an entrepreneurial organization, for that matter). There are no overlapping layers of staff. The organizational work is now your responsibility. Be sure that you maintain a simple but effective record of company, person, administrative assistant, what was said, and what is to happen next. Exhibit 25 provides a form for keeping a record of a telephone conversation. We recommend organizing these alphabetically by company name for easy access as your network grows.

Look over the following sample script. Adapt the responses with which you're comfortable, but remember that they are only script suggestions. Develop your own style, and alter that style to mesh with the personality of the person on the other end of the line.

> *You:* Good morning, Mr. Hardsell, this is [your name] calling. Fred Good-guy at TestTube Corporation suggested that I call. Could I have a few minutes of your time?

> *Mr. Jack Hardsell:* I'm very busy; I have only a minute. [That gives you license to take three minutes.]

> *You:* Ok, I will make this brief. As a result of a recent corporate reorganization at [former company], I am currently exploring opportunities for new career directions. Fred suggested that your data processing unit would double its staff this year [or that he had an extremely strong base of contacts in data processing]. [Or you read about his company's expansion plans, new product merger, or the like, in the *Wall Street Journal*.] I wonder if we might meet to discuss your needs and my qualifications and background to meet these needs [or if he'd share some of his contacts].

Give him a chance to respond, and then proceed on the basis of his comments.

> *You:* To give you a better idea of my background . . . [briefly tell him those parts that will have the most impact]. Is there a need in your [company, division, department, etc.] for someone with my skills?

Asking a question helps ensure a dialogue in which you can gain as much information as possible from your contact. Again, give him a chance to respond and assist you.

Close with an invitation to lunch or with an attempt to set up an appointment. As a minimum, get a few referral names:

> *You:* I really appreciate your taking time to speak with me. I understand that there are no immediate needs in your division, but can you suggest others with whom I may speak?

Even in this brief sample, some of the myriad options become evident. Our point is, don't script so closely that you fail to carry on a logical conversation. You want to preplan everything you say, but you don't want to memorize it. Every company, every call, every person will be different. You must react spontaneously, and you do that by practicing.

Count on the fact that some of the Mr. Hardsells on the other end of the phone line will be uncooperative. But also anticipate that a Mr. Easysell may jump at the chance to interview you and may need a new employee that day. Most people will respond somewhere between those extremes. Remember that you have immunity from those who are uncooperative; they can't hurt you. Learn to cut down their phone time to ten or fifteen seconds and move along to the next call. More likely, however, you'll find people cooperative and anxious to help. Unlike many years ago, it's not a disgrace to be unemployed in today's economy of downsizing, mergers, and acquisitions. Generally, it's an experience most of the people you'll be talking to have encountered. If they haven't personally, they probably know someone close who has, or they may even expect to be unemployed soon themselves! So don't feel that you're a deadbeat or that people will treat you like a degenerate because you're conducting a job search. If they try to do so, cut them off.

GETTING TO MR. HARDSELL

Back to Mr. Hardsell—if he's important enough to have valuable contacts, in all likelihood he's important enough to have an administrative assistant. To get to him, you must first get past her, and it's her job to see that that doesn't happen. You've probably heard advice for the best way to dodge the administrative assistant—calling before or after business hours, during lunch, and so forth. The hope is that your contact will pick up the call in person.

Those are valid tactical moves, but only as fallback positions. We always suggest that your first step should be straightforward. Although the administrative assistant's job is to protect her boss, why not consider it your job to win her as a convert to your needs? If you're really skilled on the phone and deal with her honestly, very frequently she'll feed information that will help you catch Mr. Hardsell. Don't ever dismiss that possibility without a try. For example:

> *You*: Good morning. Is Jack Hardsell in? This is [your name] calling.
>
> *Administrative Assistant:* He's in a meeting. May I tell him the nature of the call?
>
> *You:* Yes. Fred Goodguy at TestTube is a mutual acquaintance. He suggested that Jack might have some information to assist me in my job search.

We like this approach because you're limiting the information you're giving out, but you're never making a false or misleading statement. Don't try to blow smoke at the administrative assistant—inevitably, it will smother you later. At this point, she may take your name and number for a callback (don't get discouraged if you don't punch through on the first call). If you don't hear from Mr. Hardsell that day, at least you've established the rudiments of a working relationship with his administrative assistant. The next day, it's proper to call back and place the message again. Such callbacks are the times when your professionalism can really pay off. Each time, be courteous, supportive of her schedule and Mr. Hardsell's, and understanding of the delay in returning your call. Simultaneously, however, be persistent. You won't be rude, but you won't be put off, either. That's how you can subtly enlist an administrative assistant's aid.

Another possibility is that the administrative assistant will immediately instruct you to contact the human resources department. Again, don't argue the point. Do as she asks. The call to human resources will likely be unproductive. At that point, call back Mr. Hardsell's office and ask to speak with him. When the administrative assistant states that human resources handles this type of call, you can truthfully state that you're not asking him for a job—you want information, and you only want a few minutes of his time.

Notice that at no time do we recommend that you ask for an information interview (sometimes called a referral interview). First, this country has been "information-interviewed" to death. It's a buzzword with no buzz left. More important, it smacks of a technique that an amateur would use. You want to communicate implicitly to Mr. Hardsell that you're a pro—that you need help now, but that you're the type of person who can be beneficial to him in the future. The term information interview does none of that. Don't give the impression that you're stepping up in class. That's a false imagery that is especially harmful to you in job search.

The concept and content of information interviewing is fine; in fact, it's just what we're suggesting that you do. It's the terminology that drags you down with excess baggage. Stay away from it. But do get the information—and the new referrals.

Throughout this process, remember our rules of engagement in telephone lead generation. When you're talking to Mr. Hardsell's administrative person, she may resist all efforts at charm and professionalism, proving her a formidable blocker. Or Mr. Hardsell might be predisposed to be unavailable. Or the human resources department might tell you that your name has been programmed into the computer to self-destruct if your resume comes within a mile of their building.

You can't get depressed — you don't have time!

If that happens, fine. Your fail-safe position protects you. Each of those calls will take only seconds, and you will move along on your contact list. Again, you can't get depressed—you don't have time. Also, don't lose sight of the fact that in a large company, even if Mr. Hardsell and his formidable accomplice won't help you, they are only one of perhaps a dozen destinations for your cold call. If the company is one into which you are determined to network, cut off this contact and develop another within the same organization. And do it all within minutes of telephone time. The following situation will give you an idea how this can work:

John Powell had targeted a major company as having excellent opportunities to fit his background and skills. When his letter of introduction and cold calls to the Vice President of operations produced no direct response, John decided to call one of the directors who reported to the Vice President. To his surprise, the Director already had his resume in hand, routed from the Vice President. Using the referral from the Vice President to his advantage, John had no trouble setting up a preliminary interview with the Director. Had John given up on the Vice President and not placed the call to the Director, he might never have networked into that target company.

With the popularity of voice mail, you may not even get through to an administrative assistant, let alone your contact. While voice mail can be the ultimate "screening device," it can also be your ally. After all, you can leave a very professional and polished message that is designed to peak your contact's interest. This can often be more effective than a handwritten message by an assistant who may or may not get the message correct. Voice mail is private and usually permits detailed messages. Use it to your advantage. And if you do not get a return phone call, you can usually get through to the administrative assistant by entering zero in voice mail.

To cold-call hiring authorities, you first must have a company to call. Your goal is to network into a department decision maker before he or she lists a job opening with a search firm or online. To that end, you must work through your list of personal and professional contacts. We discussed in Chapter 5 what your network is and who should be on the list. You should have built a network of more than 100 names by now. Call each one, tell them your story, and ask if they can help. Most important, get three, four, or five names from each. Your contacts with search firms should also be handled as part of your networking effort. If he's a part of your network and you have helped him or her in the past, then they'll assist your networking even though there's not an immediate fee in sight. Even when you utilize online listings, if you don't get a job offer from a company, try to generate additional contacts from your interaction.

THE CLOSE

Lead generation is, of course, a selling process. If you've ever been in sales, you know that the most important part of the sale is the close. Knowing how to close the call can make the difference between another "NO" and a positive, productive call. Following are some of the many closes that can make your job search calls more effective:

> Lead generation is a selling process.

1. *Interview/meeting:* "Can we get together Monday or Tuesday to explore how I may contribute to the success of *(division)?" (Note:* Always suggest two alternative times to give your contact a choice.)

2. *Drop by with resume:* "I know you're busy, Bob, but rather than mailing my resume, I'd like to drop by with it. I'll only take a few minutes of your time to brief you on my background. Would tomorrow morning or afternoon be best for you?" *(Note:* Try to get in front of the contact rather than sending a

> By linking job listing responses to your networking process, your success ratio will rise dramatically.

resume. Ask several times in different ways to visit them—you'll get far more referrals in person.)

3. *Names of other individuals:* "I really appreciated speaking with you, Bob; I won't take any more of your time, but I wonder if there are others with whom you suggest I speak?" *(Note:* Pick up on any comments the contact may have made to help draw out names.)

4. *Identification of growth companies:* "Are there other growth companies in your particular specialty which you recommend I contact?" (*Note:* Once you get the contact thinking of companies, check whom he or she knows in them.)

5. *Do you know "so & so" in industry:* "Bob, I have a couple of names in your industry that I wondered if you might know. Jim Hart with XZY Company," (*Note:* This is a technique to get specific referrals in target companies you've selected and to get the contact thinking in terms of names he or she can give you.)

6. *Ask for advice:* "Bob, you obviously have been very successful in *(company or industry).* I'd really appreciate your advice on how to maximize my next career move. Can we get together briefly today or tomorrow?" *(Note:* People are flattered to be asked for advice and like to give it. Ask for advice and you will have an opportunity to get referrals as well.)

7. *Luncheon invitation:* "Bob, I'll be downtown on Tuesday and would like to take you to lunch. That will give us an opportunity to get to know each other without taking time out of your busy schedule. Would that time be good for you?"

8. *Members of association or club:* "Bob, if you're planning to go to our association's next meeting, why don't we plan to get together briefly then? I'll bring my resume and we can spend a few minutes getting acquainted. When will you be there?"

JOB LISTINGS

When you're reading newspapers or surfing the internet, don't stop at the ads or job listings. Other parts of the paper and on-line information sources can be far more valuable for generating job leads. Any news report about growth, expansion, sales records, new territories, new products, or mergers and acquisitions is reason enough for a networking call.

In fact, to make job listing responses pay off, you should always *integrate* them into your networking process. To do that, research the company and position. Find out who the hiring authority is by researching directories, annual reports, or by calling the company and asking who heads up the particular department to which the position reports. Don't forget to check with your personal contacts to see if they may know with whom you need to speak.

> To make job listing responses pay off, always integrate them into your networking process.

Once you've sent out resumes in response to the listing, not only to human resources, but to the hiring authority, follow up. Even if the listing states "No Phone Calls," do you always do what you're told? Just because some human resources recruiter doesn't want to be bothered, are you prepared to sit and wait for something to happen? Pick up the phone and call the hiring authority. If you get routed to human resources, you can honestly say that they asked you to call! Here are three examples:

> Barbara saw an ad for an executive assistant to the president. After responding to the listing through human resources and getting nowhere, she called the President. Her telephone introduction was so bold and professional that he asked her to set up an interview through human resources. Once she convinced human resources that the President really requested the interview (even though they had sent a rejection letter), Barbara successfully interviewed and was hired.

> Mike saw a listing for Vice President, Business Development for a manufacturing company in the midwest. He had never heard of the company, so he researched it and discovered that it was partly owned by a larger company with which he was familiar. He knew the Chairman of the larger company, so he called him about the position. Needless to say, as the result of his telephone contact, he was subsequently interviewed for the position. Had he responded "cold" to the listing, his chances for being flown in for an interview were far less.

> Bill utilized his college's on-line job listings to identify companies that were interested in new college graduates. He developed a list of companies in industries and locations of interest to him. Bill then followed the steps of professional networking by researching the companies, contacting them with cover letter and resume, and following up. He so impressed the companies he contacted that several were receptive to interviews. He received three offers from companies with which he ultimately negotiated and accepted an excellent entry-level training position.

By linking job listing responses to your networking process, your success ratio will rise dramatically. The fact is that responding to listings without follow-up is a very low payoff proposition. Certainly, include listings in your job search, but don't build your search solely on them. Like search firms, they are easier to use than networking and cold-calling, but they just don't work as effectively.

If you do respond to listings, foremost among the rules is that you conform to whatever imperatives you find in the listing. If they want a resume, don't send some hybrid mutation—send them your chronological resume. If they want a salary history, put it in your cover letter (as we discussed in Chapter 3). You'll hear a lot of advice about answering any listing with your resume, just on the theory that if a company is hiring chemists, it may need technicians or systems analysts as well. That's fine if you have the time. But don't expect too much. Remember that, at best, listings are a long shot, and this lengthens the betting odds against you.

There's always a question about when to respond to a listing. Should you respond quickly, ahead of the rush, or late, after the crush of resumes has hit the human resources department? Our suggestion is to respond immediately and mail in a resume and cover letter. In this way, there is a better chance your resume will end up in someone's hands rather than remaining in a database! And be sure to follow-up with a timely phone call.

Remember, like search firms, listings are only one source of job leads—and one that does not have a high degree of return if not integrated with your networking. So don't waste a lot of time thinking about how and when to use them. It's foolish to spend time weighing alternative courses carefully when none of the alternatives weighs much in the job search process. Spend the majority of your time with networking and lead generation.

GREAT SMALL COMPANIES OFFER GREAT POSSIBILITIES

Who's hiring?
Small companies.

Keep your eyes and ears open for small, closely held, or private companies in your networking. Specifically, entrepreneurial organizations constitute fertile ground for job campaigning. We've thoroughly refuted the notion that you can find a list of jobs and companies that are hiring, but now we'll retrench a fraction of an inch. To the question "Who's hiring?" we can safely answer: "Small companies." It's estimated that over 80 percent or more of all jobs in the next decade will be created by companies with fewer than twenty employees. Although the percentage of total civilian employment for the Fortune 500 companies has decreased from 17 percent to 10 percent as a result of the corporate right sizing trend, that's no cause to be discouraged. While the multinational corporations struggle through a transitioning world economy, remember that there's more to the job market than corporate monoliths. In fact, small entrepreneurial organizations represent the future of the job market.

That's the up side — that small companies have the jobs. The down side is that small firms are more difficult to research for a cold contact. Most are private and aren't required to produce public records for the SEC. Once again, we don't have any magic formula to simplify your task, except to stress that the reward justifies the extra effort. You must research, think, retrench, and keep sifting through information. Start on the internet using directories in your industry. Read professional journals, business periodicals, chamber of commerce publications, as well as municipal, county, and state guides to businesses registered for operation in your area. Always remember that at this point you're not only working to uncover job leads. You want to find out about the corporate culture, the environment, and the principals of these small organizations. Especially when you're dealing with newer, smaller companies, you must work smart and hard to develop your own information base before you even think about networking and cultivating job leads. To reiterate, once you hook one entrepreneur on the phone, even if you can't create a match, push your contact to the wall — max it out. Get five additional names. Remember, these are usually people who have successful corporate experience who have taken the step to independence in their career. And it's safe to generalize that they'll be more sympathetic and helpful to your networking quest.

NETWORKING/LEAD GENERATION ORGANIZATION SUMMARY

To maximize your networking/lead generation efforts, follow these recommendations:

1. Utilize the *Daily Action Plan* (Exhibit 23) or a daily calendar to list your calls. List the name of the company so you can easily recall each person. Check off the name when you have spoken with him or her. As you progress in your calling, you can look back in your calendar to identify those from whom you have not heard and follow up. You can flip forward in your calendar to list contacts you need to call at a later date to follow up.

2. Utilize the *Record of Telephone Conversation* (Exhibit 25) to record each contact. Note each call placed, what was said, and referrals.

3. Maintain a *master list of contacts* alphabetically in an electronic organizer. For each contact keep together your *Record of Telephone Conversation* along with a copy of the cover letter and *Target Company Research* form (Exhibit 19), if used. When calls come in, you can readily access all information on a given company contact.

4. Utilize the *Getting Started* form (Exhibit 1) to set your networking goals. A minimum recommended telecommunication goal is 20 to 25 calls per day, including 10 new contacts per day. This is an aggressive, but manageable goal if you use the above outlined system. Without organization, you will quickly bog down as you try to remember who you called, what was said, and when to follow up.

5. *Other forms* presented in the system are very useful and can be added to this basic organization depending on personal need for additional structure.

6. Remember to *follow up* every contact, including ad and listing responses. *Research to identify* top human resources representatives and the appropriate functional decision maker for the position before responding. This extra effort will increase your chances of being interviewed and enable you to follow up.

7. Be *persistent,* but *professional.* Although your contacts have other priorities, they are more likely to get back to you if you are persistent and have professionally represented yourself by phone, in your letter, and in your resume.

8. Be sure to maximize use of *association directories* in your field, particularly if you are a member. Remember to use *alumni directories* as well. And don't forget your *church membership.* Use other directories and databases to expand your target companies.

9. Seek *face-to-face meetings* whenever possible. The close, "I'd like to drop by with my resume" is one informal, but effective, technique. Also go to association and convention meetings for face-to-face networking opportunities.

10. Read and re-read your materials on networking and telemarketing. In particular, study the closes in this chapter. Remember, *practice makes perfect!* Try it and you will discover that people want to help you, but they can only do so if they know about you and you tell them how they can help.

THIS PROCESS WORKS

Networking is close to our hearts because we built our business from ground zero, to an extremely successful firm, living and working these same principles. Are you beginning to understand how this process eliminates the rejection syndrome that most job search consultants try to sell wholesale? Can you sense that this is a reality-based approach to creating momentum in your job campaign? We think the following chart of positive versus negative approaches to job search illustrates our point perfectly:

Approach	*Attitude*	*Decision*	*Action*	*Emotions*	*Results*
+	Learning experience	Try again	Keep improving	Enthusiasm	Success
-	Personal rejection	Withdraw	Quit	Fear	Failure

The chart's message is that when you get a no, it's not failure. It is an opportunity to analyze and improve your technique, an opportunity to isolate weaknesses in your presentation, and an opportunity to put your self-discipline to the test. In reality a no is more productive than a maybe in job search. "Maybe" means that you must maintain your records, follow-up on schedule, and continue to pursue what is, at best, a marginal possibility. "No" means that you can scrub the company and move along to more productive contacts.

We tell our transition clients that depression and failure are internally produced and, therefore, controllable. They cannot be forced upon you by the economy or the price of commodities or the heartless corporation that terminated you two days before Christmas. It is your choice to be positive or negative, your decision to succeed or fail at job search. If you can buy into that philosophy, you're a candidate for our One Percenters Club.

As our last words on lead generation, some "if . . . then" reminders:

If	*Then*
You are afraid to cold-call . . .	Get realistic. This is your career, your life. Pick up the phone and talk; each call gets easier.
You have a title . . .	Use it.
You have a company affiliation . . .	Use it.
You got the referral from a news story or report . . .	Verify the position and the name of your contact with the company switchboard or other source first.
You can't get an interview or job lead . . .	Get three to five additional names you can contact.
You ask a question . . .	Be quiet and listen; don't be so preoccupied with your script that you fail to get the answer.
You leave a callback, or voice mail message . . .	Suggest the best time for a callback and then be sure to be available – always have your cell phone charged and on hand!
You can't get past the administrative assistant . . .	Try again. Then try calling before 8:00 or after 5:00.
You can't make any progress after repeated calls . . .	Ask your original contact to help you if this company is critically important in your search. Other-wise, move along to your next cold call, with your spirits up

EXHIBIT 23
Personal Marketing Plan: Daily Action Plan

Date _____

MY GOALS FOR TODAY ARE   _____

MY ACTIVITIES TO ACCOMPLISH THESE GOALS ARE:

7:00 _____

7:30 _____

8:00 _____

8:30 _____

9:00 _____

9:30 _____

10:00 _____

10:30 _____

11:00 _____

11:30 _____

12:00 _____

12:30 _____

1:00 _____

1:30 _____

2:00 _____

2:30 _____

3:00 _____

3:30 _____

4:00 _____

4:30 _____

REMEMBER – LOOKING FOR A JOB IS A FULL-TIME JOB!
(Record daily accomplishments on Weekly Activity Summary.)

Electronic Forms are available in *The Total System Organizer*

EXHIBIT 24
Personal Marketing Plan: Weekly Activity Summary

WEEK BEGINNING: _____

RESULTS

	M	T	W	TH	F	TOTAL
NETWORKING						
Personal/Professional Contact (1)						
Target Companies (2)						
Search Firms (3)						
LETTERS						
First Contact/Cover (4)						
Ad response (5)						
Follow-up/Thank you (6)						
INTERVIEW PREPARATION (7) (research and practice sessions)						
INTERVIEWS						
Informational interviews (8)						
Job interviews for networking (9)						
JOB OFFERS (10)						

Electronic Forms are available in *The Total System Organizer*

EXHIBIT 25
Personal Marketing Plan: Record of Telephone Conversation

NAME _____	TELEPHONE # _____
TITLE _____	
COMPANY _____	
ADDRESS _____	

SECRETARY _____ OTHER NAMES _____

SUBJECT _____

DATE	CONVERSATION NOTES/REFERRALS:

Electronic Forms are available in *The Total System Organizer*

CHAPTER 8

Interviewing: It's a Psychological Tennis Match, So Hold Your Serve

First, let's do a six-question pop quiz on interviewing for a job. Answer yes or no to each question:

1. In an interview, you primarily exchange information. Right?

2. It's a chance for you to learn all about the company—products, services, philosophy, and corporate culture. Agreed?

3. Simultaneously, of course, the company will learn all about you—your strengths, weaknesses, hopes for the future, work style, and personal value system. Correct?

4. You'll be carefully evaluating the company and the interviewer during the process to determine whether you want to work at this place. Right?

5. You'll be prepared to discuss frankly the facts on your resume, paying special attention to a candid assessment of your reasons for leaving previous jobs. Agreed?

6. You'll tell the truth, the whole truth, and nothing but the truth. Correct?

That's the quiz. Before you score it, however, it might give you a clue to the answers if we tell you that those six statements incorporate much of the bromide that is peddled as advice on preparation for the job interview. Indeed, most job hunters (career counselors, too, for that matter) would answer yes to each question. Did you? If so, you're 0 for 6. More important, someone else has the job.

People think that they are preparing for the interview by merely laboring over a list of tough questions that they know they'll be asked. They struggle with the answers. They fret over how badly they'll be hurt by discussions about weaknesses or difficult situations in their work history. They expect to provide candid information about themselves and, in turn, get the same from the employer— a true exchange of information to benefit both parties in the decision-making process. Don't think us cynical, and don't assume that we're suggesting that you be deceptive—but nothing could be further from the truth.

An interview is not primarily an exchange of information. It is a contest in which you are a contender—a psychological tennis match. Your resume has captured the company's interest, proving that you have the technical skills and background to do the job. Now, in the interview, the hiring decision will be made. This is standard job search advice, and we certainly don't take exception to it. We do, however, want you to know how you can best extract the offer. To that end, you must understand that interviewing is an art form, a performance. Your task is to hold your serve by controlling — very subtly — the direction of the interview.

We don't trivialize the interview; we simply snap it into proper focus when we teach our clients that they must approach it as though they are contestants in a beauty pageant or a dog and pony show. In business terminology, visualize it as a sales call. But understand what the process is and what it isn't. We get occasional resistance on this point from individuals who protest, "That's a game. I don't play games." A game is exactly what it is. You can't change that fact; you can only succeed or fail according to your ability to grasp the reality of the scenario and turn it to your advantage.

The interaction isn't created to hurt or deceive anyone. This is a classic win-win situation. You want the job offer; and if you get it, both you and the company will profit. You're not there just to play a game—you're there to win the game. The payoff, of course, is that both you and the employer can win at the same game.

The First Great Commandment of Interviewing: Plan Every Word.

To accomplish that, you prepare. You do your homework. In fact, that is *The First Great Commandment of Interviewing: Plan Every Word.* Don't say any word that won't help you get the job offer. This is not a time for reflective, introspective responses. This is a time to *sell,* to *market YOU.* You must tell the company what it wants to hear—assuring the employer that you are confident, poised, in control of yourself and your surroundings, and with a personality that contributes to team unity and productivity. In this scenario, there really are no difficult questions, at least not for our clients. That's not an empty promise. You probably know what a devastating experience a tough interview can be, so no doubt you can appreciate what our clients typically tell us when they complete an interview. Not one or two percent but an overwhelming majority of our clients say with a grin, "I kept waiting for the tough questions. I was so confident of my responses that I was actually hoping for a chance to answer the objections. When I left, I thought it was nothing compared to the practice sessions the Dawsons put me through." Yes, we admit we're tough. But those conditions are dictated by the competitive job market. And our clients —provided that they buy into our principles— are ready to compete in any environment.

You see, each tough question is answered with a preplanned response, and it's the same for every interview. You don't pause, reflect, stammer, and then wade through an emotional response, fighting to control yourself. For each question, you've rehearsed the answer time and again, in advance. Most important, with each answer, you talk about yourself, but you do it in terms of what the employer wants to hear.

Plan and script your answers thoroughly and completely. Memorizing is a word fraught with danger in a situation like this, but we're suggesting that that's very nearly what you must do. Nevertheless, you must interact with the interviewer and respond to the changing dynamics of the discussion. For each tough question, develop an answer that meshes with your background, and ride that horse until you get a job offer. Unwavering consistency is critical. And when we say every word should be planned in advance, we mean every word. That ties in with *The Second Great Commandment of Interviewing: Positioning.*

With regard to individual questions within the interview, think of shooting a game of pool. Every pool shark in the world—and nearly every amateur—knows that the secret of success at pool is not just the shot you're attempting but the shooting position you set up for your next attempt. Ladies and gentlemen, that's also the key to unlocking the puzzle of interviewing success. With each answer, you position yourself for succeeding questions. This is how the interview becomes an exercise in control rather than a draining emotional nightmare. You allow the interviewer to rack the balls. But you make the break to control the interview. Your goal is no surprises—no questions too tough to "play."

You want to convey an image of professionalism and confident persistence. Just be careful not to be too dominant, aggressive, or rude in striving for that control. Actually, the real trick is to allow the interviewer to feel in control even through *you're* the one making the shots.

The building blocks for interviewing success are consistent with all our principles of job search—preparation, practice, research, confidence. But one imperative overrides all others in the interview—concentration. You'll probably have to develop your powers of concentration and extend the time you sustain it to a degree you've never before reached. What powers of concentration must a neurosurgeon command when he's working inside a patient's brain for eight hours? We'll never know, but it's an appropriate frame of reference. In your psychological tennis match, you must anticipate and react to every nuance of the interviewer's mental play with the same degree of intensity. Is this difficult? Without question.

IT'S NOT EASY, BUT IT CAN BE DONE

You thought cold-calling was tough! By now, you should recognize that talking into the phone is really quite simple compared to going one-on-one with the interviewer—nose-to-nose and toes-to-toes. In fact, we rank this process—especially the mandate that you concentrate, totally, completely, incessantly—as number two in degree of difficulty in the entire scope of job campaigning. In our view, only negotiating your compensation package is more subtle, complex, and difficult (and you'll learn that next, in Chapter 9).

That's the bad news. But, as always, we have good news coming along close behind. The good news is that this is the point in job search when our concept of linkage most clearly evolves from theory to reality. When you link your resume and references to your interview, you've hurdled the biggest obstacle in your path to a job offer. As we discussed in the chapter on resume writing, whenever you feel yourself getting into trouble, use your resume as an escape hatch. Moreover, you can develop most of your interview answers from the contents of your resume.

Develop most of your interview answers from your resume.

For example, the single most difficult (and inevitable) question you'll deal with in an interview is...

Q1: "Tell me about yourself."

A: It's in response to this open-ended inquiry that many people talk themselves out of a job offer. But if you structure your answer as we've suggested earlier — starting at the bottom of page two on the resume and moving up to the top of page one with a two-minute biographical sketch of who you are, where you've been, and where you're going — you'll succeed.

1. Start with your *early history*—where you were born, where you grew up. If you served in the armed forces, mention that here.

2. Part two is your *education*. Tell where you went to school and what degree you received.

3. Part three is *professional experience*—a brief description of your jobs since leaving school, explaining the transitions between jobs and notable accomplishments you achieved. Then quickly move to your most recent (or current) position, *explaining how your skills, accomplishments,* and *experience* relate to the opening.

4. Finally, part four is a career plan—a brief explanation of why you and this company would be a *good match,* reflecting facts you learned in your advance research on the firm. In closing, mention what a *first-rate company* this is and that you are *pleased to be interviewed* for a position in the firm.

Quite simply, when you follow these four steps, you've transformed a major roadblock into a positive image of yourself in the employer's eyes. And you're a giant step closer to a job offer.

YOUR TOOL KIT

Every time you go out on an interview, you will take your tool kit with you. The tool kit consists of:

- Your resume.

- References.

- Samples of projects.

- Background information.

- Documentation of accomplishments.

Your resume and references are essential. However, the latter three items are optional depending on your situation and their usefulness in documenting your accomplishments and their professionalism. Anything that is less than excellent, or that does not present you in a favorable light, or does not "score you points" should *not* be used!

These are not used to cover the interviewer with paper, but if you are asked for specific items or examples of your accomplishments, you have them in your tool kit to reinforce the points you need to make.

A very professional touch is to organize your tool kit in a presentation format using a three-ring binder and plastic protectors. Your original resume, reference letters, and work samples or proposals can be included.

Have a separate copy of your resume, references, and other supplemental data in a simpler cover to leave with the interviewer. During the interview, you can flip through the presentation binder at the appropriate time much as a salesman presents sales brochures.

WHAT IS THE GOAL OF AN INTERVIEW?

Let's pause here to clarify our position. Notice that we're not suggesting that you're after a job in the interview, only an offer. That's a critical distinction, and it's central to our approach to planning and implementing your campaign.

> Your interviewing goal is to…
> **Get the offer!**

We want you to get the best job you can locate, but if you take only one company to the point of an offer, if you have only one offer from which to choose, how can you possibly know which job is best for your present and future? To determine the best possible combination of duties and corporate culture, you must get multiple offers—at least three, preferably simultaneous—then weigh them and choose the best.

Before we move along toward helping you structure a win-win interviewing style that will generate multiple offers, let's deal with the six statements at the opening of this chapter. When we explain why each statement was inaccurate, we're confident that you'll share our viewpoint.

1. In an interview, you primarily exchange information.

   No. Interviewing is a performance by you — nothing more, nothing less. It will require six to nine months for the company to determine whether or not you're suited for the corporate culture and the position. To suppose that anyone could identify a match, for better or worse, on the basis of one or even several conversations is preposterous.

2. It's an opportunity for you to learn all about the company.

   No. You'll already know much about the company in advance of the interview, based on the information you learned from researching, networking, and cold-calling. Before you walk in, you'll understand what they do and how they do it. That's just another function of your networking. With your cold-calling skills, you learn about the company's products, services, reputation, plans for the future, and work style or corporate culture in advance of the interview.

3. The company will learn all about you.

   No. Get serious. Of course that won't happen. Think for a moment about the significant other person in your life and recall what you learned about that person during the first date of your embryonic relationship. It's a good bet that you can't even remember. Again, the employer will learn about you — your skills, abilities, ambition, personality, work style —gradually over the next six to nine months. If you try to tell the company all that during the interview, you're conducting job search death-wish style. If you get too deep into your personal business, we guarantee that you'll leave the interview feeling that it was a cathartic experience. We also guarantee that you won't get the offer.

4. You'll be evaluating the company and the interviewer.

   No. Not on your life — at least, not on your career. Remember, you're not there to make a decision; you're attempting to get an offer. You'll evaluate later and compare. If you don't have multiple offers before accepting one offer, you're selling yourself short.

5. You'll discuss your work history frankly.

   No. Never. Everyone's work history includes periods of difficulty, failure, or conflict, in varying degrees. But believe us, that is no one's business but your own. Tell the company what it wants to hear and score points in the process. You admired and respected every boss for whom you've ever worked because you learned something from each of them, everyone got along well, the company was fine, and you learned more about your profession than you could have hoped for. You're ever so thankful for all those opportunities to grow and learn.

We acknowledge that this answer is a bit flowery, but the point is that you must be totally positive in your response, even if it means leaving out the less than positive experiences you may have had with a former employer. You want the job offer. So long as your resume is factual with regard to your work history and accomplishments, the employer knows what he's getting. Once again, the interview discussion is only to confirm that you're confident, capable, positive, and a potential asset to the company.

6. You'll tell the whole truth.

No. Talk about death wishes! Tell the truth — under no circumstance should you lie to get a job. However, although telling the truth connotes honor to us, telling the *whole truth* represents stupidity. To reiterate, please don't think that we're suggesting that you play fast and loose with ethics. Never lie. Answer the questions truthfully, but do so in a manner that won't hurt you. And then stop. Don't crucify yourself with too much information. Every time, tell the truth, but when appropriate, stop short of telling the whole truth — spilling your insides all over the desk. An illustration:

> Dick Ryan was interviewing for a position as Division Marketing Manager in a major corporation. When asked about the extent of travel in a previous position, Dick proceeded to explain: "The travel was very extensive, about 90 percent of the time, which was very demanding and more than I really cared for." Although the job he was interviewing for required only 50 percent travel, Dick had raised enough doubt in the interviewer's mind about his willingness to travel that he lost his chance. Besides breaking the interviewing cardinal rule of never saying anything negative about one's former position, boss, or company, Dick offered more information than was necessary to answer the question. A better response would have been: "My last position required 90 percent travel. How much travel do you anticipate for the Division Manager's position?"

If you're asked, tell the truth — but respond only to what you're asked. People wander off mentally, say too much, realize they're in trouble, and then panic. They'll typically say something totally stupid because they're desperate and confused. If that happens in your interview, you're history. So the simple, fail-safe solution is, just don't say too much — just say the right things and keep it simple and to the point. Don't go out on a limb. Don't get into trouble.

To further illustrate the point in terms of business public relations strategy, suppose that a company is about to introduce a new product that will gain a dramatically strong market share. Also suppose that there are three lawsuits pending against the company and a projected cash flow shortage for the next quarter. What do you suppose the company will announce in their news release? This country's ingrained values about motherhood and apple pie compel us to tell the truth. Fine — just don't volunteer information that isn't requested. Leaving some information out of your answer doesn't mean that you're a liar; you're just a smart interviewee.

GREAT ANSWERS TO TOUGH QUESTIONS

We've dealt with "Tell me about yourself." Now let's inject a little truth serum into another classic tough question:

Q2:   "Tell me about your weaknesses."

A: You reply: "I have trouble getting along with people" or "I have trouble meeting deadlines" or "My spouse can't stand it if I work on weekends, and I don't like having to deal with that." Fine, you told the truth. What the employer will tell you now is good-bye. He may not speak it for another few minutes, but we guarantee that that response just clicked on in his mind. You're history.

Keeping those three weaknesses for our mythical job hunter, let's alter the responses 180 degrees without really changing the basis of the answers.

Weakness	*Why Not Respond . . .*
Trouble getting along with people?	"I do tend to get impatient with people who are deliberately unproductive."
Trouble meeting deadlines?	"Sometimes I feel so overloaded with electronic information, I have to be careful to prioritize my time."
Angry spouse?	"Sometimes I have to be careful — I get so wrapped up in my work that I don't give my family the time they need."

All we're suggesting is that you insist in your mind that you'll take a positive approach to every interviewing question. Work on it, practice, role-play, and conduct post interview self-critiques (see Exhibit 26). For the process of self-evaluation, use the technique we call the interviewing continuum to facilitate an ongoing analysis. Both during and after the interview, think of the discussion as generating positive, neutral, or negative responses. On the interviewing continuum, one end is positive, the middle is neutral, and the opposite end is negative. You can afford negative points on no questions if you plan to get the offer you really want. You can get by with a few neutral responses. But the great majority must be positive. They must weigh the interviewing continuum to the positive if you are to leave the impression necessary to receive an excellent offer.

SOME TOUGH QUESTIONS

Now let's look at some typical tough questions you'll get in an interview. But before you read on, let us caution that these questions are not included for you to merely skim over. The planning and preparation of answers is essential to maximizing your interviewing prowess. The only way to succeed is to match your background to a positive, upbeat, convincing answer for each of these questions. Start with your resume. Know every word on it. Another key part of your preparation is company research. You should know as much about the company as you possibly can before you arrive for the interview.

Now, here are the tough questions. We'll give some sample answers, but your responsibility is to construct similar positive responses that coincide with your background:

Q3:   Would you rejoin your former company?

A: Most people would say yes, but this question has a hidden agenda. The interviewer wants to be sure that you'll stay on if you're hired, so your response should be something like, "I really enjoyed the opportunity to work there — it's a fine company, and they treated me very well, but it's time to move my career along to the next level. That's why I'm so interested in your firm. I'm considering opportunities at a number of excellent companies, but yours is at the top of my list."

Q4:   What stresses you?

A: Stress is a common issue in the work place. One thing that stresses one person may energize another! Think carefully on a positive response to this question. For instance, you might say, "I am careful to manage my stress so it does not affect my productivity or others around me. One thing that does tend to stress me is people who don't pull their weight, who won't strive for excellence. That may sound like I'm intolerant, but I try to give people every benefit of the doubt, and communicate my concerns to them as appropriate." Carefully note this answer. Not only does it defuse a potentially dangerous area of questioning, but it also illustrates our positioning theory. Tolerance might be a concern of the interviewer, and if it is not addressed, it might become a negative. But by linking it to the answer, you've controlled the interview in a professional manner while simultaneously heading off a potential concern.

Q5:   Would you relocate (or travel)?

A: This is an easy one. Your answer is, "Certainly, for the right opportunity." There may be only one set of circumstances for which you would relocate —Cancun for $500,000 annually—but your answer stands as accurate. If the company makes the right offer—the right opportunity—you'll relocate. It's truthful, but it keeps control of the interview in your court. Be aware, also, of the motivation for companies to ask questions about relocation and travel. The information may have nothing to do with the position for which you're interviewing, but frequently such queries originate from a list of prescribed questions to which every new employee must respond. How sad it would be if you lost a job offer because of a careless remark about not being willing to relocate, when in fact the job in question wouldn't require a move. Of course, if you have decided you definitely will not relocate or travel, then give this answer, realizing it may preclude you from further consideration.

Q6: Were you fired?

A: No matter what your circumstance, you were never fired. Rather, you were "part of a downsizing and reorganization." Always blame your condition on the economy or on organizational restructuring, not on the company or on your former boss. Similarly, you were never laid off or cut loose, nor did you "hit the bricks."

Q7: Why are you leaving your current job?

A: Remember, no negatives. Everything about your past job and your past boss are all positive. Was there a reorganization, acquisition, or merger that caused you to leave your job? Did you quit—was it your choice to leave your job, and if so, how do you positively explain that? Was your job eliminated? Was there a new innovative technique that came in and caused your job to be obsolete? Was it a personal choice because the company no longer offered growth and challenge? Did the company reorganize, right size or go through a merger that has changed your future opportunities in the company?

The best four-part answer is:

1. A *reorganization* in the company affected my position.

2. This reorganization had *nothing to do with my performance.*

3. I have *references* that support my excellent track record.

4. My extensive research on your company suggests that you can benefit from my experience.

If you are currently employed but seeking advancement, you may simply state, "I have gained a lot in my current role, but am ready for the next step in my career. Your organization and this opportunity seem to offer an excellent match with my capabilities.

This answer can also be combined with "tell me about yourself" creating psychological leverage as you anticipate this inevitable question at the very start of an interview.

Q8: What does cooperation mean?

A: "Cooperation means working with subordinates, superiors, and peers to establish an environment of excellence as a member of the team in order to meet organizational goals."

Q9: What did you think of your boss?

A: "He was an excellent manager. I learned a lot from him, and we had an ideal working relationship. In fact, one of my letters of reference is from him, and I'd be glad to share it with you if you'd like." (By now, you recognize linkage—and there it is again.)

Q10: What books have you read recently?

A: Always keep your responses business-oriented by naming business books that are current and popular. Be sure that you've read the books you name in case the interviewer has also read them and asks more specific follow-up questions about them!

Q11: What are your strengths?

A: Your answer should address the specific agendas of the interviewer. Focus on (a) your interpersonal, supervisory or managerial characteristics, as well as, technical skills: "I am an excellent leader, decision maker, communicator, motivator. I work well with people. I'm a team player," (b) your willingness to work hard: "I do my homework. I'm willing to do whatever is necessary to meet the company's goals. I value my home life, and I'm willing to blend the needs of my family with the needs of the company," (c) your desire to do what's in the best interest of company: "I'm willing to travel, to relocate, to do whatever enhances the company's bottom line." Technical professionals often overlook these skill areas that often can distinguish them from others equally or potentially more qualified. These are skill areas in demand in virtually all companies and tend to be more difficult to apprise in the interview. You should always have examples, typically from your resume, that demonstrate these strengths.

WATCH OUT FOR . . .

In part, an abiding self-confidence is a by-product of a thorough understanding and appreciation of the following types of interview questions and cautions.

ILLEGAL QUESTIONS

How old are you? Are you married? Are you divorced? Do you plan to have more children? There's no doubt that these are illegal questions in the sense that companies can not base their selection on these factors, but don't spend time thinking about what is legal and what's not. Even if a question is inappropriate, we suggest that you not dodge it. Respond briefly; then execute a linkage maneuver, pivoting on your resume, to maintain your offensive position. You might say, following a ten-second response to a poor question: "And Mr. Johnson, what's more important to us all is how my experience in a new territory, highlighted at the bottom of page one of my resume, gives me ideal experience to assume a key role in your expansion plans." A final point: Don't assume that any question is illegal.

In reality, there are few illegal questions. Federal laws, however, do make it illegal to discriminate against candidates by eliminating them from consideration because of certain characteristics or experiences. To avoid the appearance of discrimination, therefore, many companies avoid asking questions about age, race, or nationality, and so on. To prove discrimination in the hiring process is very difficult and is counterproductive to your campaign. If a company is backward or archaic in its hiring process, imagine what it would be like to work for the company! Rather than worrying about whether a question is appropriate or not, score points by responding in a positive and general way.

Q12:   Are you pregnant?

A: "No." (If yes) "Yes, but I intend to return to work quickly. May I ask what your leave policy is?"

Q13:   Who will take care of your children while you work?

A: "I have arranged professional child care and my husband is also very supportive in assisting the children. I am very career-oriented and have always managed my job and family responsibilities so they do not conflict."

Q14:   Would you have a problem being supervised by anyone younger?

A: "Age is not a factor in my working relationships. I respect people for their position, knowledge and skill. I believe my responsibility to a company is to do my best regardless of personal characteristics of others with whom I work."

Q15:   How old are you?

A: Reveal your age and then go on to say, "As my resume reflects, I have many years of experience which I am confident qualifies me for this position. I know you would not use my age to disqualify me. In fact, I feel my years of experience and maturity are an advantage to *(Company)."*

If it is an area you absolutely want to avoid, respond, "That is an area which does not affect my ability to perform on the job, and I would not allow it to reduce my contribution to the company in any way" or "I keep my business and personal life separate and give 100 percent to the company when at work." Then take control and turn the interview back on course. That's the best message of all—you can handle adversity, and you know the law. The employer isn't dealing with a rookie.

The Federal Disabilities Act has made medical questions prior to an offer illegal. Under this law medical questions can only be asked after an offer is made. If the applicant can't do the primary parts of the job because of a medical condition and it would impose an undue hardship for the employer to make accommodations, the employer can withdraw the offer. If you are asked a medical question such as:

Q16:   "Do you have AIDS?"

Q17:   "Do you take any medication?"

Q18:   "Have you ever been hospitalized?"

Q19:   "Have you ever filed for worker's compensation?"

A: If you do not wish to answer, say, "I believe that is an area more appropriately addressed at the offer. I would be glad to answer all your medical questions at that time and I am confident you will be satisfied with my ability to perform this job at the highest level."

TWO-PART QUESTIONS

Be especially alert to two-part questions. In the interview, what you say isn't the only factor of importance. The employer is also testing your retention and confidence. He wants to see if you can answer a two-part question without stopping to ask for a repeat of the second part. This is a very basic interviewing tactic, yet many people trip over it.

EITHER/OR QUESTIONS

Q20:   Which is more important to you—money or position?

A: The important thing in an *either/or question* is to respond to both. If you say money, the interviewer will say, "Why not position?" If you say position, the interviewer will say "Why not money?" If you say money is not important, they will offer you less than what you're asking. If you say position is more important, the boss feels that you are threatening him or her. To create leverage say, "Both are important." Continue your response in a way such that you score points across the board.

Here are other examples of either/or questions:

Q21:   Do you prefer sales or operations?

Q22:   Do you prefer computer work or dealing with customers?

Q23: Do you prefer staff or line work?

Q24: Would you be happy in a smaller or larger company or environment?

HIDDEN AGENDAS

Most people will face recurring objections about parts of their background. You must custom-design your response in such cases; but in so doing, you must understand that what the interviewer asks isn't necessarily the issue to which he wants an answer.

Q25: Aren't you over (under) experienced?

A: For example, take the 61-year-old former Vice President we described earlier. He kept getting objections about too much experience. That meant that he was too old. He defused the objection with this frontal assault: "I have 35 years of experience, and if you want an executive with 35 years in the field, you're going to have to hire an older person."

Be careful that you don't threaten the interviewer—especially if he is your new boss. He may be asking, in effect, "Do you have so much experience that *you will overpower me?* Show how you can use your years of experience to make your boss look good.

Another strategy is to acknowledge that in seeking a lesser position, there may be *trade offs:* it may be more important to you to stay in Phoenix than to seek a higher salary or position. Emphasize to your potential employer that you *fully understand that trade off and have committed to it.*

Conversely, as a new college graduate or return-to-work candidate you may hear the objection, "You're not experienced enough for this position." The hidden agenda may be any number of issues—too young or too old depending on your age, or the perception that training may be required.

For example, a recent graduate, Pete, applied for a computer position requiring expertise in a specific computer language. Pete had taken a course on the language in college but had not used it on a job as yet. When the employer voiced his "too inexperienced" objection, Peter replied, "Sir, having just completed college, I'm used to learning things fast. I'll take extra time on my own to learn your specific applications, to speed the learning curve, and to contribute to your objectives more quickly."

Another example is a businessman who had closed down his entrepreneurial enterprise to reenter the corporate world. Repeatedly, he'd get questions about the nature of running a small business and his successes. Each time, he'd respond about the opportunities and challenges. Each time, he'd fail to get an offer. Finally, he realized that companies were reluctant to make an offer for fear that he'd leave to start another independent business at his first opportunity. So he altered his response to this: "I learned a great deal and treasure the experience but do not plan to return to it. The most important lesson I can bring to your company is the lesson in time management. When you're on someone else's payroll, time management is an abstract goal. But when every minute of your day either adds to or subtracts from the bottom line, you learn time management as a business imperative, not an abstract goal." On his next interview, he got an offer.

Following are examples of other hidden agendas:

Q26:   What movie have you seen recently?

A: The *hidden agenda* here is *what do you do in your spare time?* Are you reading, studying, spending time in the library researching the industry and the company, or are you out fooling around? Was the last movie you saw an intelligent movie or an idiot movie? Did you go there to escape from reality, or to improve yourself? Create a response that is job-related.

Q27:   Describe how your work has been criticized.

A: A hidden agenda to this question is -- *are you overly sensitive to criticism?* Are you going to be destroyed when the boss points out there are some things you need to improve? *Never cite criticism that might reveal actual weaknesses.* Instead, give neutral, positive responses that score you points instead of losing you points. For example, "One of the areas I would like to improve—and I have taken it upon myself to do so—is to learn more about the computer field. I believe it is important to improving my performance, and I would like to have the opportunity to learn more about it." You can construct a similar answer in engineering, human resources, or any other field related to your work experience as long as the field you want to learn more about is not critical to the job you're interviewing for. Another excellent response is to refer to educational accomplishments: "My boss wanted me to have an MBA, so I enrolled in an MBA program and got my degree in two years. He liked that a lot, and encouraged me to cross train in other areas for which my new education qualified me."

Q28:   Describe your personality.

A: The hidden issue here is often, "Are you stable, dependable, loyal, can you be counted on when push comes to shove?" You can prepare for the question by going through the self-assessment questions in Chapter One. Then you can answer, "I've been through a personality assessment, and it shows me to be a dependable, loyal individual with leadership potential," tailoring your answer to your self-assessment result.

SITUATIONAL QUESTIONS

Companies are interested in your ability to handle situations that may arise on the job. Situational questions are designed to test your reasoning, thinking, and problem-solving skills.

Q29:   When asked to describe a situation in which . . . , or to explain what you would do if . . .

           . . . an employee became angry.

           . . . you fired an employee.

           . . . you were faced with a technical problem.

           . . . a customer became irate.

           . . . a dangerous situation threatened your fellow workers.

           . . . your efforts have been praised.

A: Refer to your resume to select an accomplishment related to the particular situation. If it is a situation you have never encountered, you may respond by saying so and going on to describe your best judgment on how to handle the situation professionally and to ensure the interests of the company are protected. If it is a situation that should not be handled independently, be sure to include consultation with the appropriate staff. Remember team work in organizations is especially important in today's complex work environment. On the other hand, do not suggest that you would avoid or shirk taking responsibility for the situation when appropriate.

BEHAVIORAL BASED QUESTIONS

Unlike situational questions which are hypothetical, behavioral questions require an example from your past experience. Answers to these should be very easy for you to prepare since most can come from your resume! All of your accomplishments are excellent responses to demonstrate your various technical, organizational and interpersonal skills and competencies. Behavioral based interviewing is very popular in organizations that have a thorough and structured approach to interviewing. If you have properly prepared the answers to the questions in this list, you should be prepared for any behavioral question presented to you.

Q30:   Here are some examples of typical behavioral questions:

           Describe the most difficult work decision you made in the last year.

Tell me about a recent time you were part of a team effort.

Give me an idea of how you prepared for that presentation.

A: As with the situational question, refer to your resume, to reply with the most appropriate accomplishment that speaks to the skill or competency they are requesting. For each skill and competency that you list in your resume and in your reference letters, prepare an example to illustrate your ability and the results you have obtained.

Following are some additional behavioral questions categorized by competencies to help you prepare:

Interpersonal Skills: Tell me about a time when you took an unpopular position.

Integrity: Give me an example of when you "cut corners" to meet a deadline.

Motivation: Tell me about a challenge you have overcome.

Initiative: Give me an example of where you have exercised leadership.

Communication: Tell me about how you persuaded someone to do something he or she didn't want to do. How did you do it? What was the outcome?

Creativity: Tell me about a time when you had to be creative and use your imagination.

Analytical Ability: Tell me about a decision you made that backfired. What did you do?

Job Interest: Share with me specifically what interests you in our business.

Adaptability/Flexibility: Give me an example of how someone persuaded you to change your mind.

Planning/Organization: Describe a typical workday for you. How do you manage your time?

Technical Skills: Give me an example of a technical challenge you faced recently.

Risk Taking: Give me an example of how you have taken a calculated risk. What did you do?

Decision Making: Give me an example of an important decision you made recently.

Training Others: Give me an example of how you dealt with skill deficiencies of someone who worked for you. How did you handle it?

Managing Change: Tell me how you have managed change in your department.

Delegating: Give me an example of when you delegated an important task to someone else.

Coaching: Tell me how you coached someone whose performance was lacking.

Management: Describe your approach to managing others. Give me some examples.

Customer Service: Tell me about a difficult customer service problem you had to resolve.

Problem Solving: Give me an example of a business problem you faced and how you solved it.

WORK UP ANSWERS TO THESE TOUGH QUESTIONS

ANSWERS FROM YOUR RESUME

In keeping with our concept of linkage, remember that many answers to the tough questions come from your resume, just as we discovered with situational questions. Examples of other common questions for which your responses can be crafted from your accomplishments include:

Q31:   How have you increased sales and profits? How have you helped reduce costs?

A: Most people talk about broad, generalized responsibilities that mean nothing to the interviewer who is looking for timely, specific references to what you have actually done in terms that relate to what the company interviewing you needs. You should state specific accomplishments related to sales and profits referring to dollars, percentages, market and industry growth. Specify results not only for your company, but also for your department, section, or group. Show how you met or exceeded budgets or profit goals. For example, "I restructured the international sales and distribution organization to effectively meet the demands of the changing competitive environment, resulting in a 14 percent gain in market share."

Q32:   What are your five most significant accomplishments?

A: Your resume should state in priority order what your five most important accomplishments on your most recent job have been. State dollars, numbers, specific contributions to your job and your company. For example, "I managed salesmen and developed short and long range sales objectives for yearly sales of $60 to $70 million." "I increased efficiency by 10 percent by developing a computerized retrieval system." "I reduced administrative costs by 3 percent, by negotiating the lowest costs for suppliers."

Q33:   How have you changed your job?

A: Here you want to state how you have improved, expanded, enriched, or enlarged your job to make a greater contribution to the company. Tell how you expanded your job description, set additional goals for success and brought new members into your department who made contributions to the company. Perhaps you brought in new technology or brought in people with state-of-the-art knowledge who improved the technology or discovered new and innovative ways of doing things. Perhaps you looked at the competition and did everything you could to meet it today, tomorrow and in the future. Or you developed ways of improving departmental procedures or expanded your responsibilities and skills.

Q34:   Are you a leader? Describe situations in which you led others.

A: Go through your accomplishments in priority order. Give specific leadership examples. "I conceived, researched, and supervised the introduction of a new product line which increased productivity of our department by 15 percent." In addition, give examples from your civic or professional associations, or refer to leadership roles in the military.

Q35:   What was your greatest achievement in your most recent position?

A: Select your single greatest accomplishment in your most current position. Move from there to your second and third most important accomplishments as required by the interviewer. In addition, you may also talk about a civic or association accomplishment, or about a professional accomplishment that shows your abilities. "On my own time I have coordinated the Houston marathon." "I contribute personal time to the Boy Scouts." An answer like this shows that you are concerned about your community as well as your company.

Q36:   In what ways can you make a contribution to our company?

A: Referring to your accomplishments and skills, outline a few examples. "As you can see from my technical skills, I bring capabilities in a number of software and hardware platforms. Not only can I perform independently in these areas, I can also help others in the department to enhance their skills."

Q37:   How long would it take for you to make a contribution?

A: Your answer should be, "Immediately. I'll meet with all the key people and do a needs analysis," or "My proficiency in the areas you've outlined is such that I can contribute immediately."

Q38:   What problems have you identified in your last job?

A: Respond with problems you have resolved stating how they were identified and resolved. Consider issues such as: Was there a job description? Were goals set for success in the job? Was it a growth job? Was it too easy? Did it challenge you? Did it lead to career growth? Did you learn new and innovative approaches, techniques, ideas?

Following are additional questions with answers from your resume:

Q39:   In your present job, what problems have you identified that were previously overlooked?

Q40:   How large a budget have you been responsible for?

Q41:   How many people did you supervise?

Q42:   What are some of the most important lessons you have learned in your job?

Q43:   What are the most important contributions you have made to your present employer?

Q44:   What is your greatest potential for contributing to our company?

Q45:   Why do you feel you have top management potential?

Q46:   Describe some situations in which you have used initiative in your professional life.

ANSWERS FROM YOUR SELF-ASSESSMENT

The self-assessment in Chapter 1 is designed not only to assist in establishing your goals but consistent with linkage, can be used in crafting powerful responses to interview questions.

Q47:   Describe your ideal working environment.

A: Based on your style, you can answer this question from a number of perspectives. "The ideal environment is one in which . . . there is mutual trust; people feel free to communicate with each other; people are free to make mistakes as long as they don't repeat the mistakes; people are allowed to take risks in order to stretch themselves and do bigger and better things; people are trusted, respected, and given the opportunity to learn, to grow, and to achieve," or "The ideal working environment is one in which individual and team goals are set and met, and people are rewarded for stretching, growing, and achieving those goals." Or, "In the ideal environment, there is a career plan and a succession plan. People know where they are, where they are going, and how they are going to get there. People are given the opportunity to know where they are on their career path, and how they can improve and become better contributors."

Q48:   What are your goals?

A: Answer the question in a job-related fashion. If you say your goal is to be an Olympic runner, your interviewer may be thinking, "Runners come in late, run during lunch, and leave early to get to practice." The key here is to show that what you have done in your early career and more recent past has all led you inexorably to this company and this interview. Do not mention specific salary goals or job titles. "My future goal, based on all my past experience, is to become an excellent employee in the organization. I want to become all I can be."

Q49:   What are your five-year goals?

A: The key here is to make generic statements that do not threaten the interviewer. "I see myself as moving into the strategic planning area." "I see myself as continuing to grow in the engineering field. I hope that I might one day succeed in this company in an executive management position." Education, too, is a safe, non-threatening goal: "My objective is to get an MBA," "My objective is to cross train into the information systems field." Keep your answers growth oriented, and related to the goals of the company. Emphasize that you expect to earn any positions you may be promoted to in the future.

Following are additional questions with answers from your assessment:

Q50:   What do you look for in a job?

Q51:   What is your management style?

Q52:   What position do you expect in five years?

Q53:   How would you describe your personality?

Q54:   What are your long-range (five-year plus) objectives?

Q55:   What are you doing to reach these objectives?

Q56:   What career options do you have at the moment?

Q57:   What are some of the new goals you have recently established?

Q58:   What are your most important concerns when seeking a position?

Q59   What are five unique features about you that contribute to your success?

Q60: How would you describe success? According to your description, how successful have you been so far?

ANSWERS FROM YOUR RESEARCH ON THE COMPANY

Doing your homework on the company with which you are interviewing can make or break the offer. You should revise your answers to these questions for each company with which you interview. In each question, consider some of the alternative issues to which you may respond in your answer, such as climate, culture and style of management.

Q61: What do you know about this company?

Q62: Why would you like to work for this company?

Q63: What does it take to be successful in a company like this?

A: Would you be happy working here? Do you know any people who work here? Have they told you about the company? Is your background appropriate; does it fit with the company? Do you understand the company's needs?

These are some additional questions you must answer for yourself prior to your interview. Study the company from every perspective possible: product line, annual sales, number of employees, geophysical locations, etc. Learn all you can in advance and then practice how you will respond to these questions.

Q64: What measures do you use to evaluate a company?

A: Is the company in a downturn or upturn? Is there a hiring freeze? If so, how do you get around it? Have you studied the annual report or read other literature? Is the firm profitable? What is its reputation in the industry? How you answer this question reveals your values and attitudes. Stay positive. Customize your response to the company for which you are interviewing.

Q65: Have you targeted specific companies you would like to join? (If so, list these companies and state the factors that attracted you to them.)

A: Always be prepared to suggest a few companies similar to the company you are interviewing, including competitors since this builds psychological leverage. If you are highly marketable, the company will not want to lose you to a competitor. Be careful, however *not* to reveal names of individuals with whom you are actually interviewing or to disclose any confidential information.

Q66: What position in our company are you applying for? Why?

Q67: What is your philosophy of management?

Q68: Describe your management style.

A: Before answering these questions, you will want to *determine the style of the company* with which you are interviewing and answer accordingly. Is the philosophy of the department consistent with the philosophy of the company? Do your homework using your network and if possible, talk to the person who had the job before you. In a progressive environment, your answer should be, "I believe in participative management, in common goal setting, in creating an environment of excellence in which people feel good about their contributions to the company and in which people want to achieve and succeed and move on to bigger and better things." Once again, practice your responses and make sure you score points.

ANSWERS FROM RESEARCH ON THE JOB FUNCTION

Q69: What are the leading issues in your field?

A: The interviewer is really asking if you've done your homework. Are you reading? Are you staying current? Are you in tune with what's coming down the pike? Are you aware? Are you innovative? Are you addressing state-of-the-art issues?

An interviewer who is a long range thinker will typically ask broad, open ended questions like this. Match your response to the style of the interviewer. Study the office, the secretary, the desk. Study the environment and shape your answers to fit the interviewer.

ANSWERS FROM RESEARCH ON THE INDUSTRY

There is a *hidden agenda* for all the questions dealing with the industry. The interviewer is really asking if you have done your research. Is what you know consistent with the industry needs?

Q70: Why are you interested in this industry?

Q71: What kind of research have you done on this industry?

Q72: What in your opinion is the biggest problem in the industry?

Q73: What is the future of this industry? Short term/long term?

Q74: Where in your opinion is the greatest growth potential?

Q75: Where is the industry weakest?

Q76: How do you view the competition in this industry?

Q77:   What do you consider to be the most important skill necessary to achieve success in this industry?

Q78:   What important trends do you see in this industry?

A: Are you exploring the same industry that you are currently in? If so, what do you know about the industry? If not, what do you need to learn about the industry? Are there state-of-the-art issues? Is it a high-growth industry, a stable industry, a mature industry, a new industry? Does it have lots of ups and downs?

MANAGEMENT STYLE QUESTIONS

You probably have observed that the management style question has already appeared under the "Answers from Your Research on the Company" and "Answers from Your Self-Assessment" sections. This is a complex issue that is very important to companies. Even if you are an excellent manager, responding to questions on how and why you perform managerial or supervisory responsibilities in certain ways requires thought and preparation. Here are a few questions to assist you in your preparation.

Q79:   What do your subordinates think of you?

A: Do you get along with your subordinates? What is your leadership style? Are there letters of reference from your subordinates; if not, why not? Have you done appraisals on them? Have you had counseling sessions with them? Do you set team and department goals? Would they speak highly of you if asked? Are you a motivator? Do you create a climate of excellence? Do you bring out the best in people? Respond with all positives.

Q80:   What kind of relationship should exist between managers and those reporting to them?

A: Find out what kind of environment exists in the company before answering the question. Is it authoritative, participative, old school, or new school? Some possible responses are:

"A manager should seek to create a climate in which people get along, work well together and set specific team goals for the department. The climate should be one that is non-argumentative—one in which there is no jealousy and in which people strive toward individual goals that do not conflict in order to meet overall goals."

"There should be mutual respect between managers and the people reporting to them. Subordinates should feel that the boss is willing to allow them to grow and set stretching goals, to train and learn, and to have the opportunity to be the best they can be on the job."

Q81: What qualities must a successful manager have?

Q82: Why are you a good manager?

A: Often a company's website includes the values and qualities that it espouses in its leaders and culture. Build your answer around these as well as your personal experience with the qualities that have enabled you to succeed and be a good manager. "Successful managers must be easy to talk to, easy to relate to, and easy to communicate with. They must be honest, trusting, and respectful of their superiors, peers, and subordinates; they must be able to level with people regarding their strengths and their weaknesses and how those people need to improve; they must be willing to allow the time, energy, and money to train them; they must find the time to coach, counsel, and critique their subordinates, to help them be the best that they can be. Following these tenets is what has made me a successful manager."

Q83: What is the most difficult task of a manager?

A: "Having to terminate people." That's a neutral and positive response, much like blaming the economy. Go into the details: make sure that you don't give the impression that you're not willing to terminate people when necessary. "I understand the importance of the four-step corrective discipline process: oral warning, written warning, suspension, termination. I walk through all four steps, give the employee the benefit of the doubt; counsel, set goals, and give the employee time to improve; only as a last resort do I terminate the employee. And even with all that preparation, it's still not easy."

Another excellent response, "The most difficult task is managing in an uncontrollable situation, in an environment where I don't have control of budget, opportunities, product, service, resources or managing in a situation where possibilities for career growth for my subordinates just aren't there."

Q84: What do you look for when you hire people?

A: The trick here is not only to focus on technical skills, but on values and work ethics that are consistent with the organization. "I look for people who are team players, receptive to learning, open to constructive criticism, loyal, dedicated, and committed to excellence. I look for people who are willing to work harder, smarter, and longer to succeed." Notice the halo effect: The qualities you say you are looking for are presumed to be qualities that you also possess.

Q85: Have you fired anyone? How did you handle it?

A: If yes, "I handled it through the corrective discipline process: oral warning, written warning, suspension, termination—with counseling, goals, and an opportunity for the individual to improve at each step." Answer the question in terms of what you know an arbitrator will be looking for: "I documented all conversations, goals, and counseling sessions. I was firm, fair, and consistent. I handled it professionally." If you have never fired anyone, answer "No, but if I had to, I would walk the individual through the corrective discipline process."

TOUGH QUESTIONS TOO TOUGH TO CATEGORIZE

Some questions defy categorization. Some are off the wall, some are curve balls, but your thorough preparation will ensure your ability to respond like a pro, scoring points as you master every salvo the interviewer can throw your way. Consider your positive responses to these challenges:

Q86:   What are some important lessons you've learned?

A: "I have learned to expand my horizons, to strive to become 1 percent better every single day."

Q87:   Will you be out for your boss's job?

A: Make sure you do not threaten the potential boss in any way. When asked what you are looking for in terms of future growth, never give a title, and never give a salary. Your response should be in general terms, such as, "No—I am interested in doing the very best job I possibly can in the position I'm interviewing for, and I'm confident that the company will reward me for it."

Q88:   What do you like most about your current job?

A: Select an area of responsibility you now feel is of particular value for the position or company and expand on it as needed.

Q89:   What do you like least about your current job?

A: "What I like least about my job is having to watch employees be terminated."

Q90:   Why did you accept each of the positions listed on your resume?

A: Be sure your response is positive and focus on the learning or growth potential of each position. In addition, transition your responses by explaining promotional opportunities whenever possible.

Q91:   Why haven't you found a new position before now?

A: If you have been seeking employment for an extended period, you should be prepared to share contract, project or consulting assignment, education, training or other meaningful activities in response to the question. Family or personal commitments can also be an acceptable reason, but suggesting that you preferred to "goof off" for six months is not an acceptable explanation for an employer.

Q92: Would you object to working for a woman?

A: You may respond, "Whether male or female, I respect management and their authority." If you are a man, do not say something flip such as, "Of course not. I love women!" *Do not joke* in response to this question. Companies take this question very seriously.

COMPENSATION AND NEGOTIATION QUESTIONS

The key to successful negotiation is to delay it until you have an offer. For this reason it is important to handle early questions on compensation carefully. Also, never bring up the compensation question first—wait for the interviewer to do so. Following are typical compensation questions that the interviewer will ask early to get you to "tip your hand."

Q93: How much do you expect to make? What salary are you looking for?

A: Deflect early and general compensation questions when possible until later in the interview: "That is a question I would be glad to answer once we've had an opportunity to discuss my capabilities and the position requirements. As you can see from my resume I've had extensive experience in . . . " or "I'm open to negotiation based on the position responsibilities." Here are some additional responses to deflect early compensation questions:

"I'm sure we can come to a satisfactory agreement on a compensation package if I'm the right person for the job, so let's first agree on this."

"Compensation? Well, so far the job seems to have the right amount of responsibility for me, and I'm sure you offer a fair compensation package. So let's hold off on compensation discussions until you know you want me."

"Are you offering me the job?"

Here is a way you may preempt their compensation question: "I know it's too early to discuss compensation in detail, but could you give me some idea of the salary range you are thinking about for this position?"

"Compensation is number 3 on my list, Number 1 is making sure we have a fit, and that I can contribute to your company success."

"I've been paid fairly for my talents and responsibilities in my present (past) job, and I believe you will also provide a fair and equitable compensation arrangement for this position. Let's determine that my skills are what you are looking for before we discuss compensation."

"I'm sure we can come to a good compensation agreement when the time comes."

"With the amount of experience you see in me, and considering the functions I can handle, what would you estimate the salary range for this position to be?" Follow-up with research you have done.

If asked what your expectations are, respond that they are the fair market value or say, "perhaps you can help me here – what is the range you are considering? I'd be glad to tell you if this fits with my expectations."

"I'm sure you have established a competitive range for this position, and, given my experience and performance, I would expect to be paid in the upper portion of this range. However, let's first be comfortable that I am the right person for the job."

When you do respond with numbers, always give your range based on your research. To answer the compensation question, it is critical to do your research on salary norms in your industry, city, company, and function. Then give a range, "Based on my research, my salary and bonus requirements are in the $100,000 to 150,000 range. However, my real interest is in the total compensation package which includes benefits." Total compensation may include perquisites and stock ownership opportunities as well depending on the organization and the level of the position.

Q94:   What was your salary in your last position?

A: If you are asked directly "What were you paid in the last position," tell them honestly and directly. Then follow with an explanation of your value and your required compensation range for the position for which you are interviewing. However, do not volunteer your previous salary in answer to a general question on your salary requirements or what you are looking for in the way of compensation.

Your networking sources may be able to share inside information with you regarding compensation. The bottom of your range should be what you are currently making as a minimum. Obviously, the salary you want is at the top of your range; but if you do have to negotiate down, you haven't lost anything. The exception to this rule would be if you are changing industries, changing locations, or making a trade-off due to geographical preferences. You may be moving from a low growth to a high growth company, and may be willing to take less money now for future growth opportunities, or opportunities to train on the job or go back to school. The key point here is that you *must* plan in advance what you are going to say and *stick to your answer.*

Q95:   Why aren't you earning more at your age?

A: "I don't consider age a primary factor in determining value or job satisfaction since enjoying my job is very important to me and the company."

Q96:   What do you feel this position should pay?

A: "My research suggests a range of $60,000 to $70,000," or if the position has not been well defined, "I'd like to learn more about the company's needs before we discuss compensation."

Q97:   What is the minimum you will accept?

Q98:   How much money do you need to make?

A: You're not interested in minimums—never give a figure less than your last compensation and once again state your required range.

See Chapter 9 for more on negotiating.

If you're like most people, you've skimmed over these questions. But be certain — now or sometime before you face an interviewer — to think through and write out appropriate answers to each of them. Only then will you be prepared for an interview. Although it's a long list, don't feel overwhelmed; one answer might cover four or five different questions.

BUILD YOUR SELF-CONFIDENCE

Ironically, all the time and effort you invest in prepping for these questions will have an implicit reward even more significant than your acquired ability to respond adroitly at every turn. When you've developed answers that link with your resume and letters of reference, you will be fully prepared. That preparation builds confidence, and confidence builds excellence under pressure. You will send nonverbal signals to the employer that you're a pro, ready for anything they can throw at you in the interview. We call this the positive expectation of success. Your nonverbal communication, dress, grooming, and confidence levels will close the credibility gap within fifteen to twenty seconds of the interview opening. Everyone walks in with this credibility gap. If you don't close it within a few seconds, you'll be struggling uphill for the entire session. Our clients

> When you've developed answers that link with your resume and letters of reference, you will be fully prepared.

close it. They know that they belong there; they know that they can perform in the interview. They expect to succeed.

There's more to successful interviewing than having all the right answers to the tough questions. Consider the following cautions and recommendations.

THE ADMINISTRATIVE ASSISTANT

Your relationship with the employer's administrative assistant in the interview process is as important as it was during your cold-calling. Treat her with courtesy, use her name, and ask her a few questions if there's time and opportunity before the interview. In many offices, the administrative assistant is the first person an employer will ask for feedback following an interview. Make sure that she's on your side.

AFFIRMATIVE DELAYS

We think one of our tiniest little tricks helps our clients beyond measure in interview situations. We all know that it helps you respond better to any question if you delay for a moment before answering. But in an interview, any lengthy pause can be destructive. It suggests lack of preparation on your part, and it allows negative energy to build in the room. So take your time to gather thoughts for an answer, but do it this way: As soon as the interviewer completes his question, affirm it but do not repeat it! For example, if you are asked to list your five greatest strengths, you immediately say, "Yes, Mr. Johnson, I'd be happy to." Then you can take a couple of seconds to get your brain in gear. But to the listener, you appear to be quick, bright, prepared, and ready to go in any direction immediately. This is a key element in maintaining psychological leverage in the interview. And it's really very simple to accomplish.

GROOMING AND DRESS

Much of our job search advice is predicated on the approach of custom-designing for each company's situation. So it is with grooming. Generally, be conservative, neat, clean, and understated. If there's a choice, always go for the more muted color, the simpler pattern. But dress differently for an interview on site at a chemical plant than you would in a bank or brokerage house. We suggest that you visit a day in advance of the interview to determine corporate culture, work style, and dress code. Every place has a dress code — most often it's unwritten, but it's always there. When in doubt, dress professionally and conservatively. Also, you may want to affirm the dress code with the person who is arranging the interview.

BE PUNCTUAL, BUT DON'T BE TOO EARLY

Don't show up 30 minutes in advance of your appointment. That suggests that you're a rookie who is desperate to get this job or that you have nothing else to do. Tardiness is *always* inexcusable, however, so here's our original proposition for interview punctuality: Arrive at the location 15 or 20 minutes in advance, and determine exactly where the interviewer is located and how long it's likely to take to get through the waiting area. (Is it a private administrative assistant's office or a department full of visitors you might have to wait in line behind?) Having determined that, go to a coffee bar and spend a few minutes in last-minute preparation. Part of this preparation is a two-minute psychological drill. Tell yourself that you're the best candidate for the job because you've done your homework. You look right, you'll act right, and you feel good about yourself and about why you're there. Assert to yourself that you'll walk in with confidence. Then proceed to the interviewer's office. Time your arrival five minutes in advance of the appointment so that you'll be announced right on time. That's sharp and impressive. Again, the psychological leverage is evident. You've protected your interests by getting there in plenty of time to make the appointment. You've arrived on site only minutes ahead of time, yet you're calm, cool, collected, and ready.

INTERVIEW FORMATS

The traditional one-on-one interview continues to be the most prevalent format for interviewing in companies. However, panel or group interviews are becoming more common for selection of candidates at all levels in the organization. The flattening of the organization, the prevalence of a team approach to work, and concern over misrepresentation during an interview are reasons for this trend. In addition, on out-of-town interviews, companies will often save time in scheduling candidate meetings by using the panel approach. The dynamics of the group interview are more complex and can be more stressful than a one-on-one interview, making interview preparation even more critical to success. When an interview is arranged, be sure to ask who will be present, their titles and working relationships. This information will enable you to do some research on the interviewers. However, be prepared for changes in the interviewers and schedule for progressive interviews.

Another approach companies are using is a series of interviews including human resources, the immediate boss, team members and even subordinates, culminating with the department head or President. After a series of interviews, the interviewers will get together to compare notes — the consistency of your responses is crucial. Do not minimize the influence of any one interviewer because of level or relationship to the position for which you are interviewing.

Particularly common on university campuses is the video conference interview. Companies save on recruiting costs and have access to a broader number of campuses through this remote interviewing technique. As equipment becomes more accessible, video interviewing will become more common and will be used for recruiting at all levels when candidates are geographically dispersed. Using video to practice interview is an excellent technique for improving your interviewing skills and presentations in any situation, but is particularly important if you are asked to interview officially by video conference. Without practice, you will likely feel awkward and distracted during the interview.

Regardless of the interview format, preparation is the key to gaining the offer. Build your psychological leverage by expecting the unexpected, and preparing for every possibility.

Build your Psychological Leverage by expecting the unexpected, and preparing for every possibility.

KNOW YOUR INTERVIEWER

Let us offer a word of caution before we proceed. If you think there's enough material thus far to choke an army mule — or a job campaigner new to the task — stop now and begin digesting. Be sure that you have the basics down pat, because what follows is equivalent to a graduate course in interviewing.

Part of the process of a true commitment to excellence in interviewing is preparing and learning not only about yourself and the company but also about personality types of interviewers. If you can learn to read the person across the desk — how he lives, works, and thinks — you're really flirting with the stratosphere in the world of job search. There are four basic types:

- *The long-range planner:* Typically, this person, also known as the intuitor, is an economist, a forecaster, or occasionally a market or business developer. His job is to plan three to five years in advance, so that's how he thinks and talks. Your answers should focus on the big picture — where technology will take this industry in the next decade, how you picture yourself in that situation, and so forth.

- *The analytical, task-oriented type:* This very fact-oriented type of person is also called the thinker. Typically, the thinker is very neat, conservative, and well organized. Never use the word *about* with this person — deal in specifics, not generalities. If there are numbers in your resume, be prepared to defend them in detail. This person will tend to be very neat and controlled and immaculate in dress.

- *The people person:* This much more informal, more colorfully dressed interviewer is also called the feeler. Feelers are interested not so much in your analytical powers or skill levels but in whether you'll be a good fit for the company and the team. You're much more likely to be offered a cup of coffee, or even lunch, during the interview with this person.

- *The time-conscious, reactive type:* This person's environment is full of ringing phones and other interruptions. Also known as the senser, this individual really won't have time to allow you to create a full portrayal of your personality, skills, and background. Typically, the senser will have coat-off, sleeves rolled-up, and be harried. Always under the gun, caught up in the activity trap, with never enough people, never enough time, the senser will be looking for your ability to get things done quickly. The senser needs a doer — someone who doesn't waste time and gets right to the point.

This is typically a highly complex and sophisticated analysis, so don't deal with it unless you're ready. But if you are, you'll be able to structure your responses to mesh with the corporate style and the interviewer's frame of reference.

GO FOR THE OFFER

As we've mentioned before, we're not saying that you are going after a job during this stage of the interview. You're going all out for the *offer.* Then you will evaluate this company against the other offers you generate. If the environment is alien to you, obviously you may take another position. We're training you to survive in any interviewing situation, not push you into a corporate setting in which you can't cope and that you don't like.

THE INTERVIEW CLOSE

Be prepared to respond to a typical closing interview question:

Q99:   Why should I hire you?

A: "You should hire me because my entire professional experience to this point has prepared me for this job. I've gone to school, received my education, and worked hard at determining the needs of the job, department, and company. As my resume suggests, my accomplishments speak to each of those needs, and I'm here because I am the best qualified individual for the position. I will do an excellent job for you."

And the interviewer's possible finale:

Q100:   How long will you stay with our company?

A: Your response should resound with dedication, "For the rest of my career" or "as long as I can contribute successfully to the company's goals."

Finally, at the close of the interview, in order to show the maximum amount of interest in both the job and the company, ask three questions:

1.   Where do you see this job in one to three years?
2.   Where do you see the company in three to five years? and
3.   Where can I get more information?

That's all. We don't recommend that you ask a lot of questions during the interview since it distracts interviewers from their agendas.

Avoid the common end-of-interview faux pas of asking for the job. This is amateurish and can have the opposite effect you expect! Do let the interviewer know your interest in and excitement about the position and the company. As you depart the interview, thank the interviewer(s) for their time and the opportunity to interview. Be sure to get their business cards if they were not shared at the beginning of the interview, and ask what their time frame for the selection process is so you can appropriately follow up. If not clarified by the interviewer, verify the appropriate person with whom to follow up.

THE THANK YOU LETTER

After the interview, as soon as possible write down notes about the interview, the position and company. Then draft a thank you letter to send out no later than the next day. The letter should reinforce important issues which were discussed and cover any areas you feel are important to getting the offer which were not covered. If research is needed to address these adequately, complete it as soon as possible. Timeliness of thank you letters is as important as their professionalism. Be sure to include all of your interviewers in the thank you letter either by separately addressed letters or by copying interviewers on your letter to the hiring authority. In order to do this effectively, it is important to get business cards of all your interviewers or write down their names and titles accurately. Exhibit 27 presents a typical thank you letter.

One of the most dynamic and convincing follow up letters to an interview is called the *requirements/qualifications comparison* letter as demonstrated in Exhibit 28. Our clients have successfully used this strategy hundreds of times to win the offer and build their negotiating leverage. Potential employers are impressed by the comprehensiveness of this approach since it thoroughly states the requirements of the job much as a job description does. In many cases it reveals contributions the candidate can make which the interviewer had not considered. The thought and initiative that goes into preparing an excellent requirements/qualifications comparison letter alone can often make the difference in receiving or not receiving the offer.

In addition to writing the thank you letter, if your references were provided to the interviewer, be sure to call each reference to apprise them of a potential call and to provide them with some background on the position and the potential callers. Here's an example of why you must prep your references:

Sherry, having completed her interview and been asked for references, felt great about her chances for an offer. Unfortunately, she made two avoidable errors in the process — she failed to ask for the interviewer's business card, which made sending the follow-up letter difficult, and she did not call her references to prepare them. Later she learned that one of her references, without thinking about the consequences, had indicated to the interviewer her surprise that Sherry was being considered for the position since it was in a function and industry which was different from Sherry's experience. Sherry didn't get the offer.

Be sure too, to follow up by phone after the interview. Call within the suggested time, but if a return call is not immediate, try again within a couple of days. Waiting for a response can be frustrating, but keep in mind that the interviewer may have other priorities and the timing of the selection process often changes. In any case, never sit idle waiting for an offer! Continue networking and interviewing for other positions. Even if you get the offer, in keeping with linkage, you will want to bring as many offers to the table as possible before making a decision.

SOME LAST WORDS ON INTERVIEWING

MOST FREQUENT COMPLAINTS ABOUT INTERVIEWEES

- Poor communication — talks too little, talks too much, rambles, is evasive, and is nervous.

- Poor preparation — asks no questions, has no information about company.

- Vague interests — lacks career goals, is unsure of job goals.

- Unrealistic expectations — is too concerned about salary, is immature, is inflexible.

MOST FREQUENT COMPLAINTS ABOUT INTERVIEWERS

- Poor communication — talks too much, is unclear, rambles, and is evasive.

- Poor preparation — didn't read resume, manages time poorly.

- Judgmental attitude — draws conclusions or makes statements that are inaccurate or unfair.

- Negative attitude — spends too much time talking about negative aspects of the job.

- Dumb questions — asks questions that don't relate to the position.

Your preparation and your ability to control the interview will enable you to overcome the weaknesses of a poor interviewer. Don't allow such an interviewer to cause you to lose your psychological edge. Gently lead the interviewer through the points you want to make, without letting on that you are aware of his ineptness. Like playing tennis with a rookie, if you get frustrated by the opponent's bloopers, you can easily throw the match.

WHY PEOPLE ARE HIRED

- Positive attitude and enthusiasm.

- Good presentation of skills needed by employer for the position.

- Professional in all contacts, including letter, phone call, and face-to-face contact; excellent verbal skills.

- Good rapport with interviewer, including good discussion.

- Past experience that supports qualifications for the opening.

- Provides knowledgeable questions and statements about company and job opening, thus proving commitment to research.

- Professional appearance, including appropriate dress, neat and clean personal grooming, friendly attitude.

WHY PEOPLE ARE REJECTED

- Bitter attitude based on previous employment experience.

- Poor presentation of skills and abilities.

- Poor appearance and demeanor.

- Mistakes and misspellings in written correspondence.

- Lack of confidence during interview, including stumbling over answers and not portraying a positive attitude.

- Bad references or no positive references.

- Unqualified for the job or inability to communicate qualifications.

Look carefully at this list and observe that all of the foibles are *controllables* except perhaps the last — qualifications. Even that may be rectified with additional education or experience. The following case is an excellent illustration of how you can position yourself for the offer and success by controlling your presentation, appearance and attitude:

> Terry had been in the workplace for three years after graduation. He lost his computer programming job to a restructuring and also went through a divorce. Only 27, he felt that his whole life was falling apart. His defeatist attitude was reflected in his demeanor, body language and appearance. Long hair added to his disheveled look, even though he was particularly

proud of it. He had been looking for a new job for several months with no success. Terry's father was in our program and asked if we could help. We welcomed Terry into the program and within two weeks he was a new man. The process of learning *The Total System* rebuilt his confidence. He began to walk and talk like a true professional. We suggested that a haircut would dramatically change interviewers' perceptions of him even if it had no bearing on his performance. Reluctantly he got a professional cut and amazingly, even his own view of himself was enhanced! Terry began networking and within two weeks had two offers. He placed successfully in record time for double his former pay!

> Your preparation will ensure that you avoid the points of rejection and emphasize the winning points of acceptance.

This is just one example of how appearance and attitude affect the ability to market one's capabilities. Terry's talent hadn't changed in one month, but his outlook and marketing skills had. From head to toe, from resume to interviewing skills, he was an employer's dream candidate. Your interview preparation will ensure that you avoid the points of rejection and emphasize the winning points of acceptance. The ball's in your court so serve a winner and win the match!

EXHIBIT 26
Post Interview Self-Evaluation Form

Company _____   Interview Date: _____

Name & Title of Interviewer _____

Position Interviewed For _____

Check if you felt "OK" or "very good" about certain aspects of the interview or if you felt you could have done better and "need to improve" for future interviews. Be brutally honest with yourself – this is <u>your</u> future at stake!

	Need to Improve	OK	Very Good
(1) Personal appearance?			
(2) Professional first impression?			
(3) Firm handshake at start and end of interview?			
(4) Maintained good eye contact?			
(5) Expressed myself well by talking clearly and correctly?			
(6) Self-confident, not ill at ease?			
(7) Expressed interest in the job and career?			
(8) Willingness to start at entry level or lower level and work up? (when appropriate)			
(9) Minimized employment barriers by presenting them in a positive light?			
(10) Positive about my previous employer(s)?			
(11) Demonstrated knowledge of the company and the industry?			
(12) Described qualifications in a positive manner?			
(13) Asked pertinent questions about the job?			
(14) Presented abilities and qualifications in terms of the requirements for this job?			
(15) Thanked the interviewer and arranged for follow-up?			

Areas needing improvement for future interviews:

Electronic Forms are available in *The Total System Organizer*

EXHIBIT 27
Post Interview Thank You Letter

NAME
Address
City, State Zip Code
Cell Phone Number
Home Phone Number
Email Address

DATE

Mr. Michael Hearst
Vice President, Marketing
Energy Trading Corporation
Post Office Box
Houston, Texas 77088

Dear Michael:

It was certainly my pleasure to interview with you today. The more I learn about Energy Trading, the more impressed I am. It is obvious that Energy Trading is striving for excellence in the position of Manager of the Southeast Region.

I am confident that my skills and experience are an excellent match with Energy Trading's needs. Initial contributions would come in the following areas:

- Expand the customer base of Energy Trading by offering a full range of service to customers. This would include spot and term proposals in addition to taking advantage of gas futures, options and derivative products to meet the customer's pricing needs without exposing the company to risk.

- Create full market presence by exploring all supply options, taking advantage of transportation discounts and evaluating possible additional opportunities via split connections with alternate pipelines.

- Establish solid long-term relationships with customers by meeting their needs and solving problems quickly and efficiently.

- Continually search the market for new and profitable opportunities which will separate Energy Trading from all other trading companies.

I look forward to further discussions with you in the near future. If you have any questions or require additional information, please do not hesitate to call.

Sincerely,

Name

EXHIBIT 28
Requirements/Qualifications Letter

NAME
Address
City, State Zip Code
Cell Phone Number
Home Phone Number
Email Address

Date

Mr. Thomas W. Anderson
President
T.W. Anderson and Company, Inc.
P.O. Box
San Diego, CA 91718

Dear Tom:

I would like to take this opportunity to thank you for meeting with me on August 26th. The Institute's Executive Director position is very interesting to me, and talking about the position's responsibilities on a first-hand basis with you certainly reinforced that perception. Based on our conversation and the research that I have conducted into the plastics industry, I am absolutely confident that I can make a meaningful contribution to the industry as the Executive Director of the Institute.

After careful and thoughtful reflection on our conversation, I would like to propose that the committee consider the following points with respect to my background and qualifications for this position.

YOUR REQUIREMENTS:

- Develop and implement the Executive Board approved programs for broadening the opportunities for the effective use of thermoplastic piping. Develop and recommend programs and budgets to meet the Institute's goals.

- Manage the development and publication of technical and marketing literature. Manage technical, advertising and publicity programs.

- Manage the affairs of the Institute's Hydrostatic Stress Board, including its program for developing and listing recommended hydrostatic strengths of commercially available thermoplasticing recommended hydrostatic strengths of commercially available thermoplastic materials.

- Act as spokesperson for the Institute before code, standards, regulatory, trade and industrial groups, the public, the media, and outside organizations.

MY QUALIFICATIONS:

- Three years experience in strategic planning and implementing business plans. Full responsibility for an engineering compounds business unit, with staff budgets exceeding $300,000 per year.

- Over ten years experience developing technical and marketing literature, and publicity and market development programs.

- Three years experience as a member of the Institute's Hydrostatic Stress Board and as a member of the Extrapolations Test Method Development committee.

- Over twelve years experience as a company representative to the Institute, ASTM, NSF, FDA, UL, CSA, AGA, GRI, USP and various other industry and regulatory organizations.

EXHIBIT 28 *(continued)*

- Develop and implement membership recruitment programs

- Supervise and give direction to staff: Establish work objectives for staff; ensure compliance to relevant TPA policies and procedures; assist and guide staff training and development; and periodically evaluate staff performance. Provide assistance and direction to the Institute operating units, committees, and working groups.

- Provide excellent customer service to members, people requesting information and other TPA staff. Interface with all the Institute/TPA staff and the Institute members; regulators (code and standard) writing bodies); trade and industrial groups; manufacturers of piping materials and additives; engineers and consultants; other pipe associations and associations representing user interests; professional organizations; government organizations; and the public.

- College degree, preferably in a technical discipline. Graduate degree preferred.

- Special knowledge and skills: Understanding and appreciation of standards and code development. Demonstrated competence in effectively communicating with technical interests, special interest groups, industry members, the media, and the public. Excellent written and verbal communication skills. Effective staffing ability, conceptual (strategic) thinking, ability to delegate, enthusiasm for achieving objectives, tenacity of purpose, empathy and tact but firmness of purpose in dealing with and responding to adverse interests, and avoidance of overly ambitious or political behavior. Ability to work on a variety of projects simultaneously.

- Three years experience as membership chairman of the South Texas section of The Plastics Association (TPA) developing and implementing membership recruiting programs. Received TPA award for greatest membership growth for a large section in YEAR.

- Over six years management experience, with up to eight direct reports. Over thirteen years experience in working with task forces and quality teams. Extensive training in total quality management, team building and team facilitation.

- Over thirteen years experience in product development, technical service, marketing and sales areas where responsiveness to customer inquiries and interests was always top priority. Extensive experience in dealing with the media during the past three years while implementing publicity press releases, programs and trade show participation.

- BS in chemistry and a PhD in Chemistry. 13 years experience in thermoplastics.

- These requirements reflect on my personality and character traits and can best be addressed through my references. Copies of my reference letters have been attached for review by the committee.

In summary, my background and experience presents the committee with a candidate for this position who can provide both technical and marketing leadership for the Institute and industry. Given this scenario, the committee may consider custom designing the Institute's Executive Director position to fit my background and to take advantage of my talents and abilities.

Tom, I am looking forward to meeting with the entire search committee on September 16th at your headquarters. If you have any questions or would like additional information in the interim, please call me at either of the above referenced numbers.

Sincerely,

NAME

Negotiating the Deal You Want:
Get the Money Now

As authors of this book, we have the easy job of teaching you the art of negotiating compensation even though it took us many years to learn and master this art form. To distinguish between interviewing and negotiating, we simply end one chapter and begin another. It's imperative that you, too, make such a clear-cut distinction between interviewing and negotiating in your campaign. Your task, however, won't be nearly as simple as concluding Chapter 8 and launching Chapter 9. Not only is negotiating a tough, complex, demanding proposition—it is, we think, the most difficult of all the steps in campaigning for a job—but it is also so subtle that it takes true discernment to know when to do it, let alone what to do. Of all the facets of looking for a new position, negotiating requires the greatest measure of discipline, preparation, and confidence on your part.

Interviewing usually gets preeminent ranking among the elements of job search. Resumes, networking, lead generation, and research do nothing more than put your body in front of the hiring authority, with a chance at the job. Certainly, we agree with that. Negotiating compensation is typically considered a part of the interview process, and without question it's the most vital part of that interview. Throughout the pages of this book we have attempted to instill in you the belief that getting "a" job isn't difficult or particularly noteworthy. We want you to find the "best" job or position and career for you. But if you can not or do not negotiate the best available compensation package, what might have been "the" job may unfortunately turn out to be only "a" job. In fact, you'll probably never even know the possibilities of the position if you're not prepared to take negotiation to the limit.

THE SITUATIONS ARE REVERSED

Now that we've anointed negotiating with such an aura of significance, here's the reason we've separated it from interviewing: Despite the fact that negotiations may occur at the same time and place as your job interview, the interaction between you and the employer changes radically at this point. In fact, it represents a 180-degree position shift. Throughout all the hours of interviewing— in three, four, or five discussions—you have courted the employer with your ability to contribute to the bottom line. You've been selling, selling, selling.

When negotiations begin, the company has been sold. They want you! Now the question becomes whether the organization is willing to pay enough to get you. At least, the events should be in that sequence. Don't ever let any discussion of compensation begin until it's clear that the company is making an offer. In some cases, you'll complete the final interview, get the offer, and shake hands on a tentative deal. Then the company will set up a subsequent interview to negotiate your entire compensation package.

This is why we say that the number one tenet of negotiating compensation is to postpone the conversation until you are at the offer stage. There are several reasons for this:

- You have sold yourself to the organization and they do not want to lose you.

- Throughout the interviewing process you have likely raised your value in the company's perception as they have gained a greater appreciation for how your talent and capability will add to their bottom line.

- The company does not want to start the selection process with new candidates because it is time consuming and potentially very costly especially if they have immediate needs to fill.

This may sound idealistic and difficult to achieve and for most interviewers it is! However, there are ways that you can delay the compensation discussion and ensure the negotiations are in proper sequence. Here are a few delaying statements that you can use during the interview that work well:

> The first tenet of negotiating compensation is to postpone the conversation until you are at the offer stage.

- "Compensation is number three on my list of priorities. I would prefer to find out more about your situation and share with you how I can contribute to be sure we have a good fit. I feel comfortable that you will offer a market competitive package. Let's talk about this after we both decide the match is right."

- "I'm sure we can come to a satisfactory agreement on a compensation package once we agree that this is a good fit."

The negotiating session will take on an entirely different tone from the employment interviews. Separating the two kinds of sessions, so that both sides can work toward a mutually satisfactory goal, is often best for both job hunter and employer. Unfortunately, job search reflects life, and the best of worlds happens all too infrequently. Consequently, once an offer is made, you'll have to help orchestrate the switch from your sales presentation to negotiations. And you'll have to do that in the heat of the interview. This is where subtlety, discernment, and confidence pay off. This is also why preparation for negotiating compensation is unrivaled in its importance to your successful job search.

One point here—stop and make certain that you buy into our philosophy of negotiating compensation as well as our challenge to you to make it happen. We hope that it's evident to you that this book is about self-help; it is not designed as a "feel-good-no-matter-what-you-do" journal. Our goal is to help and advance your career, to challenge you to work hard enough to assume command of the events of your search and your career advancement. Not surprisingly, our position on negotiating is consistent with that stand. Of course, you can shake hands and smile, taking whatever first offer the company makes. That's safe, easy, and perfectly suited to the standards of mediocrity that dominate the field of job search advice. But we suspect that if you've answered the challenges set forth in this book, negotiating your own compensation package won't be such an imposing roadblock after all.

And negotiating is not reserved just for the manager or executive levels. Regardless of your level or years of experience, you too can negotiate. The following example illustrates this truth:

> Dick had graduated from college only a couple of years prior to losing his job as a computer programmer. Totally dejected and demoralized, Dick sought our help. After following the principles of *The Total System,* Dick succeeded in getting two offers, and a third possible offer. At first he wanted to take the highest offer, already 25% higher than his old job, but with our insistence, he played one against the other, creating psychological leverage and increased each offer. Ultimately, he negotiated a starting salary 40% higher than his last position, and got a signing bonus to top that!

Always remember that the level of compensation with which you begin your new position affects every dollar you'll earn with the company. When you shake hands on $80,000, your future income will be calculated from that figure. Next year at this time, if the company determines that top achievers will receive a maximum increase of 5 percent, then your increase will be $4,000 if you get the $80,000 On the other hand, if you settle for $60,000, your maximum increase just got a $1,000 cut a year in advance. Obviously, that shortfall widens every year you work at this company in this job. But arithmetic is easy. Negotiating is hard . . . unless you know what you are doing!

You don't just pick $80,000 out of thin air. If that were possible, why not ask for $165,000? The numbers are calculated from your research into the company and the industry — how your skills and experience are normally compensated, plus the demand for them in the current market. Back to the internet. Back to the telephones. Without question, the skills required to research this question and then bring the research into action in negotiating are the most complex and require the greatest degree of precision of any you'll utilize in your search. Most important, you're relying greatly on linkage to make the negotiation process work in your favor.

The skills you acquired in the preceding chapters should have that employer leaning forward in his chair, ready to leap at the prospect of adding you to the team. However, if you've merely put on an OK interviewing presentation that convinces the company that you can do the job but none-the-less leaves you grouped with four or five other finalists, you don't have an abundance of negotiating leverage. When you've enhanced your marketability with a dazzling set of interview responses, that employer wants you. Now you're in the catbird seat, ready to negotiate with the power and authority in your corner.

NEGOTIATING COMPENSATION: MONEY FOLLOWS VALUE

Your value is subjective, of course. So your interviewing performance will prove your value to the company—or at least it must convince the employer that you're as valuable as your resume and your compensation expectations promise.

Make certain, though, that you back up your newly won authority and confidence with research and preparation. The proper numbers—$80,000 or whatever—are not based on what you fancy you'd like to earn this year. And most assuredly, you won't learn the right numbers from the interviewer. So you must reactivate all your networking skills to establish a negotiating position. In advance, talk to people with or formerly with the company, people in the industry, trade associations in your profession, as well as competitors and suppliers of the company. With your researching skills, find out what your occupational skills and experience will command today at that company. As much as we've cautioned you concerning search firms, this is an area in which one you trust can help. It can be a source of accurate information about salary trends. At all costs, however, use the search firm for background information only. Do not allow the recruiter to be a surrogate negotiator. Obviously, such information has to be elicited subtly; if the search firm thinks that there is no incentive for sharing information, it won't be too open.

Besides talking directly with people who have inside or validated information relevant to your function, industries you are targeting, or specific companies from which you have received an offer, check salary and professional surveys and internet sources. Since most internet sources collect data from companies and respected providers of regular recurring market surveys, it is one of the most valid sources of market information for individual job seekers.

Your first negotiating challenge usually addresses base salary and is appropriate since many factors in your total compensation package are calculated as a percentage of base salary. Obviously it follows that the higher base salary you are able to negotiate, the higher your total compensation package will be.

Once you obtain as much information on the market as you can, take the market norms for the industry and create a base salary range within which you plan to negotiate. This strategy gives you increased psychological leverage as you go into negotiations.

Most companies (except, perhaps, very small and/or emerging companies) establish a salary range structure and assign jobs to various levels within this structure depending on the assessed value and contribution of each position. Ranges have three distinct points:

- a minimum which is the lowest amount to be paid for a given job,

- a midpoint which represents the competitive base salary for a fully qualified and experienced incumbent, and

- a maximum, which is the most the company is willing to pay and is reserved for the outstanding performers, industry experts, and those having extensive background and experience.

For example, let's say you have determined from your research that the average base salary for the position for which you are interviewing is $80,000. Following prevalent practices, a range constructed around this "fully qualified" rate would be:

- Minimum: $64,000;

- Midpoint: $80,000;

- Maximum: $96,000.

With this knowledge, you can make a determination as to where your base salary should fall based on your background, qualifications, performance and accomplishments. Of course, there is no guarantee that the company's established range for this job is identical to your range. As you gain skill at negotiating, you should be able to get the interviewer to tell you what the company's range is for the job—sometimes Human Resources will actually provide this range prior to your interview or prior to your negotiations with the hiring authority so do not hesitate to ask if this information is available at the appropriate time. Armed with this information, you will be in an even better position for implementing your negotiating strategy. If you have the exact range early on in the interviewing or negotiating process, you will still need to do your research to determine if the company's range is competitive. You can adjust your strategy for countering an offer, depending on the competitiveness of the company's range. If you don't negotiate the highest "competitive' base salary you will be leaving dollars on the table that may never be recouped!

Some job seekers are concerned about negotiating a beginning base salary close to the range maximum. Remember that things can change—adjustments to range assignments can be made after the company sees what an outstanding performer you are; there may be opportunities for promotion, and well managed companies adjust their ranges annually based on market movements. In addition, during the negotiations, you may strategize to modify the job description based on your qualifications, potentially increasing the applicable range.

Indeed, part of the negotiating process is identifying exactly what you are to do in the new company. One of the best ways to obtain the right job for yourself is to tailor it to your specifications! For example, when you're discussing a position with a firm during a sequence of interviews, you may custom-design a job description for the position based on how you perceive the company's needs. Of course, you would want to find out whether a job description already exists, but it is not unusual—even in major corporations—for there to be no job descriptions, or descriptions that are very basic. Consider this example:

> In writing such a job description, Donna Holmes was able to create her "ideal job." She first presented it to Jim, the executive who was moving into a different division and whose job was available. Jim acknowledged the accuracy of the description and was impressed. Donna then presented the description to her prospective boss, who responded so favorably that he even added some responsibilities that enhanced the position.

> It should be pointed out that Donna was wise not to assume that Jim, the executive who was leaving, would pass the description on to his boss. Had Donna not taken the initiative to do so herself, it would not have become significant in the negotiations. In this case, Donna was offered not only a job, but the precise position she had custom-designed. In addition, by clarifying the responsibilities and authority of the position, Donna was able to increase the initial salary offered on the basis of the expanded scope of the job.

In addition to base salary, when you are negotiating the cash portion of your total compensation package you should negotiate your possible short term annual bonus opportunities. Most companies offer some type of variable cash compensation opportunities for all levels of employees. If you can not come to agreement on base salary, the company may be willing to raise the level of your participation in their bonus program to make up for the difference. Small and mid-size companies in particular may have a proportionately higher variable pay compared to base pay than larger firms. This strategy enables companies to share their success in the good times with employees and protects them during down swings in the market. You share in the market risks but also have a potentially higher total compensation in the good times!

The second tenet of negotiating is never meekly accept the first dollar figure offered.

The second tenet of negotiating is never— *never* —meekly accept the first dollar figure offered. And always ask for the offer in writing. Similarly, do not accept a job offer on the spot unless the offer exceeds your wildest expectations and they must have your answer immediately. If the employer presses you, simply say that you must discuss the offer with your family or that you're evaluating several other offers from excellent companies like theirs (but never reveal who the other firms are). Offer to get back in touch as soon as possible and to let them know where you are in the decision-making process at that time. If an answer is required sooner, be flexible, of course, all the way down to a twenty-four-hour evaluation period. But under no circumstances (other than the one previously mentioned) should you be coerced into saying yes on the spot. Believe us, an employer who won't sit still for a twenty-four-hour consideration period may want you out of the marketplace where competitors can court you. Your decision time may be just the leverage you need to up the ante!

Which brings us back to the money. If you don't get it now, when your armor is spotless, when do you suppose you'll get it? The company wants you on the team, so this is your best chance—possibly your only chance—to negotiate your best deal, perhaps to transform "a" job into "the" job. And consider, if you don't get a compensation package commensurate with your skills and experience, you're more than just limiting income in the short range. Conceivably, you are retarding the progress of your career tomorrow and on over the horizon. Unless you have a sure long-range benefit in sight, a cut in salary will hurt you—and badly.

Are there exceptions? Of course—acceptable trade-offs for a reduced salary include:

- A chance to run a business (less money but more power)
- A highly visible job, perhaps one in the national or industry spotlight
- A chance to join the start-up team of a hot new company (short-range loss for long-term gain)
- A radical career change
- A chance to leave a second-rate company to join an industry leader
- A chance to leave a declining industry
- Extreme personal circumstances that dictate a geographic preference (for example, if your child has a chronic illness, and Armpit, Wyoming, has the only treatment facility in the nation, then it's Armpit, Wyoming, at almost any salary)

If you're preparing to accept a drastic salary reduction for any reason not listed, think hard. It's your career, your life—but you're making mistakes in interviewing and negotiating. And you're about to make a compensation mistake that could hurt you for years into the future and from which your career may never recover. If you're rationalizing otherwise, you're blowing smoke on your own career. Go after the compensation that you're worth. We're not suggesting that you're there for a holdup, but don't settle for a dollar figure that is so low that it could cripple your career's progress.

OTHER FORMS OF COMPENSATION

You must realize that compensation encompasses a great deal more than just base salary and bonuses. There are other ways than just dollars in the paycheck to achieve your compensation goals. Consider the following options as ways to increase the value of your total compensation package.

- *Tax Favored Benefits (Company)*: These include health, life, and disability insurance, and retirement benefits (pension plans and 401K plans). Since companies receive tax deductions for providing these programs, by law they must treat all employees the same. Coverage under these plans cannot be negotiated. At the executive level, many companies provide supplemental programs that are not tax exempt and executives may be able to negotiate coverages that are best for them.

- *Vacations/Holidays*: Many companies will adjust vacation schedules to accommodate the past experience of a new employee, even though this results in treating some new employees differently than others.

- *Perquisites*: These are non cash forms of compensation that tend to be more prevalent at the executive level, but also are found at lower levels and are fully negotiable. Included in this category are such things as cars, credit cards, first class air travel, professional association fees, educational reimbursement programs, tax preparation, membership in health, luncheon clubs.

- *Stock Option Programs*: While these compensation programs are more prevalent at the executive level, many companies are extending them to lower employee levels. These programs can be quite lucrative over the longer term and could offset lower than desired base salary offers.

- *Relocation Expenses*: These are fully negotiable and may be available even for relocation within a relatively small geographic area.

- *Sign On Bonuses*: Sign on bonuses tend to become more prevalent in tight labor markets and fall out of use when there is a plentiful supply of labor.

Exhibits 29 and 30 provide employee benefit, perquisite and relocation checklists to help you formulate a compensation package that meets your needs.

With your written offer in hand, you can utilize these forms to develop your counter offer. In fact the wise job seeker will carefully review these lists and develop a strategy before actually entering into negotiations. Each individual has his or her own unique needs depending on age, personal and family needs, and career priorities.

Our point is that almost everything is negotiable. This doesn't mean that you'll be successful on every item. But it means that whatever the company can do to increase the total value of your compensation is fair game to be placed on the table. For instance, your cost of benefits can dramatically affect how you come out overall financially. Smaller organizations may provide fewer benefits than major corporations. Here's an example of how you can use that to your advantage in negotiating:

> Kent Wilson recently moved from a large to a small organization. In nego-
> tiating his compensation, Kent was able to gain a 17 percent increase over
> his former salary because he carefully compared benefits and presented
> the differences to his new employer. On the basis of Kent's analysis, the
> new employer adjusted his initial offer to give Kent a total package that
> was substantially better than he had in his previous position.

Never assume "I can't get that" or "They have a policy against that." Remember, your challenge in the interview is to make yourself invaluable to that employer. If you've accomplished that goal, then you can approach negotiations with the mind-set, realistically, that your total compensation package should be in direct proportion to what you bring to the company's bottom line!

MAKE IT A WIN-WIN PROCESS

If you think that a tough negotiating session will alienate the employer, you're sadly mistaken—or maybe you're just copping out to evade a tough, demanding situation. In fact, the reverse is true. Our conviction is that weak, unprepared people hide behind that fear. Look at it this way: you're not out to hold up the company; you're out to join the team and contribute to a bolder bottom line for everyone. Of course, if you're rude, greedy, aggressive, and unprofessional during negotiations, you might jeopardize the offer or your future at the company. But who wants to be that way?

The whole process should be a challenge for both you and the employer, but not a bloodletting. Reach for the best, and expect the same from the employer. Attempt to orchestrate not a win-lose scenario but a win-win equation for both the company and you. Consider these additional basic negotiation tactics to achieve those ends:

- Always negotiate with the hiring authority, not with the human resources department, because it is the hiring authority's bottom line that you are impacting.

- Let the employer name a salary and total compensation package first. Then ask them to put it in writing. While they do so, you can prepare your counter offer.

- Never answer the question, "What is the minimum you'll accept?" or "How much money do you need to make?" with a lower figure than your most recent compensation. (You're not interested in minimums.) State your required compensation boldly and confidently as you also address how you will dramatically impact their bottom-line.

- Orchestrate your potential job offers so that you can consider them simultaneously. This is another delicate, subtle process, but it pays off when it's done well. If you're under consideration for three different positions, it will limit your ability to evaluate each one objectively and compare them if you don't have all the details simultaneously. Insist that the first company to offer wait until the next week for an answer. If the process is slow in the second company, you can insist that you need all the details and the offer by Friday, with your answer forthcoming the following week. And so on with the third offer. It's difficult, but it's imperative if you're attempting to select the one best job for your future. (Exhibit 31 provides a form for evaluating offers. It will assist you in weighing factors that are important in the evaluation of multiple offers.)

To appreciate how beautifully this process can be orchestrated, recall the case of Joe Williams, the engineer who entered our program with no experience in job search. He couldn't even make a cold telephone call during his first couple of weeks. By the end of three months, he was placed in a better job from among three offers. And he skillfully arranged the sequence of events so that all three offers were on the table on a Friday afternoon. He took the weekend with his family, and selected the job he wanted. Speeding one offer up while you slow another one down is not easy, but if you apply yourself, you can adapt the proper techniques and make it happen.

Look at it this way—the entire process, whether you're negotiating compensation or orchestrating job offers to bear fruit simultaneously, really constitutes what might be called your first performance evaluation. If you're weak, unprepared, and easily overpowered—if you accept the first offer put on the table—the employer will walk away with a "victory." But believe us, it's a victory he'd just as soon do without. He will not be overly impressed with your ability. You've got the job, but not much else, and certainly not his respect.

In contrast, if you strap on your seat belt and accelerate for a mutually beneficial best deal, you'll have an ally, not an enemy. Just be sure that you keep it professional and market competitive and the employer will be impressed by your performance. You've proved that you're a formidable adversary, but he's lucky enough to have you as his ally. All the complexities and subtleties that you conquered in negotiating a win-win package will now be brought to bear in the marketplace for his company. Here's an example of how your negotiating skills increase your value to a company:

> Cliff had transitioned from military officer to a corporate planning position, only to lose it to a reorganization. Still new to the civilian workforce, he was totally naïve and apprehensive about the job search process. Nevertheless, by applying our sound networking techniques, he received an offer with a small firm within one month. Feeling very lucky and really excited about working for an entrepreneurial company, he was about to accept a salary offer well below his last position. Upon hearing this, we convinced Cliff that the owner would be disappointed and would not respect him if he did not counteroffer. Skeptical, Cliff made the counteroffer, asking for a substantial increase. Without batting an eye, the owner reached over, shook his hand and said, "No problem, welcome aboard!"

If that alone doesn't convince you to get serious about negotiating, nothing will. Above all, trust in what we're telling you. This is a big step of faith, but if you do it our way, negotiating won't hurt your new relationship with the firm—it will enhance it. For proof of this, look again to our firm's success rate. For many years we've guided displaced employees to placement in an average of 3.2 months—and we're usually counseling clients why they should not be taking certain jobs, or less money, rather than pushing them into quick acceptance of any offer. Even with our rapid turnaround figure, we're pushing no one into jobs. We guide them to the best jobs. Our system works. And it's best not only for you but for your new company, as well. Remember, by utilizing our techniques, every future job should be a better job for better pay.

Once you have negotiated the deal you want, formalize your understanding with a letter of agreement.

Once you have negotiated the deal you want and have accepted your new position, it is wise to formalize your understanding with a letter of agreement. Some companies provide one automatically as part of their new employee procedures. If your new employer does not follow this practice, which we recommend, you can draft one yourself. (A sample letter of understanding is provided in Exhibit 32.) By putting in writing the agreed-upon terms, you ensure that no misunderstanding can rear its ugly head six months or a year after you have joined the company. In addition, the agreement is the foundation on which you can build future negotiations.

EXHIBIT 29
Employee Benefit Checklist

BENEFIT	COVERAGE	PREMIUM
Major medical insurance/health maintenance organization (HMO)		
Dental/optical insurance		
Annual physical		
Life insurance/supplemental life		
Accidental death and dismemberment insurance		
Disability insurance/long term care insurance		
Travel accident insurance		
Retirement/pension plans		
Vacation and holidays		
Educational assistance		
Dependent Scholarships		
Professional certification/association fees		
Bonus plan/profit sharing		
Stock options/purchase plans		
Deferred compensation (401-K)		
Tax/financial/estate planning assistance		
Low cost loan		
Legal advice		
Company car/auto expense reimbursement		
Company credit cards		
Club memberships/entertainment privileges		
Publication incentives		
Matching gifts		
First-class travel		
Signing bonus		
Sabbatical leave		
Severance/employment agreement		
Others:		

Electronic Forms are available in *The Total System Organizer*

EXHIBIT 30
Relocation Checklist

RELOCATION BENEFIT	BENEFIT LIMITATION	COMMENTS
Home purchase		
Home sale/purchase expense reimbursement		
Advance of home equity		
Mortgage interest differential		
Temporary living expenses		
Household goods shipment		
Moving allowance		
In-transit expenses		
Duplicate housing expenses		
Storage of items		
Income tax gross-up		
Spouse employment assistance		
Housing allowance (overseas)		
Income tax equalization (overseas)		
Others:		

Electronic Forms are available in *The Total System Organizer*

EXHIBIT 31
Evaluating Offers

For each offer, in column 1, rate each of the following criteria on a scale of 1 to 10 (1 low; 10 high) based on your personal needs. (Column 1 will be the same for all companies since this represents your priorities.) Then, in column 2, rate each criterion, again on a scale of 1 to 10, based on how well you feel the company satisfies those criteria. For each offer, multiply column 1 by column 2 and list that figure in column 3 (1 X 2). You can compare offers on the basis of their total scores.

CRITERIA	Offer 1			Offer 2		
	1	2	3	1	2	3
CAREER/PROFESSIONAL FACTORS Job responsibilities						
Adequacy of staff/support						
Title						
Promotion/personal growth potential						
Decision-making authority						
Other						
COMPANY FACTORS Size of company						
Company/industry history and image						
Management style (participative, directive, etc.)						
Other						
PERSONAL FACTORS Base salary						
Bonus/profit-sharing/stock options, etc.						
Benefits (pension, disability, insurance, vacation)						
Perks (car, memberships, etc.)						
Geographic location						
Amount of travel						
Commuting requirements						
Special expenses (commuting fare, taxes, relocation, etc.)						
Other						
TOTAL SCORES						

Electronic Forms are available in *The Total System Organizer*

EXHIBIT 32
Sample Letter of Agreement

PETE BLUME
Address
City, State Zip Code
Cell Phone Number
Email Address

Date

Mr. Ted Bates
Executive Vice President
Ace Company
Address

Dear Mr. Bates:

Thank you for including the executive benefits program we discussed. As I have voiced several times, I am extremely interested in employment with Ace Company as your Vice President, Operations, and particularly in working directly with you.

Upon receipt of your formal letter offering the following terms of employment, I will be in a position to conclude my negotiations with the other companies with whom I have been talking and begin the training process we outlined. Following are the terms we discussed along with several additional items for your consideration.

- Base Salary - $250,000 per year, paid in 24 semi-monthly payments.
- Bonus Plan – To be collaboratively written by Ted Bates and Pete Blume to identify mutually agreeable targets and objectives paralleling the Executive Vice President's bonus plan. Ace would guarantee a minimum bonus for the current calendar YEAR of $50,000. However, if the incentive plan in its normal operation produces more than $50,000, then the greater amount shall be paid on Ace's normal incentive plan payout cycle.
- Car Allowance - $500 per month to cover the initial cost, taxes and insurance. Gasoline and normal maintenance, (i.e. oil changes, lubrication, etc.) will be expensed items outside the allowance.
- Insurance Coverage – Effective May 15, YEAR
- Vacation Policy – Waived, to allow three weeks vacation during the current calendar year YEAR and four weeks for calendar year YEAR and beyond.
- Location Confirmation – Pete Blume will be allowed to fill this position without requiring relocation for at least 3 years.
- Employment Agreement – Will guarantee severance and outplacement including current base salary and benefits for a period of not less than 12 months after suspension of employment for "any reason" other than documented unsatisfactory performance and/or illegal activities carried on by Pete Blume.
- 401K Pension Plan – Please clarify the amount Ace matches.
- Relocation Policy – Please clarify Ace's relocation policy and finances involved for future consideration of promotions which would require family relocation either domestic or international after a 3-year period.

I look forward to your careful consideration of the above points. If you or Ace Company requires any clarification of these requirements, please contact me. I firmly believe a quick and positive resolution will ensure a solid and long-lasting relationship. I look forward to receiving your written offer confirming the provisions of this letter and clarifying Ace's pension and relocation policies.

Sincerely,
Pete Blume

CHAPTER 10
Your Curtain Call:
Make It a Standing Ovation

It's up to you, now, to play out the scenario. You're the scriptwriter, director, producer, and star. If you fully utilize the job search techniques described in the preceding nine chapters, there is no question that you will be a hit. Before you begin your creative act, let's review the essential elements of a successful search.

Linkage:
Each step of your search must be linked to the previous step and the one to follow.

- *The principle of linkage:* Each step of your search must be linked to the previous step and the one to follow. As smooth as a play's script, your job search should be planned and directed from resume to reference letters to networking to interviewing to negotiating. Link them all and increase your job search leverage.

- *Positive thinking:* If you've ever performed before an audience, you know how debilitating stage fright can be. The effect is the same when you allow negativity to dominate your job search. You alone control your thoughts, attitudes, and actions. Use whatever techniques help you to reduce stress and maintain a positive frame of mind—motivational books or CDs, meditation, exercise, proper diet, discussing your successes with your friends and family, rewarding yourself for meeting daily goals, visualizing your new job, talking with positive people you admire, reviewing your accomplishments, and so forth. Whatever it takes, be positive.

- *Flexibility and realism:* In assessing your career options, leave no stone unturned. Changing careers, starting an independent business, exploring other industries, relocating—each option should be evaluated from the perspective of your interests, aptitudes, and personality as well as from the outlook of marketplace opportunities. If you merely skimmed the self-assessment questions in Chapter 1, take time now to think them through so that you know that your job objectives are on target.

- *Keeping your resume current:* By now you probably have your resume completed—if not, return to Chapter 3 ASAP! Recognizing that employers and employees no longer share undying loyalty and life-long career commitments, it is essential that you be prepared for your next inevitable job change. Maintain a file with your resume, performance appraisals, job description, and accomplishments. You'll find this file extremely useful for salary and performance reviews and when a new career opportunity presents itself. If you're still employed and looking, start this file now.

- *Link your references to your resume:* Some people may be of the opinion that references are worthless, that no one puts stock in them, and that they are a pain to write. But if you draft reference letters which validate the accomplishments in your resume, they become very meaningful and indispensable. Have them in your tool kit for situations in which they are required and to ensure that the individuals who are your references are properly prepared for that critical reference check.

- *Be a one percenter:* Use networking techniques to the maximum. It's okay to use search firms and respond to internet listings—10 to 30 percent of jobs are found that way. But devote 80 percent of your time and efforts to networking. If you haven't started your personal and professional contact list, review your business card files, Christmas card lists, and alumni and association directories, and delay no longer.

Once you've placed yourself in your new job, be sure to send a thank you and announcement letter to your network. Maintain a networking file next to your current resume file and keep in touch with your contacts. Don't allow another five or ten years to pass—when you're in need of assistance again—before you call them. If your network is undeveloped now, vow to make it extensive for your next job search. It's up to you to be well connected.

- *Developing your personal marketing plan:* Get organized, set goals, and go for it. Pretend you're running the race of your life, because you are! You're at the starting block — on your mark! Fingers poised on the tape, you kick your legs and place them firmly in the blocks. Eyes focused on the finishing ribbon—get set! Every muscle tenses as adrenaline courses through your veins. The gun blast triggers your momentum, and you shoot off to the finish line. Can you win without training, without establishing goals, without desire? Throughout this book, we have provided forms outlining the kinds of information you must track to help you develop your personal marketing plan. Whether you use a manual or electronic system, it is essential that you develop some system with which you are comfortable — and use it.

- *Psychological leverage in the interview:* Whether you're on stage, in a tennis match, or running a race, your greatest advantage is being mentally prepared. Interviews are no different. Know your opponent. Anticipate every question. Beware of hidden agendas. Stay one step ahead, and use psychological leverage to keep the interview positive and general. Practice the tough questions in Chapter 8, and avoid the "red flags" at all costs. Interviewing success depends on your preparation and control.

- *Negotiating value:* Don't be afraid to ask for what you deserve. Whatever your concern, it won't hurt to lay it on the table. The offer is rarely "take it or leave it." If losing $25,000 on your house is what bothers you — let the company know. If your current medical insurance will lapse before the new policy comes into effect — let the company know. If your spouse would have to find a new job, perhaps the company will provide spouse relocation assistance. You are the "value"— don't sell yourself short!

- *Build a cycle of success.* Work hard, be confident, set and attain goals, be persistent, believe you will succeed. William James said it best: "Whatever the mind can conceive and believe, it can achieve."

The Total System "A+" formula:

A+ Resume
A+ Letters (Reference, Cover)
A+ Lead Generation Plan
A+ Research (Target Companies)
A+ Networking
A+ Interviewing
A+ Negotiating

Equals Better Job for Better Pay!

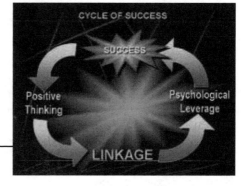

TESTIMONIALS TO SUCCESS

To attest to the effectiveness of applying the Cycle of Success and committing to "A+" implementation of each step in *The Total System*, following are several testimonials which were delivered as presentations during client luncheon events. Successfully placed clients shared their experiences with other clients who were still conducting job searches. We have selected six successful placements to share providing a cross-section of levels, functions, and experiences. If you have any doubt that what you have read in these pages works, you can believe these words—they were spoken by real-life clients of ours who found themselves in similar situations as you are facing, and who cast their doubts aside in order to succeed. (Names, titles, and companies are altered to maintain confidentiality.)

TESTIMONIAL 1

My name is Tom, and I was a Director of Manufacturing Services for over eight years. I was working for XYZ Oil and Gas Company up until May 4, 5, or 6. I don't really remember the date— one that I never thought I would forget. We knew cutbacks were coming. When your boss calls you in, you know it's not to ask what you think about the weather that day. When he got done with me, he ushered me into a conference room, and there was a Dawson Consulting Group transition consultant saying, "Well, Tom, you have an opportunity ahead of you." I thought, "Right—like 10,000 other unemployed!" But it turned out to be really true!

In the three months since I've left my job, I have found that my commitment to my industry is strong enough to get through the tough times in the business. I've spent that time, first, letting people know—individuals I knew—that I was available. That's what networking is. I spent a lot of time, also, trying to put my own contract deals together. One of the people I had been networking through, who was recently promoted to a vice-presidency, decided that he needed a few extra consultants on his staff on a retainer/commission basis. When he offered it to me, I was just in a state of shock! We negotiated back and forth on it. Fortunately, I convinced them that I am worth what I thought I was worth. I will be starting on October 15.

Most important, I think that what got me into this fortunate situation was keeping a positive attitude. Of all the things I learned from this experience, that was the most important. When I was cold-calling, I called just about every company that was in my industry, and almost everyone was real polite. Some of the people I called were more down than I was, and that was real tough. For those of you who have a marketable skill that is transferable, it won't be as bad as someone specialized in a down industry. Networking I found to be real easy. Everybody that I knew was always willing to help. I went through networking and cold-calling and responding to listings, which works to a very small degree. I was usually able to keep that positive attitude.

I just came to the conclusion that I was going to make it, and I realized that it might take a little while. There was no period that I let myself get down for more than one or two days in a row. There were days that I just said, "Okay, today I'm going to be depressed," and I would just go through the motions. That helped me get it out of my system, and I was back doing something. If you keep after it like that, something really good will happen. This really is an opportunity. I know that sounds a little hokey; I know because it wasn't that long ago somebody else was saying that to me! But honestly, *The Total System* really works.

"Most important, I think that what got me into this fortunate situation was keeping a positive attitude."

One thing that helped me was the realization that I had a niche to fill, that somewhere out there was "the position" that was just what I was looking for. I am very hesitant about going to work for a company on a regular 9 to 5 basis. What I wanted was to be a consultant, which is exactly what I found. Granted, the retainer isn't a total compensation package with benefits, but as the industry turns around, I'll be in a position to renegotiate. That's just what I wanted to do, and everything I did in my job campaign was in pursuing that goal. Whatever your goals, always keep them in mind. At the same time, keep your flexibility. What you get initially may not be precisely what you want, but if you get close, you can work your way into exactly what you want—what ever your dream, the beach house in the Caribbean, or wherever! I am very grateful for the opportunity to learn from the experts and will apply these lessons throughout my career.

TESTIMONIAL 2

My name is Dick. I am going to talk about my job search in two phases—what happened to me job-wise and emotionally. I was with St. Katherine's Hospital for twelve years. I lost my job as a pharmacist on June 13 of this year. The company made a decision that they were going to outsource my department. It didn't take long to figure out that my position would go away.

Fortunately, I learned what the "hidden" job market is from *The Total System*. The way it worked out for me is that I had five job interviews with companies. Two came from ad responses and three, including the job I got, came from networking. Next Monday I start to work for Palmer Hospital. It may surprise you that the person who recommended that I talk to this group was my former boss! The job was never advertised. As a matter of fact, the hospital has a hiring freeze! Had I not worked aggressively to ask, "Who do you know—please jog your memory—do you know anyone that I might talk to," this probably wouldn't have surfaced. So I think it's very important that you go after the "hidden" job market, both cold-calling and networking, because either way it's a percentage game. If you go for the listings, you know the jobs are open, but you also know there's hundreds of other people coming in against you. If you cold-call or network, you know you are one of only a few who are networking personally for it. And if it's a referral situation, you may come in with the endorsement which is very strong. You have a leg up on any competitor when you apply the networking techniques to gain psychological leverage.

I mostly "warm-called" in networking. For instance, one of my interviews was in San Antonio. I was referred by another man I knew in San Antonio. When I called, I didn't know this guy, but yet I was able to use the name of another acquaintance. To me that is a warm call. You are not just calling out of the blue. I had a name to drop, which got his attention, and that got me one interview. Initially, I wrote a letter of introduction to the person who offered me the job at Palmer. He didn't know me, but yet I started off with the name of my former boss, who he did know. I used other *Total System* networking techniques, but again, the "hidden" job market was my main objective. If I had time at the end of each day, I would check online to see if any new listings were appropriate for me to follow up on. That was my strategy. And it worked!

The second aspect I wanted to talk about was the emotional side of the situation. I don't know how it was for others, but the only way I can describe it is—it was hell. There is one thing in particular that I found helpful, which I'd like to share with you. Have you heard about the two frogs that fell in a bucket of milk? Two frogs one evening fell into a bucket of cow's milk down on the farm. And they were saying, "My gosh, what in the world are we going to do?! There is no way we can get up to the edge." They swam for about an hour, and they started to get really tired, and one of the frogs said, "Man, I'm so exhausted, I can't see why I should just keep swimming like this. The heck with it." He just quit swimming and sank; that was it. The other frog thought, "Well, I know what happens when I quit swimming, but I don't know what happens if I keep swimming, so I'm just going to keep swimming 'til it kills me." Well, through the long night, the frog swam so hard that the milk started to churn into butter. Finally, at dawn, he was able to get some footing and he just jumped out!

That's sort of the way I felt. In other words, I didn't know when this damn thing was going to be over, but all of a sudden I had footing and I jumped out and that was all. I knew what would happen if I quit swimming—I'd probably still be in the bucket of milk!

We all respond to rewards and recognition, so when I get home if I really had a tough day, I like to drink a beer and think about my accomplishments. At the beginning of my search, I thought, "Well I haven't accomplished a darn thing. I don't even have a job." I couldn't enjoy drinking beer or riding my bike or any of the things I like to do. Then I started to think, "I'm just going to churn as hard as I can. If I have a day when I know that I got up early in the morning and that I worked just as hard at my job campaign and churned as hard as I could—even though it didn't produce a job offer that day—then I deserve a reward." Whether it is beer, ice cream, running, or whatever, reward yourself for each day of hard work. That carried me through, and I felt the sense of accomplishment. Every day, even though I didn't have the ultimate reward—which can only be defined as a new job—I felt that I had put in my eight or ten hours that day and I deserved a small reward. Some days are worse than others, but you do deserve that reward. Hopefully, that will be of some help to you. I know that if you just keep churning, all of a sudden—bam, it's over with. I am so thankful to everyone who helped me – it will be an experience I will always remember.

TESTIMONIAL 3

My name is Jerry. This is the moment I have been looking forward to. As of Wednesday, I have accepted an offer as Vice President, Marketing with Genetics Company. I'll be working for their international division and responsible for opening up new markets for their seed productions in Africa and some in the Middle East.

It's interesting, because back in June, when we did our Dawson practice interviews, this was essentially the position for which I practice-interviewed. It just took a while to come together.

"You have a leg up on any competitor when you apply the networking techniques to gain psychological leverage."

I was trying to think of some things that might be of interest as you are just getting into your job searches. A lot of very true and worthwhile things have already been said. I know my experience in the whole job search process was a learning experience for me. I had been with ABC Company for nine years and never had really learned to do an effective job search. I feel safe to say that I would probably still be at it or would have settled for a job at McDonald's by this point! Prior to entering the Dawson transition program, I just didn't know how to go about it. I really feel that the best part of this whole process was learning about myself-- what I want to do, how to clarify my career goals, how to market myself, how to communicate effectively. Those are skills that are universal in their transferability and are going to come in very handy down the road.

I would like to share an analogy of how I think of the stages of the job search. At least in my case, it worked sort of like taking a trip on an airplane. You start out and there are the emotional aspects of departure—breaking loose from family or wherever you've been, the flurry of activity associated with getting to the airport, of boarding the plane and settling in. This is similar to the emotional turmoil you experience when you lose your job. The slow, gradual ascent is analogous to the daily routine of making your calls and writing your letters. Then things begin to level off. Along about one month into the process, you are feeling pretty comfortable with it. It gets to be almost like any other job. Then, after about two months, things began to happen for me. That's analogous to the plane beginning to descend—things start to get a little bit turbulent, and there's just a lot of activity. People begin to respond to your calls, letters or to your leads. Finally, just before landing, it gets very turbulent—and in my case, that was one of the most difficult parts of the job search. All these people start expressing interest—in my case, four or five. I started to wonder how I was going to put this guy off while I waited for these other offers to come in. But it all worked out very nicely. A few potential offers faded out of the picture toward the end, but I ended up with two strong offers—just like *The Total System* challenges us to do.

The one I accepted with Genetics Company is really the ideal job for me. It combines most of my career objectives. The one drawback is that it involves considerable travel. I had a struggle with that as I got to the point of making a decision—really wondering, thinking it through with my wife. Did I want to be gone 35 or 40 percent of the time, overseas for three-week stretches? We don't know that answer yet. I guess the only way to find out is to jump in and do it. I decided that it is better to find out now rather than later regret not having explored it, because this is an area that I have wanted to be involved in really since college.

For me, the key to success was networking. All the leads that materialized were as a result of contacts with former work associates or people that I had contact with in other companies through my previous job. My job objective was market development or projects in agribusiness, which is a narrow field. Obviously, there are not a whole lot of positions advertised in that area, so I had to rely heavily on networking. I wrote a lot of letters to major agribusiness companies here in the United States. The "cold" letter route did not really work for me. I got a lot of very nice rejection letters. The amusing part was how many different ways people can tell you "Thanks, but no thanks." There were a lot of very original letters from HR departments.

The thing that really was helpful for me was getting out and visiting companies. I took three trips to various parts of the country—one up to the Midwest, one to Virginia, and one up to the Northeast. I lined up interviews along the way. Some of these interviews were with people I had written to, and they had told me they didn't have anything. But I called them back, thanked them for responding to my letter, told them I was really interested in the company, and just wondered if I could stop by since I was going to be in the area. And I mentioned that I would like to learn more about their company. That was very helpful for a number of reasons. One, it kept me current in the interview process. I got some new contacts from doing that and occasionally got a solid lead out of those interviews. This emphasizes the importance of getting out and meeting with people. I think it is a very effective technique.

When it came time to negotiate, basically I asked for time to make a decision. I was going through a second or third interview with some of these companies, and they would say, "Well, we are getting very close to a decision stage. We would need you to make your decision here shortly." Well I became quite a bit anxious, and I wondered how I was going to hold off the other employers. Actually, that problem never materialized. The guy who said he was going to make a decision next week didn't end up making a decision 'til three or four weeks later. I think that may be practical wisdom—don't rely too heavily on what people say about when they will do something. In my case, the offers came through at least three or four weeks later than what they first told me. So just hang cool, and don't worry too much about it. The only other thing I would add along that line is, ask for time to make a decision. If they want you bad enough, they will be willing for you to make a sound decision. In certain situations, I was very up front with people. I told them I was considering several other positions; if I felt it was appropriate, I would tell them very specifically what I was doing. They understood. They said, "We are willing to wait; we would really like to have you, so we'll just wait and see what you find out."

I am very grateful for this opportunity and think it's been one of the most positive experiences of my whole career thus far. I don't know how many people there are out in the work world who probably wish for this opportunity, who are not satisfied with their jobs. I wasn't with my previous job. The opportunity to get off the treadmill and step back, look at what you want to do, and lay down some long-range plans is, I think, a chance of a lifetime. Thank you!

TESTIMONIAL 4

My name is Carol, and I was formerly with High Top Company.

I remember when I first sat in *The Total System* transition seminar, especially that first Friday; there were two or three people who got up from previous groups who had just been

> "The opportunity to get off the treadmill and lay down some long-range plans is a chance of a lifetime."

placed. They spoke to us as we are speaking to you, and some of us were a little bit skeptical. I wondered if they were paying these people to get up and tell these nice things, since this is exactly what the Dawson consultant said in our first meeting at High Top Company—insisting how great things would be. I had doubts as to whether these things really happened as clients described them, but as the weeks went by and more and more clients shared successes; I realized that everybody who spoke about their job search was just like I was. They were going through some very difficult times, but they stuck with it.

I'll tell you quickly what happened to me. I was manager of an audio/video production department for High Top. Of course, with the economic downturn— by the way I had that line down pat about the "downturn of the economy"--my whole department was shut down. I won't say it was a shock to me. In service departments, you always run the risk of something happening. Within three weeks of being here, I decided that I wanted to start my own production company. I had looked around, and there just did not seem to be an opportunity similar to what I had. I did send out resumes left and right the first couple of weeks, almost all of which were out of state. After about three weeks, I didn't hear anything back from all of the resumes I sent out. I decided that I would try starting my own production company—at least, give it the best shot I could. So for the next three months, that's about all I did, except for sending out resumes just to keep my options open. That's another thing the consultant talked about in the seminar—"Make sure you keep your options open, and don't close any door that might help you out down the road." So I kept looking on a small scale—which, by the way, also fulfilled my unemployment compensation requirements. I called on people to work on productions, individual slide shows, or whatever. And I developed a few contracts—I was at least getting some work and building that up.

Then, about a month ago, I got a call from a large bank in Florida to which I had sent a resume the week after I left High Top. About a week later, I called them and they told me that the position had been "filled." I didn't quite believe that line, since my background was perfect for the job description. Interestingly enough, they called me back a month ago and said that they would like me to interview if I was still interested. At that time, I wasn't even sure I wanted to go interview, since I was just so set on doing my own thing. Since I had started it, I was going to stick with it. But I thought, "Keep your options open. You don't know what there is out there — plus it's a free trip!" I decided to give it a shot. I went out there and interviewed with a different person every half-hour or so for about three and a half hours, one of which was an hour-long lunch meeting. That was seven interviews. The process was really an experience for me. I felt very prepared. Before I left, I reviewed my Total System notes and answers to the tough questions. I had written about five or six major points I wanted to be sure to make, and I studied those. I felt very comfortable when I was there.

After I came back, they called me a day or two later and said that they were really interested in me and asked me to return for another interview. They were interviewing someone else for the job in about two weeks, but they were narrowing it down to the two of us. I almost hoped they wouldn't call me. I had spent money on stationery and business cards and called all these people and had people call me back about possible productions that I could do independently. They invited me and my husband to come for the weekend to talk to us a little bit more and show us the area, et cetera, et cetera. I thought, "Well, okay, I'll keep my options open." I went there this past weekend, and they were just extremely nice to us.

"Make sure you keep your options open, and don't close any door that might help you out down the road."

On Monday, after I got back, they called me and offered the position. I still didn't know if I wanted to take it. After discussing it with my husband and establishing a minimum offer which could induce us to move, I told them, "No, thank you, but I can not accept the offer." They called back the next day and upped the offer. It was so good I couldn't turn it down. In fact Tuesday, when they called and upped the offer, I responded immediately. I said, "Okay, I accept the offer." The representative said, "What? You're kidding—you're taking the offer now? You don't want to think about it?" I replied, "No—you've been fair with me, I'll be fair with you."

One thing in particular about the negotiations is interesting. I had contacted a company in Chicago about a possibility of a job offer which never really came about. But since I had been talking with them, I used that as some leverage with these people. I told them I was talking to some people in Chicago. Well, when they came back on Tuesday to up the offer, the representative spent about ten minutes talking about the statistics between Chicago and Jacksonville, Florida. She told me the difference in the price of housing—that the median price was 35 percent higher in Chicago than in Jacksonville. She gave me the cost of living index of the two cities, and the relocation index difference. I mean, there were about seven or eight categories that they were using to show why this was a better deal than going to Chicago. What was really a kick was that the lady expounding on Florida was from Chicago! I felt that having a little leverage really helped me. Even though I didn't actually have an offer from Chicago, I used that as a bargaining point.

Through all this, I did learn to keep my options open. I still would like to have my own business, which I am going to keep up. I've got some things I'm involved in which I can do on weekends. So I am going to keep that going just as a small business. If, down the road, things don't work out with this job, I'll always have that to go back to.

The last thing I would like to mention deals with networking ideas. I didn't know what networking involved. I quickly learned that you talk to your friends, your acquaintances, people who were former employers and let them all know what you are trying to do. You never know when they are going to find a friend or see something that might be of interest. That gets down to how I knew about this job. A week after I left my job, a friend in the employee communications department at High Top called me and said she had seen a listing in a trade publication which I never read. My point is that you never know where the possibility of a job will come from. That's why it's important to tell all your friends, your acquaintances, people you meet—don't be shy about it. If there is anything that is going to help you, it is believing that the more people who know that you are looking for a job in a certain area and who keep thinking about you, the greater the possibility that they are going to find something and tell you about it. I hope my experience encourages you to make networking a priority throughout your career as I intend to do! Thanks for everything!

TESTIMONIAL 5

Hi. I'm Chris. Having just recently graduated from college, my plan was to enter medical school. Unfortunately, I wasn't able to start this year and was faced with a job search for the first time except for summer and part-time jobs. I was really at a loss until I had the opportunity to learn *The Total System.* I didn't even know there was a system to job search. In fact, I was so discouraged about not going to medical school I would have taken any job. Fortunately, I realized from *The Total System* that I have value to an employer, and that I can be in control of my future direction.

I had no idea how to target companies in particular industries until this experience. Once I investigated the medical research industry, I discovered that there were over 500 companies in this field. Using an online database, I produced a list of about 100 companies and began to contact them. One of the leads I got from networking was for the DeBakey Heart Institute. Well, they suggested I contact a certain person at Baylor College of Medicine. When I contacted the person, she remembered that the DeBakey Institute had contacted them about a candidate. Anyway, for some reason she was under the impression that I was being recommended by Dr. DeBakey. She already had an interview set up for me.

So, that is how I got this job. It is with Dr. Sandra Shaw at the Doctor's General Hospital—Department of Pediatrics: Baylor College of Medicine. We are research-ing a "Preemie" newborn problem. When born prematurely, a baby's digestive sys-tem does not work properly. We are researching the problem and trying to find answers leading to a cure. We actually work with the babies at the hospital which gives me clinical experience, and we're working in a lab. I cannot tell you how perfect this position is! Aside from gaining experience in both research and clinical settings, I think that Dr. Shaw will be a great help in my application for school. I plan on going back to medical school in two years, the Physicians Assistant program, which happens to be at Baylor.

As you would guess, I am very excited about the whole thing. I could not have found a better job, even if I had researched all the possibilities and chosen my ideal position. The preparation of an A+ resume, networking, and practice inter-viewing gave me the confidence I needed to begin my career in the best possible position and environment. I owe a lot to *The Total System*—it works.

TESTIMONIAL 6

My name is Bill. I started my career as a chemical engineer in a refinery in Houston. I went from refinery to refinery, from chemical plant to chemical plant. Then I left the States and spent a long time in South America building refineries and operating refineries. Eventually I worked my way to Puerto Rico, to Pittsburgh, and back to Houston. I got out of the refining business and into the coal business, which had its ups and downs. Then I got out of the coal business and went into engineering and construction, which has its ups and downs, too. I worked here in Houston with two companies, then moved to Chicago where I had a nice tour of duty in the Midwest doing engineering and construction management. Then one of the nicest things I did was move to Washington. In Washington, D.C., I was President of a company that did public sector and government contracts, both engineering and construction. The company that I headed up got restructured, and then was restructured right out of existence.

At that time my wife, Glenda, and I talked about our choices. She could come join me in Washington and starve to death or I could come back to Houston. Since Glenda is President of her own company, the latter choice seemed most appropriate. We decided it was about time we stopped commuting anyway. It was a lovely decision and I'm glad we made it. I'm real happy now that I lost my job, came back to Houston and started over again. I'm also going to tell you that it was not easy. In fact, it was very hard on me to have to start over.

I remember the first day I was in *The Total System* transition program, a consultant said, "Well, how do you feel about your situation?" That was the first time anyone asked how I felt about it and I determined at that point that I was going to be positive. So one word of advice—be positive throughout the ups and downs that you experience in your professional career. So I started off on a positive note.

> "The preparation of an A+ resume, networking, and practice interviewing gave me confidence to begin my career in the best possible position."

I've always been a very pragmatic person, and I realized that I had to restructure the way I lived and the way I worked. It was very difficult. I didn't like using the telephone. The telephone was hard; believe me it was very difficult. But it's something that you must do. You have to overcome your stage fright and you have to overcome your reluctance to talk about yourself. I've done a lot of things successfully and I didn't want to tell people that I was unemployed. The sooner you get over that and get it behind you, the sooner you can move on. The Total System helped me get my feet on the ground and head out and start doing my work. I didn't get any interviews at the beginning. But I just kept plugging away.

You need those interviews—they are good for your ego. There was a point when Glenda and I talked about the possibility that it was time for me to retire. But after a while you realize all the money is going out and no money is coming back in and you've got to decide if you are going to sack groceries or just what you are going to do. Eventually the interviews came, and the job offers came, and what do you know—some of them were so low that I wouldn't consider taking them. Some of them were withdrawn! I'm going to tell you that one of you is going to get an offer, and you're going to call back the next day to find out more particulars, and discover that there is no job. You're ready to negotiate, and they're going to withdraw the offer on you. And that's pretty hard to take. Memorial Day we had at least three jobs lined up—I just knew I would be working by July 1. Not one of them materialized. I worked with one company for weeks and I interviewed everybody from Chairman down to Project Manager level. They offered a job once and withdrew it; then later they came back to me, and started talking all over again, but nothing ever came of it. And yet you need those interviews.

You need to talk to people. One of the things that I found very beneficial when I got to a real low level was to talk to people. You need their support. There are times when you just stop and talk over your situation and it helps you get through that day.

I did a lot of job search work at night. I did a lot of work on the weekends, and you need that. It is a full-time job. Don't let anyone tell you that finding a job is not a full-time job.

> "Be positive throughout the ups and downs that you experience in your professional career".

I did some consulting work, but it didn't lead to a full-time position. I had one company that told me that they wanted to hire me but they couldn't get authorization. They wanted me to consult for awhile and then maybe they would hire me. It turned out that they took my strategic plan, which I put together for a business unit, and they are using it today. But at the end of the contract they said, "Well, I'm sorry but we can't get approval to hire you."

Another thing I would recommend is to keep in shape. You've got to be mentally in shape, but you also have to be physically in shape. Your appearance is also important. You've got to keep your wardrobe up, you've got to keep your body in good shape, and you've got to keep doing your work.

You've got to keep going—I can't emphasize that enough. Regardless of how many interviews or how many job offers you get, you still need to be digging looking for opportunities that are out there. The reason this persistence is required is that you are likely to have two or three interviews with one company and invariably in your euphoria you are going to think, "Hey, this is it," and you will start neglecting your network contacts. Then if it doesn't work out, you will have lost a lot of time. Resist the temptation, and just keep on keeping on until the offer is signed and you are in your new position!

The job that I have now is with an environmental remediation company. I selected it out of three offers. Along the way someone asked me if I had explored hazardous waste management. At the time I hadn't given it much thought, so I started working on it. As it turns out they found out about me from somebody else that eventually led to the interviews and that led to the job offer. So don't stop. Don't stop looking, don't stop working.

One of the other two offers I had was in South America and I went to look at the job. Believe me, they needed help. They had all of their operations riding on three major projects in a country that needs a lot of work. The job is going downhill, and they are going to get thrown out of there if they don't do something about it. While I was looking at that job, a third opportunity developed. It was with another company here in town, where they wanted me to take over and run their engineering construction business.

I came back from South America, and Glenda said, "You have an interview on Monday." She just told them, "Yes, Bill will be there to interview on Monday." It was Environmental Technologies, Inc., with whom I had been talking, and I didn't know if they were serious or what. As it turns out, they were very serious. I told them, "I've got to make a decision

> "You've got to keep going—
> I can't emphasize that enough.
> Regardless of how many interviews or
> how many job offers you get, you still
> need to keep looking for opportunities."

by Friday, and if you're going to play in this ball game, we've got to get with it." The Vice President said it was a bad week—there were board meetings and this and that. I said, "Fine, you've got board meetings, I'll see you. If you want to talk to me, put your offer together and let's talk about it in detail. I need an offer by Thursday morning." At that point I was tired of fooling around; I had something I wanted and I was ready to take it. As it turned out they put it together and made me an offer on Thursday morning—he actually delayed it until Thursday afternoon because we ate lunch and talked about it. Because they were playing this game, they wanted to wear me out, take me out to the very end of the day. I decided to accept the job as Executive Vice President, Business Development; I will oversee things that are happening with their construction companies, their remedial companies and with their technology company. The company has big plans and is going places, and I plan to go with them. That is my story—after all I've experienced, I feel great! Good luck and thanks for the support.

So there you have a few of the hundreds of testimonials we have heard. In a short time, you, too, will give testimony to a successful job search. Set your goal, apply the techniques, believe in yourself, and make it happen. That is how to create job search leverage. The one percent success factor is within you—use it to maximize your success. By the way, at your curtain call—when you've finished your script and attained your career goals—be prepared for a standing ovation. If you don't believe it now, perhaps then you'll know that rather than the worst thing, losing a job can be the best thing that could have happened to you!   Whether you have read this book because of a job loss or because you are seeking the next step up in your career, *The Total System* will work for you if you will work the system. We wish you success throughout your career--better jobs for better pay with each step you take. No doubt if you apply the principles we have presented, you will experience many curtain calls along the way.

A FINAL NOTE

We hope you have enjoyed reading *The Total System* as much as we enjoyed writing it. We encourage you to access and utilize *The Total System* complementary resources and services. Join tens of thousands of other successful job seekers from all backgrounds, industries and organizational levels in achieving better jobs for better pay and a better life throughout your career.

Our passion never diminishes to see people around the world apply the principles and techniques of *The Total System* as they work harder, smarter and longer to achieve their career aspirations, as well as to gain prosperity and happiness for their entire family. We welcome and encourage you to contact us with your personal success story once you land your next best opportunity! We look forward to hearing your unique story on how you have leveraged *The Total System* to gain a better job for better pay, to realize your career vision, and to harness your potential for career advancement. We wish you and your family total career success for a life time!

Ken & Sheryl Dawson

Index of Exhibits

Index

The Authors

Kenneth M. Dawson
Chairman & CEO, Total Career Success, Inc.

As a pioneer in the outplacement and career transition industry, Ken Dawson founded Dawson Consulting Group in 1977 and is now Chairman and CEO of Total Career Success. Since then he has inspired thousands of employees and executives to earn better jobs for better pay and maximize their career success. The creative genius behind *Job Search: The Total System*, Ken continues to develop practical and creative ways to optimize one's career potential. Through seminars and *The Total System* materials, many across a wide range of industries and disciplines have turned their passions into prosperity.

As an energetic, informative, humorous and motivational presenter, Ken inspires his participants to excel. His extensive career and credentials in management consulting provide a wealth of experience upon which he draws to present the best job search and career success advice available worldwide. A Marine Corps Veteran, Ken received dual undergraduate degrees prior to completing two graduate degrees with honors.

Sheryl N. Dawson
Chairman & CEO, Dawson Consulting Group

Widely recognized for her expertise in the areas of talent management consulting, program design and development, project management, and career and behavioral assessment, Sheryl Dawson is Chairman & CEO of Dawson Consulting Group. Sheryl is responsible for achieving the vision and leading the growth of this Houston-based talent management consulting and training firm. She also leads the publishing division of Total Career Success which provides career advice to the retail market.

Sheryl earned an MBA from the University of Houston - Clear Lake with honors. As author, speaker, and consultant, she serves professional and community organizations and publications by sharing her expertise on talent, career and organizational related topics. She conveys her passion for influencing the quality of life of those she touches daily in her commitment to spiritual, emotional, and intellectual aspects of personal and professional growth.